Date Due

OCT 0 5 2008			

BRODART, INC.   Cat. No. 23 233   Printed in U.S.A.

The New Financial Planner

A Guide to Client Service

The New Financial Planner

A Guide to Client Service

Cathey H. Bertot, CFP

DOW JONES-IRWIN
Homewood, Illinois 60430

ISBN 0-87094-587-4

Library of Congress Catalog Card No. 85-52442

Printed in the United States of America

1 2 3 4 5 6 7 8 9 0 BC 3 2 1 0 9 8 7 6

PREFACE

Financial planning is rapidly expanding and increasing in complexity. The key to understanding the profession is to recognize that it encompasses a number of disciplines: accounting, finance, economics, taxation, investments, risk management, and law. This book addresses these subjects, which are the basis for a systematic approach. It is designed both for those individuals entering the field and for current practitioners wishing to upgrade their skills.

The numerous topics listed in the Table of Contents may seem overwhelming at first. However, those beginning a career in the field of financial planning typically have knowledge and experience in some of the disciplines. For example, accountants and tax preparers feel extremely comfortable with taxation, but unfamiliar with risk management. Also, individuals from the insurance industry have a strong grasp of risk management, but feel uncertain in regards to time value concepts. Students and interested individuals may need to spend significant amounts of time on *all* chapters.

This book is based on the author's experience in teaching financial planning and taxation at both the undergraduate and graduate levels for the last three years. It presents information essential for financial planners. With this in mind, the book has been divided into four parts.

The first part covers the basic elements of financial planning. This includes the professional training needed to become a financial planner and a discussion of the regulatory agencies overseeing the profession. This part also gives background information planners must first obtain and analyze before a specific plan can be constructed. Once a client's current financial position is ascertained, the planner must determine what risk management strategies are appropriate. This information then becomes the basis for further analysis.

Part Two expands on financial planning in chapters on time value concepts and taxation. These quantifiable elements are essential in determining whether or not a client's short-range and long-range goals can be achieved. It is imperative that planners become thoroughly familiar with this material. This will require significant time for readers who begin without a strong background in these areas.

Part Three covers investment planning and includes a brief synopsis of economic concepts. Assets and investment vehicles such as stocks, bonds, and limited partnerships are discussed.

Part Four covers those issues that will prove to be important throughout a client's life: retirement plans, fringe benefits, and social security. Estate planning is also discussed because it is important that clients make arrangements for an orderly distribution of their wealth, rather than subject their heirs to the chaos that often results from an unexpected death.

These parts provide a practical foundation for those seeking to enter the field of financial planning.

ACKNOWLEDGMENTS

It is with great pleasure that I acknowledge those individuals who have helped me with this book. To begin, Bert Clinkston's editorial comments proved invaluable. Furthermore, his insight and perspective cannot be overestimated. Important technical assistance was received from Michael Anderson, J.D. His suggestions and evaluations in the area of estate planning were extremely beneficial. Special thanks go to Dr. Art Hansen who generously took the time to review this book and offer keen observations on its organization.

I also wish to thank Dr. Joseph Hammel, Jeffrey Higgins, Patricia Pinkos, and Stephen Bubala for their perceptive comments. Special thanks must go to Roger Blake, Yvonne Martin, Kimberly Davis, and Francisco Bertot for their tireless help in completing this book. And, finally, thanks to both my clients and my students for their helpful suggestions regarding the content and format of this book.

Cathey H. Bertot

CONTENTS

Part One
The Beginning Framework   1

1   **Introduction to Financial Planning**   3
    Objectives   4
      Risk Management   5
    Background of Financial Planning   6
      Education   6
      Research   7
      Conflicts of Interest   8
      Regulatory Restrictions   10

2   **Data Gathering and Analysis of Financial Statements**   13
    The Questionnaire   13
    Balance Sheet   27
      Sample Balance Sheet   28
    Income and Expense Statement   32
      Income   32
      Expenses   34
      Cash-Flow Management   34
      Tracking Expenses   35
      Budget   36
      Debt and Deficits   36
      Expense Patterns   37

3   **Risk Management: Insurance**   39
    Risk of Death   42
      Quantifying the Need   47
    Cost   51
    Risk of Disability   53

Medical Protection   57
Casualty and Liability Protection   59
Automobile Coverage   59
Homeowner's and Related Coverage   60

Part Two
Quantitative Elements   63

4 **Time Value Concepts**   65
   Time and Money   65
      Components of Time Value Equations   66
      Time Value Calculations Using a Calculator   67
   Interest Rates   75
   Putting It Together   78
      Educational Needs   78

5 **Investment Yield Analysis**   89
   Payback   90
   Simple Rate of Return (Simple Interest)   90
   Annual Compound Rate of Return   91
   Internal Rate of Return (IRR)   91
   Net Present Value (NPV)   93
   Adjusted Rate of Return (ARR)   95

6 **The Fundamentals of the Tax Structure**   97
   Basic Tax Doctrines   98
   Determining a Tax Bracket   99
      Combined Marginal Tax Bracket (CMTB)   102
   Four Types of Income   103
      Includable Income   104
      Excludable Income   106
   Deductions   109
      Business Deductions   110
      Nonbusiness Deductions   113
      Itemized Deductions   113
   Credits   116
   Reviewing the Federal Income Tax Return   117
   Conclusion   121

7 **Essential Components of Tax Planning**   123
   Depreciation   123
      Types of Depreciation   124

Depletion 133
Basis 134
Investment Interest Limitation 135
Alternative Minimum Tax (AMT) 136

Part Three
The Investment Environment 139

8 **The Economy** 141
Economic Theory 141
Classical Economics 141
Keynesian Theory 142
Monetarism 143
Phillips Curve 143
Supply Siders 143
Federal Reserve System 145
Banking System 146

9 **Marketable Securities** 149
Short-Term Debt Instruments 150
Long-Term Debt 151
Federal Government Securities 154
Zero-Coupon Government Bonds 156
Municipal Bonds 156
Stock 157
Trading 159
Stock Options 160
Short Sale 161
Securities Markets 161
Investment Company Securities 163
Management Companies 164
Unit Investment Trusts 168
Methods of Investment Analysis 168
Fundamental Analysis 168
Technical Analysis 169
Efficient Market Theory 170
Random Walk 170
Modern Portfolio Theory 171

10 **Limited Partnerships and Hard Assets** 174
Limited Partnership 174
Basis 176

Types of Limited Partnerships 178
Real Estate 178
Leasing Investments 182
Oil and Gas Programs 187
Research and Development 190
Cable Television 191
Movies, Master Recording, Videos, Books 192
Animal Breeding and Feeding Programs 193
Hard Assets and Collectibles 194

11 Due Diligence 196
Prospectus Review 198
Investment Selection 204

Part Four
Lifetime Planning 207

12 Retirement Plans: Qualified Pension Plans; Individual
Retirement Accounts; Tax Sheltered Annuities 209
Individual Retirement Account (IRA) 210
Tax Sheltered Annuity (TSA) 213
Qualified Pension Plans 217
Borrowing Provisions 226
Tax Considerations 226

13 Social Security and Employee Fringe Benefits 228
Social Security 228
Employee Fringe Benefits 236
Types of Benefits 236

14 Estate Planning 240
Ownership Categories 240
Tenancy in Common 241
Joint Tenancy 241
Tenancy by Entirety 242
Community Property 242
Separate Property 244
Common Law Property 244
Intestacy 245

Wills 246
  Nuncupative 246
  Holographic 246
  Formal 246
Probate 247
Trusts 248
  Types of Trust 249
Federal Estate Taxation 250
Deductions 254
Gifts 257

Summary 259

Index 261

EXHIBITS, ILLUSTRATIONS, AND TABLES

Exhibits
2-1 Confidential Financial Analysis Questionnaire, 14
6-1 Form 1040, 118
6-2 Schedule A, 120
11-1 Prospectus Analysis Worksheet, 201

Illustrations
1-1 Conflict of Interest Matrix, 10
3-1 Whole Life Insurance, 43
4-1 Value in Future Dollars, 68
4-2 Compound and Simple Interest, 69
4-3 Future Value of an Annuity, 71
4-4 Present Value, 72
4-5 Present Value per Period, 74
4-6 Educational Funding Requirement, 80
4-7 Annuity Received at the Beginning of the Period, 81
4-8 Annuity Received at the End of the Period, 82
6-1 1985 Tax Brackets, 101
7-1 Depreciation, 123
9-1 Diversification and Risk, 172
10-1 Types of Leasing Limited Partnerships, 184

Tables
2-1 Balance Sheet—Sarah Jones, 29
2-2 Income and Expense Statement—Jack and Mellisa Thompson, 33
3-1 Example of Time Value Comparison for Insurance (cash value example), 46
3-2 Example of Time Value Comparison for Insurance (term policy), 46
3-3 Determining the Amount of Insurance Needed, 48
3-4 Determining the Amount of Insurance Needed—Fred and Sharon Smith, 50
3-5 Net Cost per Thousand for Whole Life, 52
3-6 Net Cost per Thousand for Whole Life—Fred and Sharon Smith, 53
3-7 Borrowing Cash Value, 53
3-8 Disabled Working-Age Population, 1978, 54
4-1 Goal Accumulation Worksheet, 79
5-1 Recovering Original Investment, 90
6-1 1985 Tax Rate Schedules—Married Taxpayers Filing Joint Return, 100
6-2 1985 Tax Rate Schedules—Single Taxpayers, 101

6-3 Mike's Investments, 105

7-1 ACRS, 125

7-2 Depreciation of Office Equipment (five-year recovery), 125

7-3 Depreciation of Low-Income Housing, 126

7-4 Depreciation of 18-Year Real Property (18-year 175% declining balance), 127

7-5 Depreciation of Low-Income Housing, 127

7-6 Deductions for Personal Property Allowed under the ERTA, 128

7-7 Sale of Section 1245 Property, 129

7-8 Recapture of Depreciation on Sale of an Apartment Building, 130

7-9 Phantom Income, 132

8-1 Expansion of Money Supply, 148

9-1 Debt Instrument Rating System, 152

9-2 Option Transaction, 160

9-3 Net Asset Value of a Mutual Fund, 165

10-1 Investing through Different Types of Business Ownership, 175

10-2 Penalties on Incorrect Evaluation of Property, 180

10-3 Gain or Loss on Raw Land after One Year, 181

10-4 Capitalization Rate, 183

10-5 Tax Aspects of Limited Partnerships with and without Debt, 185

10-6 Inflated Value of Property, 192

11-1 Characteristics of Common Investments, 206

12-1 Basic Exclusion Allowance for 403(b) Plans (contributions to be made through salary reduction), 215

12-2 Alternative Exclusion Options, 216

12-3 Schedule 2 Vesting, 219

13-1 Social Security Tax Rates, 229

13-2 Social Security Tax Rates for Self-Employed Persons, 230

13-3 Quarters Needed to be Eligible for Social Security Benefits, 232

13-4 Maximum Social Security Benefits for Employees Retiring in 1985, 233

14-1 State of California Probate Fee Structure, 248

14-2 Unified Transfer Tax Rate Schedules for 1985 and Thereafter, 251

14-3 Unified Transfer Tax Rate Schedules for 1988 and Thereafter, 251

14-4 Unified Credit Rates, 252

ABBREVIATIONS

ACRS	Accelerated Cost Recovery System
AGI	Adjusted Gross Income
AMT	Alternative Minimum Tax
ARR	Adjusted Rate of Return
CAP	Capitalization Rate
CD	Certificate of Deposit
CFA	Chartered Financial Analyst
CFP	Certified Financial Planner
CMTB	Combined Marginal Tax Bracket
ERISA	Employee Retirement Income Security Act of 1974
ERTA	Economic Recovery Act of 1981
ESOP	Employee Stock Ownership Plan
FICA	Federal Insurance Contributions Act (Social Security)
FMV	Fair Market Value
FNMA	Federal National Mortgage Association
FV	Future Value
g	Inflation Rate (in formulas)
GAAP	Generally Accepted Accounting Principles
GNMA	Government National Mortgage Association
GTC	Good Till Cancelled
HMO	Health Maintenance Organization
HR-10	Pension Plan for Self Employed
i	Interest
IAFP	International Association for Financial Planning
IBCFP	International Board of Standards and Practices for Certified Financial Planners
ICFP	Institute of Certified Financial Planners
IDC	Intangible Drilling Costs
IRA	Individual Retirement Account
IRC	Internal Revenue Code
IRR	Internal Rate of Return
IRS	Internal Revenue Service
ITC	Investment Tax Credit

LTCG	Long-Term Capital Gain
LTCL	Long-Term Capital Loss
n	Time (in formulas)
NASD	National Association of Securities Dealers
NASDAQ	National Association of Securities Dealers Automated Quotations System
NAV	Net Asset Value
NPV	Net Present Value
OASDI	Old-Age Survivors and Disability Insurance
OTC	Over-the-Counter Market
P/E	Price/Earnings Ratio
PMT	Payment
PV	Present Value
QTIP	Qualified Terminable Investment Program
R&D	Research and Development
RIA	Registered Investment Advisor
S&P	Standard & Poor's
SEC	Securities and Exchange Commission
SEP	Simplified Employee Pension
SIPC	Securities Investor Protection Corporation
SRI	Stanford Research Institute
STCG	Short-Term Capital Gain
STCL	Short-Term Capital Loss
TDA	Tax Deferred Annuity
TEFRA	The Tax Equity and Fiscal Responsibility Act of 1982 (Public Law 97-248)
TRA	Tax Reform Act of 1984
TSA	Tax Sheltered Annuity
UBTI	Unrelated Business Taxable Income
YTM	Yield to Maturity

The Beginning Framework

CHAPTER ONE

Introduction to Financial Planning

Financial planning is a coordinated approach for determining financial goals and evaluating the strategies needed to achieve them. This dynamic process is derived from essential information obtained from clients. Equally important are the clients' attitudes and values as well as their motivation behind seeking financial analysis.

Ideally, financial planning should be a dispassionate, logical process. But it involves acquiring, maintaining, and disposing of a commodity that is usually charged with emotion: money! As a result, financial planning is often complicated by heated arguments, boastful claims, or silence. None of these emotional responses is positive.

The situation is compounded by a climate characterized by constant economic fluctuation and a continuously changing tax structure. Given this context, there is a tremendous need for a systematic approach to designing, engineering, and implementing a plan to achieve financial objectives.

Planners of financial strategies, therefore, are a welcome response to an overwhelming public need. Competent financial planners can provide important services to clients, regardless of income level or age. The most important question is not how much money clients have or earn, but how much money they retain and how it is aligned with their goals! Answering these and other critical questions is the essence of financial planning.

Financial planning entails the following key steps:

1. Identify and clarify objectives.
2. Analyze current financial position.
3. Quantify financial objectives and compare them to present position.

4. Review and evaluate risk requirements.
5. Review tax status and compute projections.
6. Examine estate plan.
7. Identify problem areas.
8. Consider how present and future assets will be positioned.
9. Determine what special circumstances may apply.
10. Recommend specific actions to accomplish financial objectives.
11. Implement requested changes.
12. Review situation periodically.

This list describes a complicated and time-consuming process. It also shows that financial planning is not a "one-shot" technique or a "quick fix" to solving financial problems. Rather it is an integrated approach that takes time, knowledge, and patience to develop and implement.

OBJECTIVES

Identification and clarification of objectives is an emotional process because it requires clients to assess values and review attitudes toward how they live. It is nonetheless an essential step, without which the planner would not know their clients' desired financial destination. The *clients'* objectives, not those of their peers, neighbors, relatives, or friends, are paramount. However, significant peer pressure must not be overlooked in helping clients determine what they need and desire.

To ascertain what clients want to accomplish, planners must undertake an extensive questioning process. This inquiry permits clients to list what is important to them, and next to assign priorities, or rank, what they want to attain. Often clients have to decide what they will give up now so as to achieve their objectives later. Planners may make observations or offer suggestions. However, there may be barriers to overcome and, consequently, planners should exercise caution. For example, clients may have problems with their spending habits or cash-flow management. It is imperative for planners to address such issues in a non-threatening manner. Ultimately, clients will decide what they wish to do about their lifestyles.

The clients' lifestyles should be reflected in accurate financial statements. A determination can be made as to the extent of assets, how they are positioned, and how they are financed. Further calculations can be used to quantify objectives and reveal whether objectives are realistic or unattainable. Frequently, clients may recognize the unrealistic character of their goals only after they have been quantified and presented on paper. Such a revelation can prove heartrending, and requires significant diplomacy and empathy on the part of the planner.

If a financial planner is the bearer of unwelcome news, some accounts may be lost, either temporarily or permanently, because the clients refuse to listen to what they do not want to hear. Experienced planners understand this response and learn to live with it. With this comes the realization that a good financial planner must also possess the elusive qualities of a psychological counselor.

Risk Management

Basic planning includes ascertaining whether clients are utilizing appropriate risk management techniques. Determining vulnerability to risk and the cost of eliminating or reducing risk can prevent unnecessary loss. This step is important to protect the client's current economic position.

Equally important is the tax status. Specific suggestions concerning taxes can be simply procedural or may involve repositioning assets. If the purchase of investment assets is recommended, it is imperative for planners to be aware of the different investment vehicles, and to inform clients of their positive and negative aspects.

Another part of the financial-planning process is determining whether clients have done any estate planning. It is quite common for clients, regardless of their net worth, to neglect making a will or having a trust drawn. Even the *titling* of assets is often ignored.

While it is not uncommon for planners to do tax preparation, handle insurance, and conduct investment analysis, not many planners are also estate planning attorneys. Financial planners who do not possess the necessary credentials and licensing requirements in a certain area must work with professionals in those fields. In fact, some financial planners have chosen to specialize in specific areas.

As the above indicates, financial planning requires attentiveness and the ability to change with circumstances. Planners recommend appropriate actions and help implement any requested changes. But their involvement does not end here. Planning is a continual process in which the client's situation is periodically reviewed. Consequently, strong and lasting relationships often develop between financial planners and their clients.

An integral part of this relationship is the integrity of the planners. Clients expect that their advisers will objectively design a course of action. Consequently, planners should not act in their own self-interest, but rather always place the concerns and goals of clients first. Ethical behavior also involves competency in addressing the client's financial planning needs.

BACKGROUND OF FINANCIAL PLANNING

The dawn and evolution of a new profession are always interesting to trace. Why did financial planning develop? How long has it existed? What is its current stage of development? Answers to those questions could generate heated discussions. For instance, some practitioners state they have been doing "financial planning" for over 30 years. Some certainly have, while others may simply have been involved with the sale of one product for that period.

The wealthy have long been involved with a coordinated approach to dealing with their financial affairs. Such planning for most people is a recent development, less than two decades old. A generally recognized need for financial planning began to grow in the late 1960s, greatly expanded during the rapid inflation of the 1970s, and exploded during the early 1980s.

This growth is evidenced by the creation in 1969 of a professional "trade" organization for financial planning. The International Association for Financial Planning (IAFP), with headquarters in Atlanta, has over 23,000 members. It promotes financial planning, sponsors educational seminars, and supports ethical standards of conduct. Local chapters of the IAFP are found in many areas of the country.

Another recognized organization in the profession is the Institute of Certified Financial Planners (ICFP). Its members have passed exams required for certification as a financial planner. Based in Denver, the ICFP has over 5,000 regular members and over 16,000 provisional members. The purpose of the ICFP is to facilitate public awareness of financial planning and to promote standards for the industry.

Education

Education is the foundation for continued growth in the field of financial planning. Many institutions across the country coordinate programs in this area. Both Golden Gate University (San Francisco) and California State University at San Diego offer a graduate degree program. Brigham Young University (Provo, Utah) has offered an undergraduate degree in financial planning for several years. The University of California, through its Extension Division, offers a statewide certificate program in financial planning. Some of the other institutions offering degree programs in financial planning include: California State University at Fresno, Georgia State University, Drake University, Des Moines, Iowa, and Wright State University, Dayton, Ohio.

The College for Financial Planning in Denver originated the Certified Financial Planner (CFP) program, which is one of the most widely recognized designations in the industry. The American College in Bryn Mawr, Pennsylvania, sponsors a series of courses leading to the designation of Chartered Financial Consultant. The designation of Chartered Financial Analyst (CFA) can be earned on completion of a three-part home study program.

Several other institutions are beginning financial planning programs. Some offer courses through the business department, others in the home economics or family science department. In addition, the American Institute of Certified Public Accountants is studying the field in terms of recognizing financial planning as an accredited specialty. Growth in the field reflects recognition of the need for technically trained planners in a complex financial world.

Responding to this need, the College for Financial Planning and the Institute of Certified Financial Planners have formed the International Board of Standards and Practices for Certified Financial Planners (IBCFP). The new board is responsible for establishing educational and testing standards for the CFP examinations, as well as awarding the CFP designation.

The CFP examination is now open to those enrolled in financial planning programs approved by the IBCFP. The board intends that these open CFP examinations will bring uniformity in national testing and provide the standard for regulating financial planners.

Research

The growth of financial planning did not go unnoticed by research and marketing institutions. In 1979, SRI International (formerly Stanford Research Institute) conducted a comprehensive study of this new field. SRI projected enormous growth for the industry, which would be slowed only by a lack of qualified planners.

The SRI research provided the first major analysis of market segments for financial services, based on net worth and income stream. It also identified the so-called "mass market" for planning, and projected an influx of new planners to support the growing need for financial services.

The report prepared by SRI indicated that banks, insurance companies, law firms, mass retailers, and accounting firms would join independent financial planners in tapping this growing market. Since that initial report, the marketplace has witnessed the entrance of giant conglomerates such as Sears, American Express, and Prudential-Bache. Additionally, banking institutions and insurance organizations routinely advertise financial planning services or products.

Each of these organizations is vying for an identifiable segment of the marketplace. This competition, in turn, generates tremendous pressure for diversified services, products, and fully automated planning systems, as well as a growing need for trained individuals.

The extent of future industry growth and who will provide these services are exciting questions. The answers will make fortunes for successful organizations and result in insolvency for others.

Furthermore, increasingly sophisticated clients will demand answers and an accurate assessment of alternatives. Inevitably, success will be determined by the knowledge, integrity, and attitude of the individual financial planner. And integrity and ethical conduct will bring the industry heightened public stature.

Conflicts of Interest

As with other professionals, financial planners are not immune to conflicts. Perhaps the most prominent disagreement is between planners who charge flat fees or hourly rates and those who are compensated by commissions from the sale of products. The question of fee-based or commission-based financial planning is the subject of extensive debate.

It is argued on the one hand that few clients can afford a truly customized financial plan. On the other hand, if planners can sell only one product, they may not plan objectively. A client once described such a company salesperson in discouraging terms: "Everything he said we needed, we already had." This "financial" salesperson did not analyze the client's present position, but merely promoted a product. This is not financial planning.

Those practitioners who charge fees and also sell products may offer a middle ground. However, full disclosure of the compensation structure must be made to each prospective client.

On both ends of the spectrum and in the categories in between, much controversy has been caused by the following major elements.

1. **Money.** How are financial planners being compensated? Is it through commission from the sale of a product, through a flat fee, or through an hourly rate?
2. **Time.** Do the planners spend sufficient time analyzing and assessing the client's position before recommendations are made? Or do the planners spend *more* time than necessary, because they are charging an hourly rate?
3. **Technical Knowledge.** Do planners have the technical education and training to handle the client's financial concerns? From what area or discipline have they entered the financial planning field?
4. **Product Knowledge.** Are planners sufficiently versed in all products that would be beneficial to clients? Also are planners aware of the track record of a specific product?

The answers to these questions can vary with individual planners. The matrix in Illustration 1.1 can be used as a self-analysis exercise for practitioners to determine their degree of objectivity. The first choice is made by selecting the specific category of planner. The next step is to review each aspect of the matrix—money, time, technical information, product knowledge—and determine how strong the conflict is. For example, in the category of fee only, planners may feel their technical knowledge is excellent and thereby place 1 point in that box because they perceive little conflict. On the other hand, the fee planner may give themselves 3 points in the box under product knowledge because of a perceived area of weakness and therefore conflict. The next step is to add all the points in each box and total the score. The scoring system is found at the bottom of the chart.

Illustration 1-1 Conflict of Interest Matrix

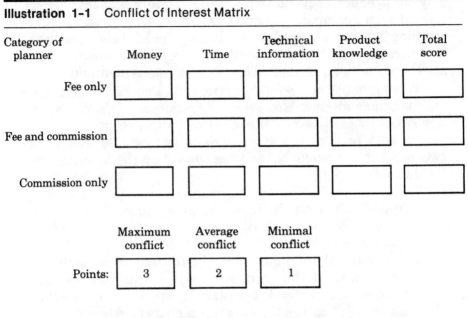

Category of planner	Money	Time	Technical information	Product knowledge	Total score
Fee only					
Fee and commission					
Commission only					

	Maximum conflict	Average conflict	Minimal conflict
Points:	3	2	1

Scoring: Each category can receive a minimum of 4 and a maximum of 12 points.

4-6 points: Minimal conflict
7-9 points: Average conflict
10-12 points: Maximum conflict

This matrix of conflicts reveals that most planners are involved in controversy and inherent contradictions. One category of planner is not innately positive or negative. Rather, the key points to remember in minimizing potential conflict are:

- Integrity.
- Awareness and sensitivity to client needs.
- Acting in the client's best interests.
- Possessing the appropriate education, training, and licenses.
- Full disclosure.
- Remaining in contact and staying abreast of changes.

Regulatory Restrictions

To charge fees for analysis, a financial planner, or his or her firm, must be a Registered Investment Advisor (RIA) listed with the

Securities and Exchange Commission (SEC). State registration may also be necessary. To become an RIA requires a fee, filling out form ADV in triplicate, and submitting both to the SEC. At this time (1986), there are no specific testing requirements. Charging fees for specific investment advice without being an RIA is a violation of the Securities Act of 1940.

For those who sell products, it is essential to possess the appropriate license. For example, to sell securities it is necessary to pass one of the exams administered by the National Association of Securities Dealers (NASD). There are numerous categories of tests that must be passed, depending on the type of product one wishes to sell. A Series 7 exam enables planners to sell stocks, bonds, mutual funds, real estate investment trusts, and limited partnerships. The other exams are more limited in scope and allow only a specific product to be sold, such as mutual funds (Series 6), commodities (Series 3), and limited partnerships (Series 22). A word of warning: Planners should not attempt to circumvent these registration requirements by selling products that they do not *personally* classify as securities. However, determining whether an investment should be classified as a security is not always easy. According to one official from the California Department of Corporations, "when in doubt, consider everything to be a security." Thus, if financial planners wish to sell products, they must be properly licensed.

To take the securities exam, an individual must first be associated with a *broker/dealer*. Broker/dealers are individuals or organizations that have met the SEC's financial and regulatory requirements. They are engaged in buying and selling securities, both for their own accounts and for those of others. As a matter of course, the NASD will not allow individuals the opportunity to sit for most of the exams unless they are sponsored by a broker/dealer. (Note: an exception is provided through the Series 2 exam, which is for non-broker/dealer members.) On successful completion of the test, the individual is then a registered representative of the broker/dealer.

To promote high ethical standards, broker/dealers are required to join the NASD, which is a self-regulating organization. The NASD oversees the professional conduct of its members. Furthermore, all broker/dealers must become members of the Securities Investor Protection Corporation (SIPC). The SIPC is a nonprofit corporation created by Congress in 1970. It offers certain protections against financial loss to the clients of broker/

dealers that fail. Protection limits are $500,000 per client, with the exception of cash accounts which are limited to $100,000 per customer.

Broker/dealers are important to financial planners. They serve as the first screening level for products. If a security is not on the broker/dealer's list of approved products to sell, it is illegal for a financial planner to sell the investment to clients.

There are many legal restrictions on selling products or charging for financial advice. However, government regulatory bodies are uncertain as to their overall responsibility in terms of financial planning. Compounding these legal issues is the fact that, although warned against earlier, some planners claim immunity from security laws and therefore do not register.

Against this background, many states have introduced legislation to regulate financial planning. Regulation is becoming a hotly contested issue, with certain industries seeking to be excluded. However, it appears legislation may eventually require that individual financial planners:

- Pass an examination.
- Possess at least minimum education or training.
- Have a certain level of experience (as through an internship).
- Participate in continuing education courses.
- Provide written disclosure of commissions, fees, or special interests.

These regulations indicate that, as with all emerging professions, financial planning is undergoing dramatic changes. Currently, there are no "typical" or "required" methods of performing services. But, as fiduciary responsibilities are better defined and the industry achieves more recognition, financial planners will need increasing knowledge. The basic information financial planners must possess is the subject of this book.

CHAPTER TWO

Data Gathering and Analysis of Financial Statements

The first step in financial planning is gathering the necessary data. This information must be sufficient to obtain a clear picture and pattern of the client's current situation. In turn, the value of this process will be directly related to the accuracy and completeness of the information obtained.

Data gathering is often a painstaking process because clients either may not see the significance of certain information or may not wish to reveal everything. It is especially important to be aware of any essential hidden facts. If the planning is for a couple or a family, planners must verify the objectives of each person involved and clarify important discrepancies before proceeding to the analysis stage.

To facilitate data gathering and analysis, it is essential to use a data intake form or questionnaire. The questionnaire should be as brief as possible while obtaining all necessary information. Few people appreciate a 40-page document which, realistically, could be condensed to a dozen pages. Specialized questionnaires may be used to handle specific needs such as business planning.

THE QUESTIONNAIRE

Exhibit 2.1 (Confidential Financial Analysis Questionnaire) shows the type of basic information that must be obtained. Because clients often tend to give inaccurate responses to tax questions, other documentation will also be necessary. It is essential for a planner to obtain copies of the client's last three years' tax returns. A tax return, unless it is fraudulent, contains a great

---

Exhibit 2-1 Confidential Financial Analysis Questionnaire

PART I.   PERSONAL DATA

Name _____ SS# _____ Age _____

Birthdate ____/____/____ Birthplace _____ Occupation _____

Employer _____ Salary payment mode _____

Spouse's name _____ SS# _____ Age _____

Birthdate ____/____/____ Birthplace _____ Occupation _____

Employer _____ Salary payment mode _____

Home address _____
Street   City   Zip

Home   Work ⎱ Client: _____
phone _____ Phone ⎰ Spouse: _____

Business   Client: _____
address   Spouse: _____

Name of child	Age	Dependent	Date college begins	Cost (today)	Amount in place
		Yes ____ No ____			
		Yes ____ No ____			
		Yes ____ No ____			
		Yes ____ No ____			
		Yes ____ No ____			
Other dependents	*Age*	*Relationship*		*Amount of support*	

Advisors	Name	Address	Phone
Attorney			
Accountant			
Insurance agent			
Securities broker			
Other			

Exhibit 2-1   (*continued*)

Tax Information:	Last year	Prior year	Prior year
Federal tax paid	$_____	$_____	$_____
Federal taxable income	$_____	$_____	$_____
State tax paid	$_____	$_____	$_____
Estimated quarterly tax (this year)	$_____	$_____	$_____
Was the alternative minimum tax paid?	Yes _____		No _____

PART II.   PENSION AND RETIREMENT INFORMATION

	Client	Spouse
1. Type of current pension plan	_____	_____
2. Years of coverage	_____	_____
3. Percent vested	_____%	_____%
4. Annual contribution	$_____	$_____
5. Value of account	$_____	$_____
6. Rate of return	_____%	_____%
7. Number of social security quarters	_____	_____
8. Amount in IRA account	$_____	$_____
9. Amount in TSA account		
10. Amount in any deferred compensation plans	$_____	$_____
11. Balance of previous pension plans	$_____	$_____
12. How many years before retirement?	$_____	$_____
13. Desired monthly income (today's dollars)	_____	_____
14. a. Name another source of retirement income	$_____	$_____
b. What is the amount this will provide?	_____	_____
15. Amount of retirement income needed for surviving spouse	$_____	$_____
	$_____	$_____

Exhibit 2-1 (*continued*)

PART III. INCOME AND EXPENSES

1. Do you expect a significant change in income? _____ What is the amount? _____
2. Are you interested in reducing your living expenses to better achieve your financial goals? _____ Do you have a formal monthly budget? _____
3. How much do you think you should save and invest annually? _____
4. How much money would you want in a highly liquid form for emergency reserves? _____

Annual Income	Client	Spouse
Salary, bonus, commission, etc.	$_____	$_____
Self-employment (net)	_____	_____
Pensions, social security	_____	_____
Interest and dividends	_____	_____
Net rents/royalties	_____	_____
Investments	_____	_____
Alimony/child support	_____	_____
Other	_____	_____
Combined total:		$_____

Annual Living Expenses

Fixed Category	Amount	Discretionary Category	Amount
Housing (rent/mortgage)	$_____	Clothing and cleaning	$_____
House insurance	_____	Gifts	_____
Car:		Charities	_____
Oil and gas	_____	Education	_____
Insurance	_____	Personal care	_____
Repairs	_____	Household expenses/repairs	_____
Other transportation expenses	_____	Furniture and appliances	_____
Telephone	_____	Yard/pool maintenance	_____
Utilities	_____	Housekeeper	_____
Water, sewer, garbage	_____	Restaurants	_____
Groceries	_____	Entertainment/recreation	_____
Life/health/disability insurance	_____	Vacation/travel	_____
Medical/dental fees	_____	Pet care	_____
Alimony/child support	_____	Miscellaneous	_____
Child care	_____	Other (specify)	_____
Debt repayment	_____	Saving and investing	_____
Income taxes	_____	Unaccounted-for cash	_____
Social security taxes	_____		
Retirement contribution	_____		
Other (specify)	_____		
Total:	$_____	Total:	$_____
		Combined Total:	$_____

Exhibit 2-1 *(continued)*

PART IV. INVENTORY OF ASSETS

Cash and cash equivalents

Type of account	Amount	Interest rate	Date of maturity	Location	How titled—ownership
Checking					
Savings					
Certificates of deposit					
Money market funds					
Treasury bills					
Series EE and HH					
Other					

Total: $ _____

Exhibit 2-1 (continued)

Stocks, bonds, mutual funds

Name of company	Number of shares	Date acquired	Cost or basis	Current value	Annual yield (percent)	How titled— ownership

Total $_____

Real estate	Date acquired	Cost or basis	Fair market value	Mortgage balance(s)	Interest rate	How titled—ownership
Personal residence						
Second Home (cabin, etc)						
Rental						
Rental						
Other						

Total: $_____ $_____

Limited partnerships (leasing, real estate, oil and gas, etc.)

Type of program	Name of general partner	Amount invested	Date acquired	Tax write-off	Current value or income	How titled—ownership

Total: $_____

Exhibit 2-1 *(continued)*

Long-term miscellaneous assets	Date acquired	Cost or basis	Fair market value	How titled— ownership
Business assets				
Trust deeds				
Collectibles/antiques/art				
Receivables				
Employer stock options				
Annuities				
Others (specify)				

Personal assets	Date acquired	Cost or basis	Fair market value	How titled— ownership
Household furnishings				
Automobile(s)				
Recreational vehicles				
Jewelry/furs				
Other (specify)				

PART V. INVENTORY OF LIABILITIES

Outstanding obligations	Name of creditor	Original amount	Current balance	Interest rate	Maturity date	Repayment schedule
Credit cards						
Banks/S&Ls/Credit Union						
Family loans						
Investment liabilities						

Exhibit 2-1 (continued)

Outstanding obligations	Name of creditor	Original amount	Current balance	Interest rate	Maturity date	Repayment schedule
Securities margin loan						
Income tax liability						
Pending law suits						
Other (specify)						

Total: $ _____

PART VI. INSURANCE PROTECTION

Life insurance

Name of Insured	Name of company	Face amount	Cash value	Policy loan	Date issued	Annual premium

Present health status: Client _____ Spouse _____ . Any health concerns which may affect insurability? _____

Smoker/non-smoker: Client _____ Spouse _____

Explain: _____

Disability income insurance

Name of insured	Name of company	Monthly income benefit	Elimination period	Benefit period	Annual premium

What is the minimum amount of income needed if disabled? Client $ _____ Spouse $ _____

Health insurance

Name of insured	Name of company	Date issued	Maximum limits	Deductible	Annual premium

Do you have any unusual health problems? Describe: _____

Exhibit 2-1 (continued)

Automobile insurance

Auto	Name of company	Liability/collision/comprehensive	Deductible	Medical amount	Annual premium

Homeowners insurance

Property	Name of company	Fire Ins. (amount)	Extended coverage	Liability (umbrella coverage)	Deductible	Annual premium

Do you have replacement coverage on personal property? _____

Exhibit 2-1 (*continued*)

PART VII.   ESTATE PLANNING
1. Will: Client   _____ _____   Date of will   _____/_____/_____
           Spouse _____ _____   Date of will   _____/_____/_____
2. Trust: Client   _____ _____   Date of trust _____/_____/_____
           Spouse _____ _____   Date of trust _____/_____/_____

   Describe type of trust(s) and purpose(s) _____

   _____

3. Do you expect to receive gifts or an inheritance? _____

   Amount $_____ When? _____

4. Have you named a guardian for your minor children? _____

5. Do you have a basic estate plan? _____ Describe _____

   _____

   _____

6. Would you wish for your spouse to work if you died prematurely? _____

PART VIII.   FINANCIAL OBJECTIVES
1. What would you like to accomplish via this financial planning process?

   _____

2. What is your greatest concern about money? _____

   _____

3. Is there a major obstacle in reaching your financial goals? _____

   _____

4. Which of your present investments meet your objectives? _____

   _____

5. Are you presently considering any financial proposals, i.e. investments,

   insurance, tax shelters? _____

6. For what specific items do you wish to save your money?

Goal	Approximate dollar amount	Date desired
a. _____	_____	_____
b. _____	_____	_____
c. _____	_____	_____
d. _____	_____	_____

Exhibit 2-1 *(concluded)*

PART IX. RISK/RETURN PROFILE
1. Rate the following instruments of *savings* and *investment* with a circle indicating the *degree* of your preference.

	Low		Medium		High	
Savings accounts/money market funds	0	1	2	3	4	5
Government securities	0	1	2	3	4	5
Municipal bonds	0	1	2	3	4	5
Stocks and bonds	0	1	2	3	4	5
Annuities	0	1	2	3	4	5
Cable TV	0	1	2	3	4	5
Oil and gas	0	1	2	3	4	5
Cattle feeding and horse breeding	0	1	2	3	4	5
Research and development	0	1	2	3	4	5
Equipment leasing	0	1	2	3	4	5
Real estate (direct ownership and	0	1	2	3	4	5
partnerships)	0	1	2	3	4	5
Commodities	0	1	2	3	4	5
Gold and silver	0	1	2	3	4	5
Coins, diamonds, collectibles, art	0	1	2	3	4	5
Foreign currencies						

2. Circle the number to the right of each of the items below that most accurately reflects *your own* financial concerns.

	Low		Medium		High	
Current income	0	1	2	3	4	5
Future income	0	1	2	3	4	5
Liquidity	0	1	2	3	4	5
Safety of principal	0	1	2	3	4	5
Expanding standard of living	0	1	2	3	4	5
Investing and accumulating wealth	0	1	2	3	4	5
Inflation protection	0	1	2	3	4	5
Reducing or deferring taxes	0	1	2	3	4	5
Retirement planning	0	1	2	3	4	5
Providing an education fund	0	1	2	3	4	5
Insurance protection/cost	0	1	2	3	4	5
Developing an estate plan	0	1	2	3	4	5

---

deal of valuable information. It is also important for planners to obtain any booklets describing pension plans and fringe benefits received by the client. And of course, insurance policies should be analyzed and estate-planning documents examined.

Once the data are complete, the planner can synthesize important information and present it to the client for review. The basic tools for a financial assessment are often called *financial statements*. They include a *balance sheet* and an *income and expense statement*. It is also essential to obtain a budget profile to ascertain how a client manages cash flow.

With these tools, the financial planner can begin to see whether assets reflect objectives, to ascertain the type and extent of debt, and to determine whether lifestyle and income match. The planner can also determine whether emphasis has been placed on current consumption or accumulation objectives. These financial statements are simply decision-making tools. It is the planner's role to assess, analyze, and align the client's objectives and financial position. To accomplish this end, the first analysis tool is the *balance sheet* or *net worth statement*.

BALANCE SHEET

This statement lists the value of assets owned and the extent of outstanding debts. After subtracting liabilities from assets, the remaining value is *net worth*. Net worth then is really the equity clients have in their assets.

The purpose of the balance sheet is to allow clients to easily review where they stand and to decide whether to make any changes based on recommendations of the financial planner.

A balance sheet is needed for any of the following reasons: to obtain a loan, to determine insurance requirements, to plan for a divorce, or to prepare an estate plan. This net worth "picture" should be taken at least once a year for comparison and evaluation purposes.

With a balance sheet assets can be catagorized for clients to better understand the information and make any necessary decisions. Also, the format may change in relationship to an individual or an organization for whom it is designed. For example, a banker may require assets and liabilities to be classified in a certain manner in order to obtain a loan. One key point to remember is the end purpose for which the statement has been constructed.

Assets. Most individual balance sheets list assets according to their *liquidity*. This enables the planner to know which items can be used in an emergency or for repositioning the client's assets. *Liquid assets* include cash and assets that can be readily converted to cash at their current listed value within a short period (30 days or less). Marketable securities are included within the category of liquid assets, as is the cash value of life insurance which can usually be tapped within a couple of weeks.

Liabilities. Liabilities can also be categorized as short term or long term. Short-term liabilities include all debts due in one month or slightly longer, and which require use of liquid assets for payment. Debts that will be paid over more than one years' time are classified as long term.

It is interesting to note that one major difference between a corporate and a personal balance sheet is the valuation of assets. Generally Accepted Accounting Principles (GAAP) require corporations to list their assets at their original or *historical cost,* and there is also a reserve for depreciation. However, GAAP allows individuals to list their assets at *current* fair market value. GAAP requires reduction for the amount of taxes to be paid if all the assets were liquidated at this fair market value.

Sample Balance Sheet

Balance sheets come in many forms and styles. Table 2.1 is a sample.

This is the first piece of information for analyzing the client's position. The statement indicates that as of December 31, 1985, Sarah has a net worth of $78,000. The date is important for comparison purposes because situations are constantly changing. In the future, it will be important to see how Sarah's assets have grown and what specific changes she has chosen to make. Yearly net worth statements will verify whether Sarah has followed her planner's recommendations or chosen other alternatives. After reviewing the client's assets, the planner must determine whether the assets are aligned with the client's overall objectives.

Reconciliation of objectives. To determine whether a client's balance sheet matches stated objectives, or at least reflects lifestyle, the planner must ask the following questions:

1. Are the majority of assets in one category? (e.g., all real estate—no cash.)
2. Which assets are treasured and cannot be traded?
3. Which assets are liquid or nonliquid?
4. Are all the resources meeting the client's financial and tax objectives?
5. What resources can be repositioned?
6. Are investments producing tax problems or benefits?
7. How does converting assets to cash affect total assets and liabilities?
8. Is fair market value readily determinable and accurate?

Table 2-1

Balance Sheet
SARAH JONES
December 31, 1985

Assets

Liquid
Cash	$ 1,000	
Money market fund	15,000	
Marketable stocks	4,000	
Mutual fund	2,000	
Cash value life insurance ...	1,500	
Total liquid assets ...		23,500

Nonliquid
Residence	$100,000	
Automobile	6,000	
Personal property	15,000	
IRA	4,000	
Total nonliquid assets		125,000
Total assets			$148,500

Liabilities

Short Term
VISA	$ 100	
Master Card	200	
Total short-term liabilities		300

Long Term
Residence	$ 65,000	
Auto	3,200	
Bank loan	2,000	
Total long-term life liabilities		70,200
Total liabilities			$ 70,500
Net worth			$78,000

9. Which assets tend to be more risky?
10. Is the size of personal assets consistent with what the client can afford in relationship to their overall objectives?
11. What portion of assets can be used to meet maturing obligations?

Answering these questions will present a clearer picture of the client's situation. For example, if a client has all her investment assets in either money market funds or certificates of deposit, then she is receiving interest that is taxable as ordinary income. If she is in a high tax bracket, this is only compounding her problem.

Another key is to determine which assets can be repositioned if they are out of line with stated objectives. At this point, if a client's aims remain ambiguous and vague, a financial planner must help clarify them. Clarification is the predecessor to qualification of these objectives. To avoid any resemblance to an inquisition, the purpose of the assets and their relationship to the various types of risks and rewards must be reviewed.

Risk factors. One of the most important factors in analyzing assets is determining the degree of risk they involve. Risk is often defined in terms of loss or injury, or the degree of uncertainty of the outcome.

Assets may be associated with different types of risk.

Economic risk. Assets will react to various economic changes. During inflationary periods, costs increase and consequently, purchasing power declines. The opposite occurs during depressions or severe recessions because prices decline. Thus, the value of assets can increase or decline during economic cycles.

For example, with inflation the value of real estate increases. On the other hand, in a depression, real estate prices decline. When the price of a parcel of real estate falls below its outstanding debt, the owner will often walk away from it. This happened many times during the depression.

Interest rate risk. Many interest-producing assets, such as bonds, CDs, and preferred stocks, pay a fixed return over a period of time. As interest rates increase or decrease, the market value of these assets changes. For example, a 10-year, 12 percent government bond is assured of a 12 percent annual return over the life of the bond. But a sharp rise in prevailing interest rates would batter its resale value in the bond market. Of course, the bondholder in this case would suffer no loss of principal if he held the bond; but he would forego the higher interest return.

Business risk. Exposure to competition in the marketplace—or simply an unforeseen event—can dramatically affect a company's operations or a specific industry as a whole. When this occurs, net cash flows and profits can decrease and the potential for default on the company's outstanding debt can increase. An example of a very competitive industry is computers. Some investors obtained high profits by investing in new companies in this field, yet others lost money when a major industry shakeout took place in 1984.

Liquidity risk. Liquidity is the ability to quickly sell an asset at its current market price. Marketable securities are an example of a liquid asset because they can easily be traded at the current market price. (This, of course, does not mean that the securities won't be sold at a loss.) Compare this situation to the sale of a nonliquid asset such as real estate or an art collection. It may take several months or more to find a buyer who will pay the current market price. This type of asset could probably be sold quickly if the current market price were greatly reduced.

Taxation risk. Some assets will generate no tax liability, such as the sale of personal residence by a person age 55 or over. Other assets, such as certain tax shelters, can generate enormous problems at the time of acquisition or sale. Knowing the potential or incurred tax liability is essential in matching assets to objectives and in considering repositioning assets.

Political risk. Government actions can have a negative impact on assets. Through regulations, tax code changes, excise taxes, etc. the government can change the profitability of companies and the market value of assets.

Market risk. The mood of the investing community often fluctuates in dramatic and unpredictable ways. The market values of real assets and marketable securities are subject to these moods. For example, when the economy goes into a recession, investors become pessimistic about the future, and the stock market value of most companies declines—even of companies that are showing record profits.

Debt. To obtain an accurate financial picture, the planner must analyze the client's liabilities. Debt is an important aspect of personal financial planning. It is important to see whether individuals are averse to using debt or, conversely, whether they borrow money whenever they can.

The following set of questions will be helpful in assessing a client's attitude towards debt.

1. Which assets are debt financed—consumer durables or appreciating assets?
2. What percentage of leverage is used?
3. What is the repayment schedule of the debt and the interest rate?
4. What are the sources of repayment? For example, are they from asset conversion, cash flow from income, or creation of new loans to pay off old debt?

5. What trends can be observed in the client's liabilities? What habits have been established?

Debt ratio. One method of analyzing debt is to compute the ratio of total debt to total assets. Refer to Table 2.1, illustrated earlier, for the figures used in this calculation.

$$\text{Debt ratio:} \frac{\text{Total debts } \$\ 70,500}{\text{Total assets} \$148,500} = 47.47\%$$

The debt ratio reveals the extent to which assets are financed through borrowing. In the above case, for every dollar of assets, there is approximately 47 cents of debt. There are no hard rules on what is the perfect proportion of debt. Low debt reduces the degree of risk of loss in an economic downturn. It also reduces the potential of gain in a boom cycle. The key element is that leverage is favorable when assets earn more than the cost of debt. Net worth will be reduced when this is not the case.

Financial planners frequently see clients borrowing money by using credit cards. The finance charges for this type of credit can be as high as 20 percent. In addition, clients often do not use their cash savings to pay off this monthly debt, instead claiming a tax deduction. This is expensive because more is being paid in credit card interest than is earned on saving accounts.

INCOME AND EXPENSE STATEMENT

The income and expense statement is another financial document that reveals the economic health of the client. This statement determines whether there is any excess discretionary income (i.e., does the client consume all income or is there some left over for asset accumulation?)

Table 2.2 is a sample of this type of statement.

Income

The source of income is important. Is income from work, from investments, from a trust fund, or from relatives or friends?

Whatever the source, it is essential to know how stable and consistent it will remain. For example, a government employee with 25 years of service has a consistent salary source. The opposite would apply to an individual who just opened a new business. Also important is the length of time a client has been at a given income level.

Table 2-2

Income and Expense Statement
JACK AND MELLISA THOMPSON
For the year ending December 31, 1985

Annual Income	Client	Spouse
Salary, bonus, commission, etc.	$42,000	$45,000
Self-employment (net)	—	—
Pensions, social security	—	—
Interest	800	—
Dividends	—	—
Net rents/royalties	—	—
Investments	—	—
Other	—	—
Combined total		$87,800

Annual Living Expenses

Fixed Category	Amount	Discretionary Category	Amount
Housing (rent/mortgage) . . .	$14,000	Clothing and cleaning	$ 3,000
Real estate taxes	1,900	Charities, gifts (personal)	2,000
Home insurance	300	Education	2,000
Car insurance	1,300	Personal care	500
Transportation		Household expenses and repairs . . .	1,500
(commuting)	500	Furniture and appliances	2,000
Utilities and telephone	3,000	Yard/pool maintenance	—
Groceries	2,400	Housekeeper	1,000
Life/health/disability ins. . . .	1,120	Restaurants	4,000
Medical/dental fees	500	Entertainment/recreation	1,000
Alimony/child support	—	Vacation/travel	3,000
Child care	—	Pet care	—
Debt repayment	11,000	Miscellaneous	—
Income taxes	16,000	Savings and investing	—
Social security taxes	5,940	Other (specify)	—
Retirement contribution . . .	—	Unaccounted-for cash	9,840
Other (specify)	—		
Total	$57,960	Total	$29,840

Combined total $87,800

If income is from investments, how reliable and predictable is it? What, if any, is the potential for income growth? This is especially important during retirement, because income requirements increase with inflation. And regardless of a client's stage in the life cycle, does the income stream match his or her lifestyle? In other words, are a client's spending habits too high?

Finally, how does the level of investment asset accumulation compare with the level of income? Table 2.2 shows an annual income of close to $90,000. How much is set aside for investments?

Does a comparison with the net worth statement show that investment assets have been accumulated? To make an accurate assessment, it would be important to know how long this level of income has been earned.

Expenses

This is the section of the income and expense statement that many would like to forget. In the example, it appears the clients have certainly forgotten a great deal of their expenses. For instance, Jack and Mellisa are unable to account for almost $10,000 of expenses. In analyzing the statement, a planner would want to consider the following questions:

1. Which expenses are fixed and which are discretionary? Can some expense be switched to another category?
2. Have all expenses been included and accurately recorded?
3. Are any expenses excessive, given the client's overall objectives?
4. To what extent is future income being tied up?

Through analysis, the financial planner can fill in another piece of the puzzle—namely, how well the client manages cash flow. This is essential for predicting or anticipating future needs.

Cash-Flow Management

An important and integral segment of financial planning is knowing where a client's money goes. This is really very fundamental, because spending habits cannot be approved or changed without this knowledge. Who enjoys tracking their expenses? Probably no one. But it is very difficult to make good decisions on future investments, retirement goals, or major purchases without going through this process.

One purpose of cash-flow management is to determine the amount of discretionary income. In this context, it is *not* up to financial planners to specifically determine how clients should spend their money. Nor should they impose their value judgments on the lifestyles or spending habits of their clients. Rather, the role of a planner is to point out aspects of spending patterns that positively or negatively affect financial objectives. It is up to individual clients to determine whether they will continue in a wrong direction or seek to change.

Assisting clients in determining whether their cash-flow management is aligned with their objectives is the first step. To begin, planners will note when income is received and when it is disbursed. Timing is critical. A client could have a significant sum in a low-interest or no-interest account until the expenses are paid. For example, if Sarah sold stock in a taxable transaction, how long does she have before the taxes are due? During this time, she should earn the highest rate, not leave the funds in a low-yielding savings account. Consistently managing income in this manner will produce significant benefits over time.

Some people constantly borrow from the future to cover current living expenses. Most commonly, they borrow against future salary increases or bonuses to pay for daily spending. If this is happening, planners must intervene and help the client recognize the impact of this behavior on his or her financial objectives. In this situation, the client's values must be clarified before any further decisions can be made.

In sum, if clients are living beyond their means, what will encourage them to change this pattern? The answer lies in their values, such as fear of bankruptcy. Clients must not become so attached to borrowing that they feel borrowed money belongs to them. Money borrowed is meant to be paid back.

Tracking Expenses

Regardless of where clients are on the cash flow continuum, it is necessary for them to review expenses. Although this is basic, many individuals cannot specify either their annual or monthly expenses. There is a middle ground between tracking every cent spent and having unaccounted spending of hundreds or thousands of dollars each month.

If a client has sufficient excess discretionary income to achieve objectives, then reviewing a budget statement may not be necessary. Or the client may already be setting aside a specific percentage of income for saving and investments. Whatever legal methods clients use to meet present cash-flow needs and long-term objectives is fine. For those who have budget problems, however, a systematic approach to tracking expenses is essential.

Tracking expenses involves a number of steps:

Step 1. Record all expenses. The process can be quantified if there are checks, receipts, charge card statements, and an entry log for cash expenses or checks written for cash.

Step 2. Categorize expenses. By subdividing expenses, it is easier to see patterns and spot problem areas. It is especially important to observe debt service and determine whether it is appropriate or excessive.

Step 3. Evaluate and rank expenses. Clients at this point have to decide whether they like what they see in their spending patterns, or whether they must alter their behavior. Planners can assist clients in ranking expenses and determining which ones might be eliminated, if reductions are essential.

Step 4. Revise and plan expenses. Revising and planning at this stage allow clients to follow through with objectives they have set. This plan is not considered to be locked in concrete. Rather, it begins a new cycle, which will be repeated until the objectives are achieved.

In the final analysis, the responsibility for changing expenses rests with clients. Financial planners can only use the art of persuasion, which may include showing clients their potential, with and without change.

Budget

Budgeting is one area clients will try to avoid because it is tedious and time-consuming. Nevertheless, for many clients budgeting is an essential step, and for others it should be mandatory before they begin a comprehensive financial plan. There are specific instances in which a budget is needed. A good example would be planning for retirement. Retirement planning can be long range or short range. However, at least one year prior to retirement, a client should have an "ACT AS IF MONTH." A budget is drawn, based on known sources of income *during* retirement. Then the client spends one month living on that income. If long-range planning was done, there should be no rude awakenings. If problems develop during the month, it is imperative to review all expenses to see which ones can be reduced or eliminated. It would be unfortunate if, after retirement, an individual could not make ends meet and therefore had to return to work.

Debt and Deficits

Wisely utilizing debt—"other people's money"—can assist in creating enormous wealth. However, *overleveraging* or borrowing too much can lead to prolonged poverty. To determine the appropriate level of debt for a specific client, financial planners will:

1. Look at the client's stage in the life cycle.
2. Calculate the client's debt ratio.
3. Determine what percentage of debts are used to finance appreciating versus depreciating assets.
4. Determine the interest rate on each debt.
5. Determine whether the client is borrowing to pay current living expenses.
6. Ascertain whether the client budgets in advance to pay for large expenses such as real estate taxes, insurance premiums, or large items.

Expense Patterns

The key to identifying expense patterns is to determine how a client handles both everyday and unusual expenses. If there are problems, realignment of assets will not be easy and will probably take time. To get back in financial shape, the client should consider changing his or her debt level by:

1. Determining whether the net yield on savings and investing is less than the net cost of borrowing. If it is, the client should utilize as much of savings as possible to pay off the highest interest rate charges first.

For example, Dave and Margaret had $6,000 in a money market account yielding between 8.5 and 9.5 percent. They also had VISA and MasterCard bills of $3,500 at 19.5 percent interest. In this case, they were going backward on their net worth. The reason for this is that it cost them more to borrow than they were receiving from their money market fund.

2. Establishing a habit of paying off all high-interest loans as quickly as possible, unless the asset is increasing more than the cost of borrowing.

3. Attempting to borrow only for appreciating assets. If this is impractical, searching for loans with the lowest interest rate and up-front interest charges.

4. Not collateralizing loans with savings. There will always be an out-of-pocket net cost in this instance. And savings cannot be withdrawn in case of an emergency if they are pledged as collateral. Conservative clients should pay cash rather than finance purchases in this manner.

5. Obtaining a preapproved line of credit. There is usually no charge for obtaining this type of loan until the money is borrowed. It is important to establish lines of credit before they are necessary.

6. Not borrowing simply to obtain a tax deduction for the interest paid. No one is in a 100 percent tax bracket. (To determine the tax consequences of borrowing and saving, turn to Chapter 6.)

Although the federal government has enormous deficits, individuals cannot maintain the same type of standard. Government budgets, deficits, and debts can be explained by analysts, politicians, and economists. However, planners cannot explain away a client's debt structure, which may prevent a client from reaching his or her objectives.

CHAPTER THREE

Risk Management: Insurance

Many things are managed in life, such as emotions, time, money, talents, and of course, taxes. One thing that financial planners help their clients manage is risk. There is a potential for significant financial loss if the concepts of risk management are ignored. It would be truly pathetic to see a client's hard-earned net worth fall apart because of improper risk management.

Obviously, it is impossible to plan for every potentially damaging situation. However, there are categories under which loss can be defined and quantified: death, disability, health, accident, casualty, and liability. It is in these areas that planners must operate.

To manage risk, there first must be an awareness of it. The type of loss must be definable and manageable.

Second, the magnitude of a risk must be known, as well as the degree and extent of potential damage. How costly can it be? Third, various methods of managing risk must be reviewed to determine which are most appropriate.

The ultimate goal, of course, is to control risk. If control is impossible, then determining the best way to manage risk is essential. The following techniques help clients reduce the risk of loss.

Avoid Risk. Refraining from doing certain things can minimize risk significantly.

Reduce Risk. Clients can lessen risk by taking specific precautionary steps.

Retain Risk. Full responsibility for a loss is assumed. This is the concept behind *self-insurance* where people use their own funds to cover any loss rather than purchasing insurance. Caution must be exercised when utilizing this technique, because inability to pay for the loss could be disastrous. Also, the potential frequency of loss must be considered to determine whether this technique is feasible.

Transfer of Risk. In this instance, the risk is shifted to another. This frequently happens when waivers of liability are signed, for example when going on a rafting trip or for children on a Scouting expedition. However, the most frequent method of transferring risk is to purchase insurance.

Insurance minimizes or eliminates a financial loss due to the uncertainty of future events. However, not all risks are insurable. The following are the principles on which insurance is based:

Nonspeculative. If a risk, such as gambling, produces either a profit or a loss, it is not insurable.

Nonintentional. The potential risk is not premeditated. It must be accidental, and not deliberate. An exception is suicide, usually if committed more than two years after a policy is purchased. In this case, suicide is classified as a mental illness, and all illnesses are considered accidental and, therefore, insurable.

Insurable Interest. One must have a specific relationship to the insured, say a wife insuring the life of her husband.

Definite Loss. The loss must be real, not counterfeit. It must actually occur, as in death verified by an attending physician or a coroner's office.

Measurable Loss. The cost of the peril is quantifiable. For example, the hospital costs can be determined and matched to the type of coverage purchased. Of course, it is impossible to measure the value of a human life. In this instance, the face value of the insurance coverage will determine the loss.

Economic Hardship. The peril causes substantial economic concern. It would not be financially feasible to cover minimal losses because of an insurance company's actual costs, expense margin, and profit margin.

Large Groups of Homogeneous Exposure. The cause of loss or peril must affect a significant portion of the population because risks faced by large groups can be statistically predicted. It then becomes economically feasible to offer protection through an insurance policy, because the odds are low that everyone in the covered population will suffer the same loss at the same time.

Furthermore, no change in a policy is valid unless approved by the executive officer of a company. Consequently, any verbal agreements made by an insurance representative are not binding on a company. On the other hand, any misstatement or concealment on the part of the insured can cancel the contract. However, there is a *incontestability clause.* This states that after a given time, usually two to three years from issuance of the policy, the insurer cannot void a contract because false information was given. (A misstatement of age is rectified by crediting the insured with the amount of protection the premium would have purchased at the correct age.)

The purpose of the contract is to *indemnify* the insured against any covered losses. This concept means the insured should be placed in the same financial position after the loss as before the event occurred. Exceptions include life insurance, replacement cost insurance, and valued insurance. Life insurance is not an indemnity contract because the value of a lost life cannot be precisely measured. Replacement coverage is a special feature often found in a homeowner's policy. With this insurance, no deduction is taken for wear and tear on the property. Instead, the cost of replacing the loss is paid by the company. Valued insurance will pay the stated amount of loss. These policies are generally limited to objects for which the market value may be difficult to determine, such as collector's items and art objects.

Another important aspect of indemnity is *subrogation.* This right permits the insurance company to take measures against a person or company responsible for the insured's losses, thus preventing the insured from collecting from two sources—his or her own insurance company *and* the party responsible for the damage.

Insurance is an acceptable, and certainly the most common, form of risk management. However, caution must be exercised when using this or any other technique for managing risk. The criteria for selecting insurance should include the following:

1. Applicability of coverage—does the insurance fit the client's needs?
2. Nature of coverage—under what circumstances will a company pay?
3. Cost of coverage—is premium expense in line with potential benefits?
4. Financial status of the insurance company—what is the rating of the company with regard to its financial reserves? (Best's ratings are often used for evaluation.)

RISK OF DEATH

Although humans are not born with an expiration date, the inevitability of death becomes more obvious with age. Death can prevent people from reaching their financial destination. However, if the deceased has no dependents or beneficiaries and wishes to make no charitable bequests, then there may be little need for risk management in case of death. On the other hand, if there are dependents, loved ones, or favorite charities, then death could bring financial disaster.

Insurance protection provides a solution to this financial dilemma. As a matter of course, insuring a persons's life is one of the most common forms of coverage. There are many different types of life insurance, but all are based on mortality tables which list the statistical number of deaths that will occur in each age group. They also show that the older a person becomes, the greater the chance of dying.

Besides mortality rates, insurance companies must charge for overhead expenses and their cost of money, as well as a profit. These elements comprise the premium cost for a prespecified amount of life insurance.

To determine the type of life insurance to buy, the insured would want to consider several factors:

1. For how long is the protection needed?
2. For whom and for what specific purpose is the coverage?
3. What is the cost of the protection, both now and over time?

The following common categories of life insurance will answer these questions.

Term. This type of insurance simply provides coverage based on the face value of the protection purchased. For example, if the face value of the policy is $100,000, then this is the amount paid at death. Most term insurance policies are periodically renewable until age 99. However, during each renewal period (annually, every five years, etc.), the cost increases. Term protection is the least expensive type of insurance for younger people, but the cost dramatically increases for those above age 50. This coverage is often used if the insured wants to purchase significant protection at younger ages or for short periods of time.

Decreasing term. In this instance, the premium does not increase, but the face value or benefits decrease each year. The most common type of decreasing term is mortgage insurance. In many instances caution should be exercised in selecting decreasing term. For example, if inflation is increasing costs, do clients want protection that decreases each year? If a client's needs are decreasing, the coverage would be suitable. Regardless, purchasing this type of insurance through a mortgage company may not provide sufficient overall protection and may be more expensive than if the policy is bought directly through an insurance company.

Deposit term.   Here a deposit is made in the first year to obtain a guaranteed premium rate over a specific period, usually 10 years. At the end of the period, the deposit plus interest is returned. This is an example of an initial overpayment to achieve a perceived benefit, namely lower yearly premiums. Actual premium costs and the time value of money should be used to verify if the premiums are lower.

Whole life.   This category of life insurance is also known as *ordinary life, permanent life,* and *cash value life.* There is a significant difference between term insurance and whole life insurance. In the latter, the premiums stay the same. Thus, one is overpaying for pure protection in the early years and underpaying for coverage in later years. The overpayment is sufficient to cover a company's experienced mortality rate and overhead costs and provide a cash value benefit. The cash value is often referred to as a *forced savings plan.* Illustration 3.1 shows how the money placed in whole life increases over time. However, when the insured dies, the beneficiaries receive only the face value. The cash value belongs to the insurance company on the death of the insured.

Everyone's needs are different. Thus, there may be times when one type of insurance is more beneficial than another. Many analogies have been used to describe the various types of insurance. Term insurance has been compared to renting a

Illustration 3–1   Whole Life Insurance

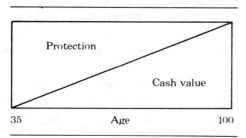

35   Age   100

house, while whole life has been compared to owning a house and building up equity. However, analogies often fail to set the picture straight. It is important to remember that in the case of whole life, individuals do not receive a tax deduction for buying the insurance. Also, the cash value of the policy can only be realized while the insured is alive.

On the other hand, overpayment of premiums will subsequently build up cash value that can be used to pay future premiums. Or the cash value may be borrowed. However, this aspect must be viewed from the perspective of the time value of money, as money is worth less in the future.

Initially persuasive arguments have been made for the savings feature in whole life policies. If money goes through a client's hands like water through a sieve, then a compulsory obligation such as whole life insurance may be suitable. However, a client without any financial discipline rarely follows through with the financial planning process.

Endowment. It is an extremely expensive form of whole life insurance. The premiums are very high, so that at the end of a specified period, say 20 years, the cash value equals the face value of the policy. This type of policy is often used for retirement. However, the cash value increases slowly, and the premiums are paid using aftertax dollars.

Interest-sensitive life products. As the economic climate rapidly changed and the need to stay competitive increased, insurance companies began to introduce new types of life insurance contracts. These products differ from traditional whole life policies because the cash value buildup is sensitive to current market rates of return. These interest-sensitive policies also offer more diversity in selecting premium payments and face value coverage. Another key characteristic of these innovative policies is that insurance companies have transferred the risk of interest rate fluctuations to the insured. The following are examples of interest-sensitive policies:

Universal life. The policy has a flexible premium that accumulates cash value which is used to purchase renewable term insurance. The term insurance premium is deducted from the cash fund. Thus, universal life separates the protection element from the savings portion. And the savings or cash-value element is responsive to current interest rates.

Variable life. Whereas universal life offers payment flexibility, variable life offers investment flexibility. Under this type of coverage the premium is fixed, but the insured may select such vehicles as stocks, bonds, or money market funds for the accumulation of cash value in his or her policies. The investment results are credited directly either to the policy reserves or to the cash value account. Thus, the investment risk is transferred to the insured. Overall death benefits will depend on investment results, but there is a guaranteed minimum amount of protection.

Adjustable life. With this type of coverage, the insured chooses the death benefit and makes premium payments corresponding to the benefit chosen. The flexibility offered allows the insurance to be purchased based on the insured's ability to pay. However, once selected, the face amount and the premiums are fixed.

Individual interest-sensitive life insurance policies should be examined because the terms vary from policy to policy. For example, does the entire cash value earn the new current money market yields, or only amounts above $5,000 or $10,000? Are the rates competitive? If current interest rates are used, how long are they guaranteed? And what is the risk tolerance of insureds who select investments for the cash value element in their insurance policies?

The previous questions will not be sufficient in analyzing all cash value or interest-sensitive policies. Insurance companies have significantly different contracts. Consequently, it is important to obtain a concrete picture of benefits in relationship to premium payments. To accomplish this comparison, the cash values and premium costs of whole life insurance and term insurance are calculated. An example of this procedure is shown in Table 3.1. The specific steps require using the financial functions of a calculator which reveal the cost of coverage in present value terms. (Note: These time value concepts are explained in Chapter 4. For purposes of the following calculations, the insured's discount factor or conservative after-tax rate of return on investments is 8%.)

FOR CASH VALUE LIFE INSURANCE

Step 1
The present value benefit of the 11th year's cash value is $5,973. The formula is future value *(FV)*: $13,926; interest *(i)*: 8%; time *(n)*: 11; Press: present value *(PV)*, Displays: $5,973.

Table 3-1 Example of Time Value Comparison for Insurance (cash value example)

Year	Premium	Cash Value
1	$1,858	$ 118
2	1,858	1,194
3	1,858	2,340
4	1,858	3,552
5	1,858	4,836
6	1,858	6,190
7	1,858	7,613
8	1,858	9,101
9	1,858	10,649
10	1,858	12,258
11	1,858	13,926

Assumptions:
Male, age 53.
Smoker.
Good health classification.
Discount rate is 8 percent.

Table 3-2 Example of Time Value Comparison for Insurance (term policy)

Year	Premium	Present Value of Premium
1	$ 409	$ 409
2	478	443
3	561	481
4	659	523
5	791	581
6	1,018	692
7	1,316	829
8	1,708	997
9	2,155	1,164
10	2,726	1,364
11	3,411	1,580
Total		$9,063

Assumptions:
Male, age 53.
Smoker.
Good health classification.
Discount rate is 8 percent.

Step 2

The present value *(PV)* cost of paying $1,858 in premiums over 11 years is $14,325. The formula for this equation is as follows:

To find the Present Value (Note: Beginning of the period):

PMT: $1,858 (premium)
n: 11 (years)
i: 8% (discount factor)
=
PV: $14,325 (present value)

Step 3

Subtracting the net cash value of $5,973 from $14,325 leaves a present value cost of $8,352.

Table 3.2 shows the present value cost of a term insurance policy. The present value of this type of protection is $9,063.

In using this method of comparison, one sees that it is only in the 11th year that the cash value policy is less expensive. Therefore, how long does the client need this insurance? Also, what is the cross-over point in cost comparison if the cash value earns at a lesser rate?

If a client dies during the 11-year period, it would have been less expensive to have term insurance, because beneficiaries do not receive the cash value of the whole life policy. The whole life policy would be beneficial if a client needed the protection for more than 11 years. Also, if the need ended after 11 years, the client would receive the cash value from the insurance company. In that instance, the net present value would be the least expensive with the whole life policy. The key is the date of death.

It is interesting that if an older client discovers a new need for insurance protection, a cash value plan will often be less costly over a relatively short period of time. It is important to compare not only the cost, but also the length of the client's need. For young clients with a great need for protection it makes sense to purchase the largest amount of insurance for the least cost. The difference in premium between cash value and the term policy can be invested, perhaps in a qualified plan to reduce taxes and help improve cash flow.

Quantifying the Need

It is not wise to use rules of thumb or to pick figures from national averages to determine how much life insurance is required. Even the often-used method of adding a zero to the insured's salary (with a $30,000 annual salary, the estimated life insurance need would be $300,000), is not satisfactory. Rather, it would be more appropriate to use the form in Table 3.3 to determine how much life insurance a client needs. The purpose of the form is not to make the beneficiaries rich, but simply to enable survivors to maintain a standard of living that an untimely death can reduce.

The manner of death should not be a factor in determining the level of benefits. A beneficiary's needs are the same regardless of whether death is the result of cancer, heart attack, or an accident. Thus, coverage for accidental death would *not* be appropriate.

In completing the form it is important to observe the following steps: (NOTE: The numbers correspond to lines on the form):

1. Probate and administration fees vary from state to state.
2. The specific computations involving federal estate taxes are handled in a subsequent chapter. There may also be state death taxes.

Table 3-3 Determining the Amount of Insurance Needed

Immediate Cash Requirements
 1. Probate and administration fees   _____
 2. Estate taxes   _____
 3. Funeral expenses   _____
 4. Home mortgage debt   _____
 5. All other debts   _____
 6. Emergency and readjustment fund   _____
 7. Education fund   _____
 8. Other   _____
 9. Total fixed requirements   _____
Survivor Income Needs

	Period A with Children	Period B to Retirement	Age ____ to Life
10. Number of months	_____	_____	_____
11. Income required	_____	_____	_____
12. Income sources:			
Salary	_____	_____	_____
Social security	_____	_____	_____
Pension benefits	_____	_____	_____
Investments	_____	_____	_____
Other	_____	_____	_____
13. Surplus (deficit)	_____	_____	_____
14. Present value of deficit	_____	_____	_____
15. **Total present value of income deficit**			_____

16. **Total capital need**   _____
17. Less:
    Present life insurance   _____
    Value of assets which would be sold   _____
18. Net insurance surplus (deficit)   _____

3. Funeral expenses should be based on client objectives and local cost.
4. At death, home mortgage repayment should be based on the amount of debt, consistency of the interest rate, and the beneficiaries' cash flow. The results of this analysis will reveal if it is appropriate to pay off the mortgage.
5. Installment debt, bank notes, and any other miscellaneous debts should be included in this category.
6. To cover unexpected contingencies, a client may want to provide from two to six months of living expenses.
7. This amount should closely reflect the type of education parents desire for their children.
8. Any unique categories are included here.

9. This is the first portion of the total amount required.

   The next calculations deal with the ongoing income needs of the survivor(s). Each period can be divided according to the specific requirements of the clients. In this instance, period A's income need includes the surviving spouse with the responsibility of providing for the children. Period B is prior to the survivor's retirement, and period C is after retirement. The number of time periods can be increased or decreased as the situation warrants.

10. Each period can be segmented according to the client's needs. The number of months in each period is essential.

11. A realistic calculation of living expenses for each period must be made. The expected rate of inflation can be built into the model.

12. All sources of consistent income should be reflected.

13. The income sources listed in 12 are subtracted from the income required in 11. The resulting answer may be a surplus or a deficit.

14. The insurance need is also dependent on the present value of any future deficits.

15. The deficits in line 14 are added together.

16. Then lines 9 and 15 are added to find the total capital need.

17. The current amount of life insurance coverage is subtracted, as is the value of any assets to be sold. These assets should not be included in line 12 since they will not be available for income.

18. This shows whether the client has excess or insufficient protection.

Table 3.4 illustrates how the life insurance requirement is determined.

Fred and Sharon Smith are both age 52. They have one child, Amy, who is 19 and has just finished her freshman year in college. Fred has a $60,000 whole life policy he bought 18 years ago, but no life insurance through work. The Smith's estimate the following costs: remaining college costs of $12,000, emergency fund of $5,000, mortgage balance of $90,000, administrative fee of $2,000, no estate taxes, and funeral expenses of $1,000.

For simplicity, it is assumed Fred dies first, and Sharon has indicated the following: income requirement of $35,000 for the

Table 3-4 Determining the Amount of Insurance Needed (Fred and Sharon Smith)

Immediate Cash Requirements
1. Probate and administration fees	$ 2,000	
2. Estate taxes	-0-	
3. Funeral expenses	1,000	
4. Home mortgage debt	90,000	
5. All other debts	9,000	
6. Emergency and readjustment fund	5,000	
7. Education fund	12,000	
8. Other	-0-	
9. Total fixed requirements		$119,000

Survivor Income Needs

	Period A with Child	Period B to Retirement	Age 65 to 90
10. Number of months	36	120	300
11. Income required	$ 2,917	$ 2,853	$ 4,430
12. Monthly income sources:			
Salary	$ 1,917	$ 2,283	-0-
Social security	-0-	-0-	$ 1,000
Pension benefits	-0-	-0-	$ 2,494
Investments	300	300	300
Other	-0-	-0-	-0-
13. Monthly surplus (deficit)	(700)	(270)	(636)
14. Present value of deficit	22,013	16,458*	24,720
15. **Total present value of income deficit**			$ 63,192

16. **Total capital need**		$182,192
17. Less:		
Present life insurance	$60,000	
Value of assets which would be sold	-0-	
18. Net insurance surplus (deficit)		($122,192)

---

*This is a two-step process:

	PMT	i	n	PV
Step 1	$270	.75	120	$21,314
	FV	i	n	PV
Step 2	$21,314	9	3	$16,458

---

next three years; after Amy is out of school Sharon wants the equivalent purchasing power of $30,000 per year. Sharon currently earns $23,000 per year, and expects a 6 percent annual salary increase, until retirement, when she is scheduled to receive a monthly benefit of $2,494. The estimated social security benefit in 13 years is $990 per month. The example assumes: a 4.5 per cent inflation rate, an aftertax rate of return of 9 percent, no employee pension benefits for Fred, and $300 per month for investment income, without using the principal.

The example is only an estimate that must be revised periodically. However, it can be used as a starting point to clarify a client's overall goals and objectives. For example, the mortgage debt may not be paid in full. Then its effect on the income requirement must be reevaluated. Also, the category "age 65 to 90" may not be sufficiently long, and the impact of inflation may have to be recalculated. The figures will change, based on the assumptions—inflation rate, discount yield, salary, and retirement income projections—selected. Financial planners must point out the advantages and disadvantages of the assumptions used.

COST

Once the insurance projection is completed, a review of the client's current policies is in order. A client's health and smoking status is important because the cost increases if the client's health is poor. The rate the client is paying must be compared with all available potential alternatives.

Life insurance costs are quoted in terms of the price per thousand dollars of coverage. Therefore, to readily identify the cost of various policies, it is essential to reduce each policy payment to the cost per each thousand dollars of protection.

The following examples will illustrate the cost.

Comparison cost for term insurance. Comparing the cost per thousand of term policies is not difficult. Simply divide the total cost per year by the per-thousand face amount of coverage:

Face amount of coverage	$120,000
Net coverage in thousands (amount/1,000)	120
Premium (include policy fee)	280
Divide line 3 by line 2	($280/120)
Cost per thousand	$2.34

Comparison cost for whole life. Table 3.5 can be used in analyzing the cost of a whole life policy. It can also be used to determine the cost after borrowing the cash value. (Note: In choosing the interest rate or the discount rate—usually referred to as the opportunity cost, that is, the cost of deferring the use of money to a later date—consider selecting a *conservative* aftertax rate of return. In case of death, it is important that insurance proceeds can be invested at that rate.)

Table 3-5 Net Cost per Thousand for Whole Life

1. Face amount of coverage	_____	
2. Less: current cash value*	_____	
3. Net coverage		_____
4. Net coverage per thousand (Line 3 divided by $1,000)		_____
5. Premium	_____	
6. Less: increase in cash value†	_____	
7. Plus: interest lost on cash value (Line 2 plus line 6 × opportunity cost, e.g., 8 percent yield)	_____	
8. Real cost		_____
9. Net cost per thousand (line 8 divided by line 4)		_____

*To find the *current* cash value, simply refer to the cash value chart in the client's policy. The cash value is based on age at the time the policy was purchased and the length of time the policy has been owned.

†The *increase in cash value* is the amount of interest earned over the present year.

Table 3-6 Net Cost per Thousand for Whole Life (Fred and Sharon Smith)

1. Face amount of coverage	$60,000	
2. Less: current cash value	16,500	
3. Net coverage		$43,500
4. Net coverage per thousand (Line 3 divided by $1,000)		43.5
5. Premium	$ 1,700	
6. Less: increase in cash value	1,500	
7. Plus: interest lost on cash value (Line 2 plus line 6 × opportunity cost, e.g., 8 percent yield)	1,440	
8. Real cost		$ 1,670
9. Net cost per thousand (line 8 divided by line 4)		$ 37.70

The case of Fred and Sharon Smith, Table 3.6, will once again illustrate this example. Fred's $60,000 whole life policy was purchased over 18 years ago. The annual premium is $1,700, and last year's cash value was $16,500. The cash value is scheduled to be $300 per thousand this year.

Before a decision is made to terminate or change the whole life policy, another calculation must be made. Planners must know what the cost per thousand is if the insured borrows the cash value. The format for this calculation is given in Table 3.7.

Table 3-7 Borrowing Cash Value

1. Annual premium   _____
2. Less: cash value increase   _____
3. Less: annual dividend (if applicable)   _____
4. Less: taxes saved from interest paid   _____
5. Plus: loan of $____ × net interest ____%   _____
6. Equals net premium cost   _____
7. Face amount   _____
8. Less: current cash value   _____
9. Less: cash value increase this year
   (and dividends if applicable)   _____
10. Net coverage   _____
11. Net coverage per thousand   _____
12. Net cost per thousand (divide line 6 by line 11)   _____

With comparison of the present cost per thousand and the previously mentioned measurement tools, financial planners can appropriately analyze a client's insurance requirements.

Human lives can never be replaced, and insurance has never been intended to accomplish that feat. Life insurance can only protect against financial disaster. To minimize this devastating loss, the maximum amount of affordable protection should be purchased. The appropriate coverage should be based on a client's overall objectives and the results of time value calculations.

RISK OF DISABILITY

Recognizing the need to protect against disability is often difficult. Although most people realize the inevitability of death, few consider the odds of becoming disabled. Table 3.8 shows that the probability of disability is higher than the probability of death for many age groups.

Typically with disability, the income and the standard of living decrease. Consequently, in financial planning it is essential to reduce the effects of this type of risk. The most common way to minimize the danger is through purchase of disability insurance.

This type of coverage is meant to ensure an income stream. It also provides a source of funds for making up any deficits caused by reduction or cessation of income from inability to work. However, the purpose of disability insurance is not to provide more

Table 3-8 Disabled Working-Age Population, 1978 (in thousands)

Characteristic	Total Population	Severely Disabled	Disabled, but Not Severely*	Not Disabled
Total population	127,086	10,771	10,519	105,796
Race				
White	111,212	8,818	9,256	93,138
Nonwhite	15,212	1,953	1,263	12,657
Sex				
Male	63,120	4,610	5,339	53,171
Female	63,966	6,161	5,180	52,625
Age				
18 to 34	58,213	1,485	3,215	53,513
35 to 44	24,887	1,585	2,016	21,286
45 to 54	23,681	2,670	2,915	18,095
55 to 64	20,305	5,031	2,372	12,901

*Includes occupationally disabled and disabled with secondary work limitations.
SOURCE: Social Security Administration's Survey of Disability and Work, 1978.

income than would be available if a client were working. In fact, clients can only insure a portion of their income, because insurance companies believe earning a full salary is an incentive for returning to work. Thus, insurance companies have "double coverage" clauses. This means if a client has policies with several companies, each company will pay a proportionate amount of the prespecified percentage of salary. For example, Kelly earns $2,000 per month and has two policies, each designed to pay 60 percent of his monthly wages in case of disability. On being disabled, Kelly will receive $600 from each company for a total of $1,200. This combined limit is 60 percent of his salary.

Selecting the most appropriate disability coverage is not easy because a number of important characteristics must be taken into account. Perhaps the most important aspect to consider is the definition of disability: Is protection based on injury, sickness, or accident? Where does the disability have to originate? Must the disability occur at work, or will the client also be insured during nonworking hours?

The next distinguishing factor is the basis for coverage. This is usually divided into two categories: *own occupation* and *earnings only*. The own occupation contract insures against disability when clients are medically unable to resume work in their previous occupation. The earnings only, or residual contract, insures against a loss of income because of disability.

There are pros and cons to each type of contract. An important question is whether the insured's occupation is readily definable. It would be easy to ascertain whether a surgeon could perform surgery. However, it would be more difficult to determine that administrators or managers could not perform their duties. In the latter case it is more easily measurable if there is an earnings loss.

Other differences include the cost of coverage. The occupation contract is more expensive, but pays full benefits regardless of whether a client returns to work. (However, the work must be in another occupation to earn full benefits.) Conversely, an earnings-loss contract will not pay if a client is able to return to another line of work and earn the same amount. It would pay a proportionate amount if earnings from the new employment were substantially lower.

To determine the best type of coverage, it is important to focus on specific definable requirements of each occupation, as well as cost. If a client is partially disabled in one occupation but able to work in another, the earnings loss contract would pay a percentage of the lost income. Own occupation coverage would pay full benefits. A decision must be made as to whether income or lifestyle is being protected. In addition, several points must be considered. Can the client pay for more costly protection? Are the client's skills specifically definable? If the disability forces a job change, will the insurance company recognize the change as a different occupation?

If a brain surgeon switches to teaching, the insurance company will recognize the change. If a manager switches to a less-demanding management position, the insurance company can argue there has been no change in occupation. If the manager has own occupation coverage, a percentage of lost income would be paid, but not 100 percent of benefits.

Disability costs. Many important factors besides the age of the insured and the amount of the benefits determine how expensive disability insurance will be. The following contract provisions must be considered to determine the expense.

Elimination period. This is the time during which no disability benefits are paid to the insured. The longer the waiting period chosen, the less expensive the cost. Rates do not always go down proportionately, therefore a cost comparison must be made. The elimination period is comparable to self-insurance in that the insured is "covering" himself for that time. Hopefully, the client has sufficient assets to select a waiting period of between 90 and 180 days, depending on cost. However, the waiting period chosen may be as short as several days or as long as a few years.

Benefit period. Once the elimination period elapses, disability benefits will be paid for the length of time selected. The most common benefit periods are five years, to age 65, and life. The shorter the benefit period, the less expensive the cost of the insurance.

Guaranteed renewable. An insurance company must continue coverage as long as premiums are paid. The company may increase the cost of the premium, but only for a specific group or class of people, and not for selected individuals because of prior claims or current health.

Noncancelable. An insurance company may guarantee that the policy will be renewed. Specific rates may also be guaranteed. Therefore, the insured knows what the future cost of coverage will be. Premiums may be stable throughout the benefit period, or may increase at a predetermined rate and time. This type of policy is more expensive than guaranteed renewable.

Cost-of-living adjustment. The provision allows for increased benefits once the insured has been disabled for a specific period of time. However, there is no automatic increase provision prior to disability. Benefits can be adjusted upward or downward, based on the inflation index used. Benefits can never be adjusted below a base amount.

Zero day qualifies. With this provision, the insured does not have to be *totally* disabled for a certain period of time. It is essential if someone is suffering from a slowly debilitating disease. With this type of coverage, there would be no period of total disability before payments were made.

Maximum benefit. Benefits received under all group and individual policies and under government programs must be coordinated. For example, most contracts indicate how their benefits will interrelate with other disability benefits. This will vary from contract to contract. However, benefits usually will be reduced by:

1. Workers' compensation programs.
2. Proportionate amount of benefits from other disability policies.
3. Social security benefits.

Social Security benefits are based on a stringent definition of disability. Payments will not be made during the first five months of the disability and the disability must be projected to last for at least one year. The benefits are based on the amount of the insured's wages subject to social security. The maximum amount of disability coverage is usually 50 to 70 percent of a client's salary. Income from investments or interest from savings is not taken into account. Often, there is an overall benefit maximum of between $2,000 and $3,000 per month for various occupations.

MEDICAL PROTECTION

Most people are aware that sickness, injury, and disease, whether catastrophic or not, can devastate their financial future. Consequently, medical coverage is obtained through employers, government programs, medicare, or prepaid insurance plans. Regardless of the source, the purpose is to cover expenses due to ill health.

Common providers of this type of protection include health maintenance organizations (HMOs)—Kaiser-Permanente, INA-Cigna, or Family Health Plan, for example. Under an HMO plan, premiums are paid directly to the organization, which provides medical services and hospital facilities. A program can be sponsored by an employer or individuals can participate on their own.

There is usually an additional nominal charge per doctor's visit or for a prescription. Those enrolled in an HMO may usually use only that HMO's facilities and doctors. Some HMOs, however, allow limited exceptions for special types of illnesses or for accidents occurring outside their service area.

Other commonly used medical plans are Blue Cross and Blue Shield. Participants can join through an association such as an employee group or a fraternal organization. Individual coverage is also available.

With Blue Shield, the cost of doctors services are covered. This plan contracts with participating doctors who will accept payments according to a preplanned schedule. If a doctor is selected who does not participate in the plan, Blue Shield will pay the insured according to the fee schedule. The insured then pays the doctor and must make up any difference. Blue Cross plans cover hospital costs, both surgical and general medical services. Under both plans, participants or their employers pay a monthly fee for coverage.

Blue Cross and Blue Shield are the largest providers of group health insurance. The next largest are commercial insurance companies. There are also labor union and consumer cooperative medical coverage plans.

It is important to remember that medical insurance is based on indemnifying the insured against specific losses. Therefore, in theory, an individual would not receive reimbursement for more than actual expenses. To accomplish this, insurance companies attempt to coordinate any reimbursement payments with those of other companies.

The main determinant of the expense of medical coverage is the type of protection offered. The following are some of the more common aspects of medical insurance plans.

Hospital and surgical. Under this category, hospital room and board, surgery, physician nonsurgical services, laboratory expenses, X-ray expenses, and miscellaneous hospital expenses are covered. It is essential to know whether the period covered is determined by ailment or whether separate hospitalizations are treated individually even though the same illness is treated. Having to meet the same deductible for each hospital stay can be expensive. For example, Patrick is hospitalized twice within a nine-month period for the same knee injury. If his hospital deductible is $400, does it have to be paid twice? Or will the deductible apply only to the first visit, since the second visit was within a certain time period—e.g., a calendar year.

Also, limits on miscellaneous expenses should be reviewed. The policy will define which costs are reimbursable. Either a specific amount will be covered or a guideline of coverage will be provided. The key is to determine whether the coverage is reasonable.

Major medical. This type of policy is specifically designed to cover catastrophic illness. It is important to determine which specific services are covered and what the maximum benefit will be. For example, are maximum benefits paid per illness, by calendar year, or for the life of the policy? The significant aspects of major medical coverage include:

Deductible. The insured will have to pay a certain amount before any benefits are paid. The deductible can range from $100 to a few thousand dollars, and can be on a calendar year or a per-illness basis.

Coinsurance. The insured will also share the medical expense. In most instances, after the deductible has been reached, an insurance company will pay 80 percent and the insured will pay 20 percent, up to a prespecified limit, and the insurance company will pay 100 percent of the remainder.

Comprehensive medical. It covers medical expenses prescribed by a physician, whether in or out of a hospital. Again, the insured must be responsible for the deductible and the coinsurance costs.

While it is necessary to purchase protection against a catastrophic loss, attempting to cover all smaller injuries would be expensive. In addition, even major coverage should be considered carefully. The coinsurance clause in some policies could cause a significant financial hardship for some clients. For example, an extended hospital confinement could easily cost over $25,000. The insured could be liable for 20 percent of that figure or a lesser predesignated amount. Each insurance program also has various exclusions. Knowing which are applicable is important. The following are some of the common circumstances under which *no* medical benefits will be received:

- War, covered by government plans other than medicare.
- Services rendered were not reasonable and necessary, or not available in the United States.
- Cosmetic surgery, except if required by a physician.
- Preexisting conditions.

CASUALTY AND LIABILITY PROTECTION

With this category of insurance, clients are able to protect their homes, personal property, and cars against fire, theft, and various other types of damage. Liability coverage can also protect against lawsuits, which are proliferating at the moment. Most casualty and liability coverage is based on indemnity, that is, the insured cannot be compensated in excess of his or her economic loss.

AUTOMOBILE COVERAGE

Automobile insurance protects against the following losses.

Liability.

Split limit. With this coverage, the insurer pays legally obligated damages on behalf of the insured; legal defense for civil damages is also provided. Bodily injury protection usually is purchased in limits of $5,000/$10,000 to $500,000/$1 million. The first figure in each category is a limit per individual, the second is a limit per accident. Property-damage liability losses range from $5,000 to $50,000. These limits are quoted per accident without any limits in terms of specific items or persons.

Single limit. More realistic than the split-limit liability coverage ($100,000/300,000/50,000) is the single-limit protection. With this type of policy, a single maximum limit covers all losses, whether bodily injury or property damage. More and more policies are being written to include this type of protection.

Liability protection extends to other members of a household. It can also cover the insured while driving another individual's automobile. Therefore, the protection should be as broad as possible to cover other vehicles, such as rental cars or trucks.

Collision. The purpose of this insurance is to reimburse the insured for actual damages after the deductible has been paid. The actual cash value of a loss cannot exceed replacement cost minus depreciation of the car. Consequently, if a car is demolished in a collision with another car or a telephone pole, the amount recovered may not be sufficient to replace the destroyed car with a comparable one.

Comprehensive. Here the protection insures against damages that do not involve a collision. Examples include fire, theft, windstorm, smashed windows, and vandalism. Again, the maximum benefit is the cash value less any deductible.

Uninsured motorist and medical payments. These are two of the more common additional features the insured can purchase. Most states now require uninsured motorist coverage because of the large number of accidents involving motorists who drive without insurance. Medical coverage can be especially beneficial for passengers and minimize chances of personal litigation over medical bills.

HOMEOWNER'S AND RELATED COVERAGE

The classification includes homeowner's protection and renter's insurance, which covers the personal property of the renter.

There are several categories of peril to insure against. They are usually classified under the cause of the loss, such as fire, lightning, smoke, theft, explosion, vandalism, etc. Because it covers both real and personal property, the type of protection most commonly purchased is *homeowners.*

With this coverage, it is important to know whether there is an 80 percent-of-value requirement. If damage occurs, this clause would allow an insurance company to pay a proportionately smaller amount of benefits. Homeowners should also purchase the personal property replacement value benefit. With this feature, if a chair were destroyed in a fire, the insured owner would receive its replacement value, not its depreciated value. For example, the original cost of the chair was $600 and its current depreciated value is only $250. Without replacement protection, the insured would only receive $250, even though the same chair would now cost $750.

Finally, an umbrella liability policy can be attached to a homeowner's policy that would provide protection against a significant loss in which the insured was held personally liable. Limits of up to $1 million can be very inexpensive; a cost range of $100 to $300 is not uncommon for this type of coverage.

It is mandatory in financial planning to make sure clients have sufficient protection by determining the adequacy of their current policies. The cost of replacing possessions can prove overwhelming for the underinsured.

PART TWO

Quantitative Elements

CHAPTER FOUR

Time Value Concepts

TIME AND MONEY

Time is money! So goes an old saying, and many people consider time their most valuable asset. Some even gauge their lives by it. Without the parameter of time, financial planners could not measure their clients' objectives or compare their progress in reaching them.

Viewing time from the perspective of a child is occasionally helpful. For example, children think in terms of today. They will always take *now* for an answer in responding to a wish list. Financial planners should emulate a child's perspective when calculating and quantifying their client's goals, objectives, and investment yields. The concept of "now" being better than "later" is understood intuitively by children.

The concept of assessing the value of time is reduced to this: Money is worth more today than it will be tomorrow. If clients give up the use of money today, they must be compensated. This is imperative, because by keeping their money they could earn interest on it. Also, the dollars given up may never return, and even if they do, any future inflation would certainly decrease their purchasing power.

Compensation for dollars given up today is commonly referred to as the *opportunity cost*. Another standard term in valuing this cost is *interest*, which could be viewed as a "rental" charge for the use or receipt of money. The concept itself is readily understandable, but determining the degree of this compensation and the risk level is not always as easy.

Much financial decision making revolves around the appropriate use of money. Common concerns include whether to save, borrow, lend, or invest. The decision to either give money out or receive it is related to the time factor and the rate of interest. In its most basic form:

1. Take money now and give back more money later.
2. Give money now and expect to receive more money later.

Time value calculations enable planners to systematically measure the results of these financial decisions. The computations can also tell clients the dollar amount needed to reach their objectives or the amount of the current deficit. Consequently, time value calculations can help clients: (a) determine whether their goals are attainable or simply pipe dreams, (b) set priorities, (c) revise goals when necessary, and (d) evaluate investment yields.

To accomplish this evaluation, financial planners have various tools, including: algebraic equations, mathematical tables, interpolation, and calculators. The last device is proving increasingly popular because of the decreasing cost and ready availability of calculators with financial functions. These sophisticated calculators are easy to use and enable financial planners to quickly assess the impact of the time value of money—a factor that should never be discounted.

The end result of time value calculations is the beginning step in making certain financial decisions. The mundane procedure for computing these figures may seem unnecessarily time-consuming. However, it is essential for financial planners.

Computing these figures will enable planners to review assumptions and determine what is realistic. Without a thorough familiarity with how the time value numbers are derived, it will be difficult for planners to understand how goals should be changed or what an investment yields.

Components of Time Value Equations

The components of these calculations include the following:

- *Interest*—This is the price of using money. The term is also used to denote the inflation rate, or the investment yield and the discount rate which is the cost of exchanging money now for money later.
- *Time*—The duration of a span or period—how long the money is used.
- *Present Value*—The value of an amount today—how much it is worth right now.

- *Payment*—A specified amount of money that is paid or received at regular intervals over a specific period.
- *Future Value*—The value of an amount of money in the future, the opposite of present value.

Time Value Calculations Using a Calculator

If any three of these variables are given, the unknown variable can be found. Corresponding to these components are the financial functions available with a calculator or a computer.

i	interest
n	time
PV	present value
PMT	payment
FV	future value

For ease of use, a calculator should be selected that includes these financial functions as part of its program. Several models have financial function keys, including those made by Hewlett-Packard and Texas Instruments. Regardless of the model chosen, it is essential for financial planners to become thoroughly familiar with how the calculator operates. Effectively using this tool is simply a matter of repetition. The actual calculation sequence, memory functions, storage, and clearing sequence may differ. The operator's manual will explain the procedure. It is important to note that many calculator errors stem from improper clearing of the calculator as well as malfunctioning batteries.

The following time value calculations were computed on a Hewlett-Packard Model 12-C calculator. Other calculators may produce slight numerical differences due to different method of rounding numbers.

Planners can use six basic mathematical formulas to assess a client's present financial position and future objectives. Knowing when and how each category is used is the essential first step in this quantification process. Practicing the calculations is the next step in understanding and ensuring the reliability of the figures. In other words, repetition will minimize errors and increase knowledge.

First equation: Future value of a dollar.   This computation reveals the increased value of a single sum of money over a specific future time period. The question is often asked: If money is invested today, what will it be worth tomorrow? In Illustration 4.1, $1,000 invested today at 10 percent for three years is worth $1,331 at the end of that time.

Illustration 4–1 Value in Future Dollars

$$\begin{array}{cccc}
& & & \$1,331 \\
\$1,000 & & & \uparrow \\
\vdash & \vdash & \vdash & \vdash \\
0 & 1 & 2 & 3
\end{array}$$

Periods in years

CALCULATOR KEYSTROKES

Input:

PV: $1,000—The lump sum available today.
i: 10—Interest earned on the money.
n: 3—Length of period for compounding the money.

Press: FV

Displays: $1,331—The future value of the $1,000.

(Note: Many financial calculators would display $1,331 as a negative number. Consult your calculator manual.)

This calculation automatically computes a compound rate of return. The concept of *compound interest* is important. In contrast, with simple interest, if $100 is placed in an account paying 10 percent, then $10 would be received at the end of each year. After three years, there would be an accumulation of $30 in interest for a total value of $130. The following illustrates the increase in value:

Year 1 $100 × 10% = $10
Year 2 $100 × 10% = $10
Year 3 $100 × 10% = $10
                          $30 + $100 = $130

Had the investor placed the $100 in an account paying 10 percent *compound* annual interest, the individual would have received interest on the interest. At the end of three years, the account would have been worth $133.10

The following illustrates compounding:

Year 1 $100 × 10% = $10
Year 2 $110 × 10% = $11
Year 3 $121 × 10% = $12.10
                          $33.10 + $100 = $133.10

Illustration 4-2 Compound and Simple Interest

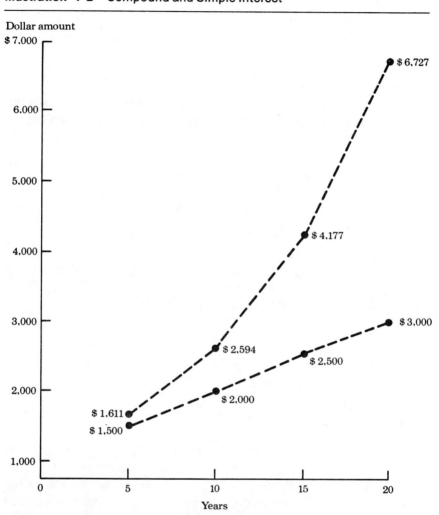

Assumptions: Present value is $1,000. Interest is 10 percent. Time is 20 years. Numbers are rounded.

Notice that the annual interest was added to the principal on which interest was paid. (Compounding can be done annually, semiannually, monthly, weekly, or daily.) The dramatic difference between simple and compound interest is revealed in Illustration 4.2.

APPLICATIONS

1. What will be the purchase price of a $10,000 car in 10 years, if the inflation rate is 9.5 percent?

Input:
PV: $10,000
i: 9.5
n: 10

Press: *FV*

Displays: $24,782

2. Jack Saenz invested $22,000 in a venture which is projected to grow at the rate of 13.25 percent per year. What will it be worth in four years?

Input:
PV: $22,000
i: 13.25
n: 4

Press: *FV*

Displays: $36,189

3. Katie Thompson is currently earning $21,000 per year. She expects to receive a 5 percent pay increase each year. How much will her income be in seven years?

Input:
PV: $21,000
i: 5
n: 7

Press: *FV*

Displays: $29,549

Second Equation: Future value of one dollar per period.   With this calculation, planners can determine the increased value of multiple payments over time. Often this accumulation is called an *annuity.* An annuity is defined as a series of fixed payments over a specified number of years. If the payment occurs at the end of every period, it is called an *ordinary annuity.* All payments made at the beginning of each period are called *annuity due.*

Over time, the difference between the future value of a payment made at the beginning of a period and those made at the end of a period is significant. This information is especially important for procrastinators. For example, $2,000 placed in an individual retirement account (IRA) each year for 25 years and earning 13 percent will amount to:

$351,700—beginning of period.
$311,239—end of period.

Illustration 4-3 Future Value of an Annuity (end of period)

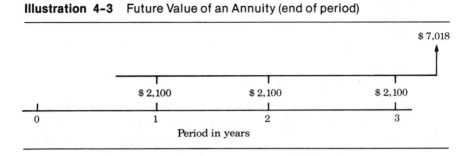

Unless otherwise specified, payments are received (or made) at the *end of a period*. For example, Fred is willing to save $2,100 per year for the next three years to buy a car. If he can earn 11 percent on his money, how much will he be able to afford? The problem is shown graphically in Illustration 4.3.

CALCULATOR KEYSTROKES

Input:
Payment (*PMT*): $2,100—Periodic amount.
        i: 11—Interest earned on savings.
       n: 3—Number of periods.

Press: *FV*
Displays: $7,018

APPLICATIONS

1. Sam invests $2,000 in an IRA every year and earns 12.8 percent. What is the value of the account at the end of the 18th year?

Input:
  PMT: $2,000
     i: 12.8
    n: 18
Press: *FV*
Displays: $120,954—End of period.
                 $136,436—Beginning of period.

2. Trice pays $300 each month for four years to buy a boat. The stated interest rate is 12 percent, compounded monthly. How much will she have paid for this boat? (Note: Time periods are calculated in months, four years × 12 months = 48. Interest is compounded monthly, 12%/12 months = 1% per month.)

Input:
>   *PMT:* $300
>   *i:* 1
>   *n:* 48

Press: *FV*

Displays: $18,367—End of period.
> $18,550—Beginning of period.

3. Becky intends to go to school for the next four years. Her annual costs are $3,200, increasing at the rate of 6 percent. How much will she have paid for her education?

Input:
>   *PMT:* $3,200
>   *i:* 6
>   *n:* 4

Press: *FV*

Displays: $13,999—End of period.
> $14,839—Beginning of period.

Third Equation—Present value of one dollar.   Present value is simply the reverse of compounding. By knowing what something is worth in the future, it is possible to find out its value today. This is often referred to as *discounting a future amount* to determine its current worth. For instance, receiving $2,000 in one year at a 10 percent rate is the same as receiving $1,818 today, as Illustration 4.4 shows.

CALCULATOR KEYSTROKES

Input:
>   *FV:* $2,000—value of the amount in the future.
>   *i:* 10   —interest rate or discount rate.
>   *n:* 1   —period of time.

Press: *PV*

Displays: $1,818

Illustration 4-4   Present Value

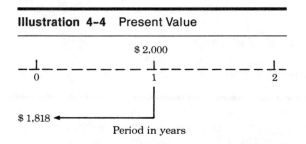

Period in years

The above illustration compares the value of future funds with current cost. With this formula it is possible to see whether a client's future one-time goals are realistic. For example, a budget may be devised to purchase a $9,000 car in five years. However, if the inflation rate were as high as 11 percent, a comparable car today would cost $5,341. If a client would not accept a $5,341 car today, he would not want a $9,000 car in five years. The more devastating examples do not deal with consumer purchases, which can be changed, but with the projections for retirement or education.

APPLICATIONS

1. A client wants $125,000 in 10 years. She can earn 9 percent on her money. How much should she invest this year?

Input:
   FV: $125,000
   i: 9
   n: 10
Press: *PV*
Displays: $52,801

2. John Duffy is scheduled to repay $21,000 at the end of the year. The discount rate is 12 percent. How much would be required to pay off the loan today?

Input:
   FV: $21,000
   i: 12
   n: 1
Press: *PV*
Displays: $18,750

3. Chris will receive a $50,000 settlement from an insurance company at the end of five years. If the inflation rate is 9 percent, what is the present value of this settlement?

Input:
   FV: $50,000
   i: 9
   n: 5
Press: *PV*
Displays: $32,497

Fourth Equation: Present value of one dollar per period. This equation is necessary to value a series of payments that extend

---

Illustration 4-5 Present Value per Period

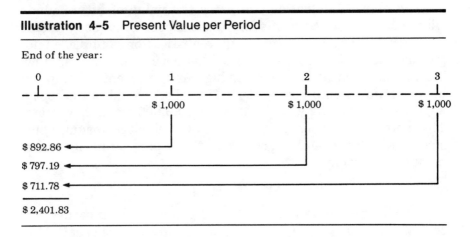

End of the year:

into the future, that is, an *annuity*. The present value of an annuity is simply the opposite of compounding. Thus, in calculating the present value of a future series of payments, planners discount the value back to today.

For instance, as shown in Illustration 4.5, Rita will receive $1,000 at the end of each year for three years. What is the present value of these payments if the *discount* (interest) rate is 12 percent?

CALCULATOR KEYSTROKES

Input:
   PMT: $1,000—periodic amount, occurs more than once.
      i: 12—interest rate or discount rate per period.
      n: 3—compounding periods.
Press: *PV*

Displays: $2,401.83

If payments were *received* at the *beginning* of each period, the present value would be $2,690.05.

APPLICATIONS

1. George is taking back a second trust deed on the house he is selling. He will receive $5,000 at the end of every year for seven years. The discount rate is 9 percent. What is the present value of this stream of income?

Input:
   PMT: $5,000
      i: 9
      n: 7

Press: *PV*

Displays: $25,164.76—End of period.

$27,429.59—Beginning of period.

2. Jasper takes a leave of absence for three years. He needs $10,000 per year to supplement his expenses. How much would he deposit to cover these expenses if he earns 12 percent?

Input:
    PMT: $10,000
        i: 12
        n: 3

Press: *PV*

Displays: $24,018.31—End of period.

$26,900.51—Beginning of period.

3. The terms of a divorce agreement include a monthly payment of $1,000 for five years. If the discount rate is 12 percent, how much is the settlement worth today?

Input:
    PMT: $1,000
        i: 1
        n: 60

Press: *PV*

Displays: $44,955.03—End of period.

$45,404.59—Beginning of period.

All the preceding examples assume that the compounding period is equal to the payment period. Before proceeding to the next level, it is essential to discuss equivalent relationships. Here, it is important to know the real interest rate when compounding periods are different from payment periods.

INTEREST RATES

The first distinction is between nominal and effective interest rates. The *nominal rate* is the stated interest rate in borrowing or lending. The *effective rate* is the real rate of interest earned based on allowing interest to accumulate each year, compounded at intervals during that year (daily, monthly, quarterly, etc.).

The following shows the effective rate of 9 percent compounded monthly:

Input:
    n: 12   The number of compounding periods
                          per year.

i: 9.0/12 = .75   The interest rate per compounding period.

PV: 1   Enter 1 for present value.

Press: FV

Displays: 1.0938

Input:

 n: 1   Enter 1 for the number of compounding periods.

Press: i:

Displays: 9.381   The annual effective interest rate.

It is important to remember that the H-P 12C calculator was used for these computations. Other calculators may display the numbers as positive or negative. The numbers are also rounded.

APPLICATIONS

The following examples further illustrate how often it is necessary to calculate the effective rate.

1. A bank is advertising 10 percent interest payments compounded quarterly. What is the effective annual yield?

Input:

 PV: 1

 i: 10%/4 = 2.5

 n: 4

Press: FV

Displays: 1.1038

Input:

 n: 1

Press: i

Displays: 10.381

2. Francisco deposits $1,000 at the *beginning* of each quarter for five years. He earns 9 percent annual interest compounded monthly. How much will he have after five years?

Step A

Calculate the equivalent interest rate.

Compounding Periods per Year	Rate per Compounding Period (percent)	Enter 1 for PV	Compute FV
n	i	PV	Press FV
12	9/12 = .75	1	Displays: 1.093806898

Payments per Year	Compute **Equivalent Interest** *Rate*
Input: *n*	Press: *i*
4	Displays: 2.266917195

Step B
This step completes the calculation. There will be rounding differences between various calculators, if the calculator is not cleared before proceeding.

Input:
  n: 20 [total number of payments (5 × 4)]
  i: 2.2669 (rounded equivalent interest rate)
  PMT: $1,000

Press: *FV*

Displays: $25,519.39   Beginning of period.
        $24,953.71   End of period.

3. How much will $10,000 grow to in 15 years with an annual rate of 6 percent compounded monthly?

Step A
Calculate equivalent interest rate.

Input:
  n: 12
  i: 6/12
  PV: 1

Press: *FV*
Displays: −1.061677812
Input:
  n: 1
Press: *i*
Displays: 6.1677812

Step B
Calculation formula

Input:
  i: 6.1677812
  PV: 10,000
  n: 15

Press: *FV*

Displays: $24,540.94

PUTTING IT TOGETHER

As previously stated, the purpose of these exercises is to give planners a working knowledge of the actual computation process. Now these equations can be used to calculate a client's objectives. This quantification process can demonstrate how close clients are to achieving their goals.

Table 4.1 shows the Goal Accumulation Worksheet and indicates the necessary calculator steps. *After* the answer is displayed in Step 6, 0 must be entered on the *PV* key, and *PMT* must be pressed. Then the calculator will display the annual contribution necessary for a client to reach a specified objective.

Now comes the difficult part. Can these goals be met? The clients in the above illustration will have to set aside $34,842 today to reach their goals over the next five years. If this is not possible, they can set aside $12,562 the first year, and as each goal is achieved, reduce the annual savings by a like amount. For example, after the first year, when the video recorder is purchased, they may reduce the $12,562 annual contribution by $1,050. The second year's savings will then be $11,512, and so on, as each year's goal is achieved.

This type of worksheet can be used to answer a few key questions, including:

- Does the client have sufficient funds to cover expenses?
- What other items must be given up to gain the possessions desired?
- Can any of the purchases be assigned a priority or delayed?
- Is the client willing to reevaluate objectives?

Educational Needs

The present and future value functions can be readily used to calculate education needs, as shown in Illustration 4.6.

The calculation for a client's educational funding requirement can be accomplished in a two-step process:

Table 4-1 Goal Accumulation Worksheet

Item desired:	Step 1 Input Present Cost	Step 2 Input Time Factor	Step 3 Input Inflation Factor		Step 4 Calculate Future Cost	Step 5 Input Investment Yield	Step 6 Calculate Lump Sum Amount	Step 7 Calculate Annual Amount
	PV	n	i 7%	=	FV	i 9%	(PV)	(PMT)
Car	$10,000	5	7%		$14,025.51	9%	$ 9,116	$ 2,344
Vacation	4,000	2	8		4,665.60	9	3,927	2,232
Furniture	6,000	3	8		7,558.00	9	5,836	2,306
Pool	15,000	4	9		21,174.00	9	15,000	4,630
Video recorder	1,000	1	5		1,050.00	9	963	1,050
Lump sum	$36,000			=	$48,472.11		$34,842	$12,562

Total needed today: $34,842
Total needed annual contribution: $12,562
(Note: The $12,562 amount is for the first year only.
Each subsequent year's cost is reduced when the goal is achieved.)

Illustration 4-6 Educational Funding Requirement

$5,000	$5,300	$5,618	$5,955	$6,312	$6,691	$7,093

```
  .__ l_____ l_____ l_____ l_____ l_____ l_____ l_
     0       1       2       3       4       5       6

$  4,598 ◄──9%──────────────────┘       │       │       │
$  4,472 ◄──9──────────────────────────┘       │       │
$  4,349 ◄──9──────────────────────────────────┘       │
$  4,229 ◄──9──────────────────────────────────────────┘

$ 17,648
```

Assumptions:
Today's cost: $5,000 per year
Years in school: 4
Years to start: 3
Inflation factor: 6%
Investment yield: 9% after tax

Step 1
   Input:
   PV: 5,000
     i: 6
     n: 3
   Press: *FV*
   Display: $5,955

By simply changing *n* to 4, 5, and 6, the total future value will be displayed.

Step 2
To determine the present value cost or the annual contribution necessary to fund this objective, the following keystrokes are used. It is important to remember that after *PV* is calculated, a 0 is entered in *PV* and the *PMT* key is pressed.

Input

FV	i	n	Press PV	*or* PMT
$5,955	9%	3	$ 4,598	1,817
6,312	9	4	4,472	1,380
6,691	9	5	4,349	1,118
7,093	9	6	4,229	943
Total			$17,648	$5,258

The lump sum needed today is $17,648. The annual investment made at the end of each year is $5,258. As in the previous calculation, this annual contribution is reduced as each year of education is funded. For example, the $5,258 is reduced by $1,817 when the education costs for that year are paid.

Fifth equation: Future value of a growing annuity. The future value—inflation factor equation reveals how a constant percentage increase affects a series of cash flows. (This is also known as a *growing annuity*.) It is an essential computation when the rate of inflation is different from the rate earned on the investment. With most calculators, it is easier to work by first finding the present value of a growing annuity. Then the future value can be ascertained.

Sixth equation: Present value of a growing annuity. Once again, present value is simply the reverse of compounding. However, the format will be changed slightly for input into the calculator. In this instance, the series of outflows or inflows is growing at one rate and the discount rate is growing at another.

The first step involves solving for the present value. In Illustration 4.7, Samantha just won a state lottery. She can accept $5,000 today or receive $1,000 per year, increasing at the rate of 12 percent, over a five-year period. If her discount rate is 10 percent, which alternative should she take?

Planners must be especially concerned with when Samantha receives her annual payment. Illustrations 4.7 and 4.8 show the difference between receiving the annuity at the beginning or the end of a period.

Illustration 4-7   Annuity Received at the Beginning of the Period

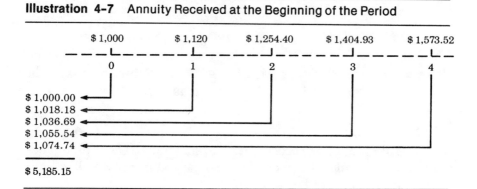

If Samantha receives her payment at the end of the period the numbers are:

Illustration 4-8 Annuity Received at the End of the Period (increasing with first payment)

| | $ 1,120 | $ 1,254.40 | $ 1,404.93 | $ 1,573.52 | $ 1,762.34 |

```
        $ 1,120      $ 1,254.40    $ 1,404.93    $ 1,573.52    $ 1,762.34
  _|_ _ _ _ _|_ _ _ _ _|_ _ _ _ _|_ _ _ _ _|_ _ _ _ _|_ _
   0         1         2         3         4         5
```

$ 1,018.18
$ 1,036.69
$ 1,055.54
$ 1,074.74
$ 1,094.27

$ 5,279.42

By using the following keystrokes, this problem can be solved quickly. The future value can also be ascertained using this sequence.

Step 1

In this equation it should be noted that the discount rate can be defined as the yield or the investment rate of return. The growth rate can be described as the inflation factor. The first step is to find an equivalent interest rate for this calculation.

$$\frac{1 + \text{Discount rate (investment yield)}}{1 + \text{Growth rate (inflation)}} - 1 \times 100 = i$$

or:

$$\frac{1.10}{1.12} = .9821 - 1 = -.017857 \times 100 = -1.7857$$

The equivalent interest rate is now -1.7857. (Note the answer is a *negative* number and must be inputed as such).

Step 2

Now the planner can proceed with the solution to the problem because the equivalent rate or yield per period is known. The keystrokes can be entered as follows:

Input:

$\quad\quad i:\quad -1.7857$

$\quad\quad n:\quad 5$

$\quad PMT:\quad \$1,000$

Press: PV

Displays: $5,279.43 (end of period value)

Press: BEGIN PV

Displays: $5,185.15 (beginning of period value)

Step 3

Continue with the following keystrokes, the calculator should not be cleared.

Input:

$\quad PMT:\quad$ 0 (no more payments are added)

$\quad\quad n:\quad$ 10 (growth rate)

Press: FV

Display: $8,350.74 (When payments are made at the beginning of a period.)

To find the future value of the payments with an end-of-period calculation, one must reenter the present value.

Input: PV $5,279.42

Press: FV

Displays: $8,502.56

These steps sometimes seem difficult, but financial planners are often called on to resolve problems involving the time value of money. Applying time value concepts to a client's concerns will take the client one step closer to achieving them.

The following applications of time value concepts are routinely handled by financial planners. They should be studied carefully.

APPLICATIONS

1. Gail wants to retire from her teaching job in 20 years. She has estimated her benefits as $20,000 during her first year of retirement. How much will that $20,000 be worth in today's dollars if the rate of inflation is 9 percent? Answer: $3,568.62.

2. Fred would like to receive a lump sum of money each year. How much will he pay today for an annuity yielding 12 percent per year, paying $30,000 at the *end* of each year for six years? Answer: $123,342.

3. You want to invest $5,000 today and in each of the next five years for a total of six equal investments. How much will you have accumulated after six years, assuming an 11 percent per year return? Answer: $43,916. (These payments were made at the *beginning* of each period.)

4. Your client will have accumulated $750,000 of investment assets by the time she retires in 20 years. Upon retirement, she plans to use this sum to purchase an annuity that will provide monthly income over 25 years, and earn 10 percent per year. What would be the size of each monthly payment? (Note: Payout is at the beginning of every period.) Answer: $6,758.93.

5. Debbie is obtaining a $45,000 second trust deed to be amortized over 15 years. If the interest rate is 15 percent compounded monthly, what is her monthly payment? Answer: $629.81.

6. Should Fernando buy or lease a car which he intends to use for pleasure only? The discount rate is 9 percent. (Note: Ignore tax aspects and simply find the present value of the lease option and the buy option).

Buy option. The purchase price is $7,000, the down payment is $400, and the remainder to be financed at 12 percent, compounded monthly for three years. Residual value of the car at the end of three years is $3,500.

Step A
Present value of down payment is $400.

Step B
Loan amortization for purchasing car:

> Input:
>   PV: $6,600
>   i: 12%/12 = 1
>   n: 36
> Press: *PMT*
> Displays: $219.21

Step C
Present value of car loan payment, using a discount rate or the client's 9 percent rate of return on investments:

> Input:
>   PMT: $219.21
>   i: .75%
>   n: 36

Press: *PV*

Displays: $6,893

Step D

Present value of residual value of the car. (Note: clear calculator or enter 0 in *PMT.*)

Input:
  FV: $3,500
  i: .75%
  n: 36

Press: *PV*

Displays: $2,675

Step E

Add the present value cost of the $400 down payment and the present value of the loan repayment ($6,893) for a total of $7,293. Subtract the residual value of $2,675. The present value of buying the car is $4,618.

Lease option. The down payment is $400. Monthly payments are $150 for three years. At the end of the third year, there is no further obligation.

Step A

Present value of down payment is $400.

Step B

Present value of lease payments:

Input:
  PMT: $150
  i: .75
  n: 36

Press: *PV*

Displays: $4,717

Step C

Both figures are added together and the total present value cost of leasing the car is $5,117.

7. Ceci carried a second mortgage on a home she sold. The $10,000 loan was at 8.5 percent for 10 years, and the monthly payment was $123.99. After 24 months, she needs money. What would she have to sell the loan for if current investors want a 9 percent yield, compounded monthly, and she had already received 24 payments?

Input:

> n: 96} 120 − 24 = 96 (number of periods remaining).
> i: .75} 9/12 (current yield investors require).
> PMT: $123.99 (amount to be received each month).

Press: PV

Displays: $8,463.36 (what an investor would pay).

8. Mr. and Mrs. Anxious are retiring now. They require a monthly income in today's dollars of $2,000. For their 30 years of retirement, project a 6 percent inflation rate and an aftertax investment rate of 9 percent. What lump sum should be available today? (Note: The monthly payments begin immediately.)

Known variables:
$$i = 9\%$$
$$\text{Inflation rate } (g) = 6\%$$
$$PMT = \$2,000$$
$$n = 30$$

Step 1

$$\frac{1 + .09}{1 + .06} = 1.0283 - 1 = .0283 \times 100 = 2.8302$$

Input:

> i: .23585 (2.8302/12)
> n: 360 (30 × 12 months)
> PMT: $2,000

Press: PV

Displays: $484,846

Press: BEGIN PV

Displays: $485,990

The following is another way to calculate a retirement need, based on completely liquidating the principal over the projected retirement life. Consequently, the length of time chosen for retirement should be realistic or changed periodically. Since clients are not born with an expiration date, it is imperative not to have their money run out before they do:

Step 1
Establish the amount of monthly income needed if the client retired today.

Step 2
Determine how many years until retirement, and choose an inflation factor.

Step 3
Calculate equivalent monthly income at retirement.

Step 4
Determine the length of retirement and consider selecting an interest rate factor or investment yield that surpasses inflation by no more than 3 percent. (Some financial planners believe that retired clients will be less affected by inflation because they will not be buying a more expensive home or a car, etc; this may or may not be the case.)

Step 5
Calculate the present value of the sum needed. (Note: this is the amount that must be on hand at the beginning of retirement. A 3 percent discount factor can equate to the net yield of investments over inflation.)

Step 6
a. Bring this lump sum back to today to see whether current assets are sufficient. (Use the investment rate as the discount factor.)
b. Calculate periodic contributions necessary to reach goal. (In this example, it is a monthly contribution.)
   Note: Both numbers would be greatly reduced by other retirement benefits.

EXAMPLE

The following example will assist in understanding the steps previously described. Remember, the length of retirement is arbitrary.

Step 1
$2,000 (today's dollars).

Step 2
15 years to retirement, 6 percent inflation factor.

Step 3
  Input:
      n: 15
      i: 6
    PV: 2,000
  Press: *FV*
  Displays: $4,793 ($2,000 in 1985 dollars)

Step 4

Length of retirement 20 years, inflation rate:

$(1.09/1.06 - 1 \times 100 = 2.8301887/12 = .235849058)$

Step 5

Input:

n:	240
i:	.2358
PMT:	$4,793

Press: *PV*

Displays: $877,668

Step 6

a. Input:

n:	15
i:	9
FV:	$877, 668

Press: *PV*

Displays: $240,953 (lump sum amount)

b. Input:

n:	180
i:	.75
FV:	$877,668

Press: *PMT*

Displays: $2,319 (monthly retirement contribution)

In lieu of Step 6, above, a present value analysis of future benefits from the client's pension plan would be in order. As each pension plan is unique, it is difficult to make generalizations. Hopefully, the client's pension plan will provide at least 50 percent of retirement needs. Other sources of income, such as social security, deferred compensation, an IRA, and investments will have to be looked at closely.

Inflation over time can only be approximated. Investment yield is also difficult to project with accuracy. It is reasonable to think the spread between the inflation rate and the investment yield will invariably change over time.

It is important for planners to remember that the numbers can only be exact when the assumptions are accurate. However, projections should be viewed as a place to start. Projections are not set in concrete. Rather, they give direction and gain the client's attention. Projections reinforce the concept that nothing is static in financial planning. Consequently, a client's status must be periodically reviewed and necessary changes made.

CHAPTER FIVE

Investment Yield Analysis

Further applications of time value concepts include determining potential yield. This is an important calculation because investors are always concerned with how much return there is from any one investment.

There are many methods for measuring the financial success of investments. Regardless of which analysis is used, the time element must be considered as essential. Remember the analogy to children and their constant demand for *now*. If a child (or a client) gives up something now, he or she will demand more later.

Evaluating investment yields should be reviewed from this perspective. The purpose of these evaluations is to efficiently rank investments according to their track records or projections for a given investment. The steps involved in evaluating investment yields are as follows.

1. Determine the amount to be invested, whether a single sum or periodic payments.
2. Calculate the benefits to be received on an ongoing basis—tax savings, cash flow, etc.
3. Determine the proceeds from the sale or disposition of the investment.

Once these figures have been obtained a method of evaluation must be chosen. How investments are ranked will depend on the method of analysis used. The following are some of the more common methods.

Table 5-1 Recovering Original Investment

	Return		
	Investment A	Investment B	Investment C
Year 1	$ 2,000	$ 5,000	$10,000
Year 2	1,000	6,000	5,000
Year 3	12,000	4,000	0
Totals	$15,000	$15,000	$15,000

PAYBACK

The payback method simply shows how the cash flow was received over a given period. This type of analysis was frequently used for measuring capital investment only a few decades ago. It does not take into consideration the value of receiving more money now versus later. Furthermore, it ignores cash flows beyond the payback period. This is an unacceptable method of evaluating investments in that it is not enough to choose the investment with the fastest payback. However, it is interesting to compare this method with the other forms of calculating yield, and to see the development of yield analysis.

The elementary example of the payback method in Table 5.1 shows how many years are required for investors to recover an original $15,000 investment. The cash inflows can be derived from a combination of tax savings, interest or the proceeds from a sale. In the example given, investment C would be preferable because it has the fastest payback.

SIMPLE RATE OF RETURN (SIMPLE INTEREST)

With this method, the yield on investments is computed by simply dividing the profit by the amount of time involved. This is also referred to as the *average annual rate of return*. Even the Internal Revenue Service (IRS) does not accept, or pay, simple interest. However, a few years ago one bank was advertising the "Best IRA in Town." Its stated interest rate was 18 percent on individual retirement accounts (IRAs), while all the other banks were advertising approximately 13.5 percent. In reality, there was little difference. The first bank's advertisement was based on a simple rate of return. The other banks were indicating a compound rate of return. The key in any analysis is to make similar comparisons.

EXAMPLE

Mike invests $10,000. Fifteen years later he receives $25,000. What is the yield? Based on a simple rate of return:

Amount received	$25,000
Amount invested	10,000
Profit	$15,000/15 years = $1,000

According to this calculation, the rate of return is 10 percent per year ($1,000/10,000 = 10%).

This method is more suitable than the payback evaluation, but it shows a higher return then the other methods presented. These high yields may unduly influence investors or give them a greater expectation of profit.

ANNUAL COMPOUND RATE OF RETURN

Using the example above, this yield calculation produces a different result:

Input:
  PV: $10,000
  FV: $25,000
   n: 15
Press: *i*
Displays: 6.299

Although compound rates of return are more commonly recognized by the general public, simple rates of return give the appearance of more profit. To lessen any confusion, it would be appropriate for investment sponsors to show their track record with compound rates of return.

INTERNAL RATE OF RETURN (IRR)

One objective of any financial evaluation is to determine whether the rate of return is acceptable to an investor. This can be done using the internal rate of return (IRR) which equates net cash flows received with original capital invested. The cash flows, or cash receipts, can be comprised of tax savings, income from investment, interest earned on an investment, or proceeds from the sale of an investment. It is important that cash flows are computed as the net amount an investor keeps after paying any taxes. The IRR is then calculated by arbitrarily selecting an interest rate that discounts all the cash flows to equal the initial cash invested.

The IRR is actually found by trial and error. Each interest rate must first be selected and then discarded if it does not discount the cash flow to equal the original cash outlay. It is a tedious computation to perform with a calculator that lacks an IRR function.

As an example of how the IRR is calculated, if the cost of money is 10 percent, then for every $100 invested, a minimum of $10 must be received. Thus, if an investor received $110 after one year on a $100 investment, the IRR would be 10 percent.

The calculation reveals the interest rate that will discount the future cash flows to equal the $100 investment.

Input:
  FV: $110
  PV: 100
   n: 1
Press: *i*
Displays: 10

The following example goes a step further by showing what the IRR would be if an investor had to wait two years to receive the $110.

Input:
  FV: $110
  PV: 100
   n: 2
Press: *i*
Displays: 4.88

This illustrates that the longer investors must wait to receive their cash flow benefits, the lower the IRR is.

The previous two examples show that the relationship between the present value of an investment and the future value of a single cash flow is determined by the discount rate. This discount rate is also the IRR for these elementary examples. To demonstrate the complexity of an IRR calculation, an investment that produces a series of cash flows must be shown. In the next example the question is, what interest rate will discount the cash flows back to present value to equal the original capital contribution?

Take an initial capital contribution of $1,000. If an investor receives the following aftertax cash flows, what is the aftertax IRR?

Year	Cash Flows	Present Value at 10 percent	Present Value at 20 percent	Present Value at 15 percent
1	$550	$ 500	$458	$ 478
2	$400	331	278	302
3	$335	252	194	220
Total		$1,083	$930	$1,000

The example shows that selecting an interest rate of 10 percent is not sufficient. On the other hand, an interest rate of 20 percent discounts the cash flows too much. Choosing a discount rate of 15 percent produces a present value of a $1,000, which equals the original investment.

As shown, calculating an IRR is a tedious task, based on trial and error. Using financial tables will not be any quicker, as interpolation is necessary. The easiest approach to this problem is to select a calculator with an IRR function and let it compute the answer internally.

There are two major problems in using IRR analysis. First, the calculation assumes that when cash flows are received they can be reinvested at the same internal rate of return. This is not always feasible.

Second, there is the possibility of having more than one IRR for a particular investment. This can occur when additional money is placed in an investment and money is received from an investment in years other than the initial investment year.

NET PRESENT VALUE (NPV)

An investor has to choose between investment alternatives because no one has an unlimited supply of money to invest. When choosing among mutually exclusive investments, selecting the one with the highest net present value will produce the greatest rate of return.

The net present value (NPV) calculation indicates the present value of future cash flows by allowing investors to select the discount rate or the rate of return they want their investments to achieve. The answer is then subtracted from the initial cost of an investment. If the net present value is positive, then the desired rate of return has been surpassed. If the answer is negative, the investment would be rejected because the investment yield has not been achieved.

EXAMPLE

Katie is looking at two investments. Each requires a $1,000 capital contribution. Her alternative use of this money would yield 10 percent. Katie thus expects her new investment to yield at least the same return. (Once again, in this example the discount rate is on an aftertax yield.)

Investment A

Year	Cash Flow	PV(10 percent)
1	$600	$ 545.45
2	$375	309.92
3	$275	206.62
Present value of cash flows:		$1,061.92
Less cost:		– 1,000.00
Net present value:		$ 61.92

Investment B

Year	Cash Flow	PV(10 percent)
1	$275	$ 250.00
2	$600	495.87
3	$375	281.74
Present value of cash flows:		$1,027.61
Less cost:		– 1,000.00
Net present value:		$ 27.61

In this example, both investments produce an increase in value. However, with investment A, Katie is ahead by a greater amount. Therefore, investment A would be chosen first.

Net present value and IRR methods of evaluating investment returns have some things in common. Both can be used to rank mutually exclusive investments to determine which have the highest returns. And both take into account the *timing* of cash flows. But the planner should be aware of the differences in these two tools. These differences occur because:

1. Initial cash flows differ.
2. The size and timing of cash flows vary.
3. The expected lives of competing investments often differ.
4. IRR assumes that all cash flows are reinvested at the internal rate of return. Unfortunately, investors often either use cash flows for personal consumption, or receive a lower yield on cash flows.

At any rate, the net present value calculation simply involves finding the present value of future cash flows. When in doubt, using the net present value to determine an investor's return would be most appropriate.

ADJUSTED RATE OF RETURN (ARR)

This calculation also involves the amount and timing of cash flows. Nevertheless, there is a significant difference between this method and IRR. With the adjusted rate of return, an investor selects the yield at which cash flows can be realistically reinvested. These cash benefits are calculated using both an aftertax rate of return and a conservative yield. The following demonstrates this concept.

EXAMPLE

Carlos invests $10,000 into a real estate partnership. His cash benefits are derived from tax savings, cash distributions, and sale of the property. Sean's discount rate for reinvesting the cash flows is 8 percent (aftertax yield).

Step 1

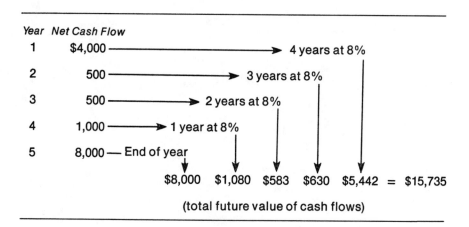

Year	Net Cash Flow					
1	$4,000	→ 4 years at 8%				
2	500	→ 3 years at 8%				
3	500	→ 2 years at 8%				
4	1,000	→ 1 year at 8%				
5	8,000 — End of year					
		$8,000	$1,080	$583	$630	$5,442 = $15,735

(total future value of cash flows)

Step 2

Input

Original investment—*PV:* $10,000

Total cash flow benefits—*FV:* $15,735

n: 5

Press: *i*

Displays: 9.49

The yield obtained is a compounded rate of return, based on net cash benefits being reinvested at the chosen discount rate. Consequently, when planners are calculating the yield on investment cash flows, it would be more appropriate to compute an ARR than an IRR. The ARR can produce a reasonable yield, because the reinvestment rate is chosen on the basis of an investor's most conservative personal experience. Typically, the ARR will produce a lower, though more realistic, rate of return than the IRR.

CHAPTER SIX.

The Fundamentals of the Tax Structure

Taxation is a fundamental element in financial planning because it is an obligation that may be adjusted but usually cannot be avoided. So it is essential for financial planners to understand the federal tax structure and how it operates. With this knowledge, planners can help clients reduce taxes and improve their financial position.

The current federal tax structure is based on the Internal Revenue Code (IRC) of 1954, which Congress continues to amend. The most recent revisions have been:

- 1981—Economic Recovery Tax Act.
- 1982—Tax Equity and Fiscal Responsibility Act.
- 1984—Tax Reform Act.

The U.S. Treasury Department interprets tax laws through regulations written by the Internal Revenue Service (IRS). These regulations are binding on both the taxpayer and the IRS, unless they are contrary to the law, unreasonable, or exceed the Treasury Department's power.

The same numbering system is used for the Internal Revenue Code and IRS regulations. The number "1," followed by a period, indicates a regulation. For example, 212 is the code section dealing with the production of income, while regulation 1.212 is the IRS interpretation of that section.

The IRS is also responsible for enforcing tax laws and collecting revenues. However, any dispute between a taxpayer and the IRS that cannot be resolved is handled by the judicial system.

Over the years, interpretations by both the IRS and the courts have resulted in producing several key tax doctrines. These perspectives not only clarify the intent of the revenue code, but are also useful in designing tax-planning strategies.

BASIC TAX DOCTRINES

Income realization. All income from whatever source (such as salary, proceeds from the sale of stock, or gambling winnings) is taxable, unless the Internal Revenue Code cites a specific exception.

Income recognition. This deals with the timing of income. Although a client may make a profit, the code may not recognize it. For example, tax-free exchanges and installment sales in real estate may minimize the gain included as taxable income.

Constructive receipt. Income is taxable when the right to receive it is established. A taxpayer does not have to actually receive the funds. That is, if an individual is entitled to receive a certain amount which is made available, or the taxpayer has control over the money, then the amount is taxable. This limits arbitrarily shifting income from one year to the next in an effort to reduce taxes. One such example would be not cashing a December bonus check until January of the next year.

Cash equivalent doctrine. The fair market value of all compensation, whether in money, property, or services, is considered income. For example, if a person is a member of a bartering club, the value of services and products received is recognized as income.

Assignment of income. The person who earns the income is taxed on it. In a Supreme Court case, the analogy of the "fruit and the tree" was used to clarify this point. Whoever owns the income source (the tree) cannot assign the right to the income (the fruit) to another. For example, a mother cannot assign stock dividends to her children without first giving them the stock. It is not always easy to determine who is the taxpayer, or who really owns the "tree." However, the IRS has been quite successful in numerous court cases involving this point. Thus, a person who generates income through work, luck, capital, or property is legally entitled to receive the income and the ensuing tax liability.

Claim of right doctrine. Various court cases have shaped this doctrine which has now evolved into IRC Section 1341. Under this section, taxes are levied on income in the year it is received, even if the money is subject to dispute or is mistakenly received. The law allows a deduction in subsequent years if the money is repaid.

Substance over form. This could also be called illusion versus reality. The tax reality will not be overlooked because a transaction superficially conforms to the law. For example, this doctrine is often used by the IRS to disallow inappropriate deductions taken by certain tax shelters.

Based on the principles described, financial planners can help clients determine which tax planning strategies are feasible. The first step is to ascertain whether income has been realized. Is the income taxable or excluded by a section of the IRC? For example, if a retired person waits until age 55 to sell a personal residence, the first $125,000 of profit is not taxed.

The next question is *whose* income is it? Identifying the taxpayer is important, as well as knowing for what year the money is taxable. This information is essential for financial planners to coordinate other strategies, such as selling a profitable stock or recognizing a loss.

Shaping overall tax planning is the doctrine of substance over form. Tax strategies will usually not be successful if they are devised merely to comply with the letter of the law, while attempting to circumvent its intent. Clients who wish to reduce taxes at all costs, must be advised of the current IRS position and relevant court cases. Because tax penalties and interest are expensive, helping clients concoct illusionary tax strategies is unwise.

Appropriate application of these tax doctrines can prevent clients from falling into higher tax brackets. Without systematic planning, the tax structure ensures that as income increases, a higher percentage of taxes will be paid. Taxes are paid on the *marginal tax bracket,* that is on the last dollar received, after adjustments and deductions. In other words, an increase of $1 of income could move a taxpayer into the next (higher) bracket.

DETERMINING A TAX BRACKET

Although ascertaining a tax bracket is a fundamental process, it has caused some taxpayers much confusion. The following will help clarify this procedure. To begin, all sources of income are added, all adjustments are made, and all deductions are subtracted. The resulting figure is *taxable income,* and corresponds

Table 6-1   1985 Tax Rate Schedules—Married Taxpayers Filing Joint Returns (and qualifying widows and widowers)

If Taxable Income Is		Then, Tax Is			
Over:	But not over:				of the Amount over:
$ 0	$ 3,540	$0.00			
$ 3,540	$ 5,720	$0.00	+	11%	$ 3,540
$ 5,720	$ 7,910	$239.80	+	12%	$ 5,720
$ 7,910	$ 12,390	$502.60	+	14%	$ 7,910
$ 12,390	$ 16,650	$1,129.80	+	16%	$ 12,390
$ 16,650	$ 21,020	$1,811.40	+	18%	$ 16,650
$ 21,020	$ 25,600	$2,598.00	+	22%	$ 21,020
$ 25,600	$ 31,120	$3,605.60	+	25%	$ 25,600
$ 31,120	$ 36,630	$4,985.60	+	28%	$ 31,120
$ 36,630	$ 47,670	$6,528.40	+	33%	$ 36,630
$ 47,670	$ 62,450	$10,171.60	+	38%	$ 47,670
$ 62,450	$ 89,090	$15,788.00	+	42%	$ 62,450
$ 89,090	$ 113,860	$26,976.80	+	45%	$ 89,090
$ 113,860	$ 169,020	$38,123.30	+	49%	$ 113,860
$ 169,020	. . . .	$65,151.70	+	50%	$ 169,020

to line number 37 of the 1985 IRS 1040 form. (The line number may change in future years, but the term taxable income will remain the same.) The next step is to take this amount to the tax tables (such as those shown in Tables 6.1 and 6.2) and determine among which set of numbers it lies. *The corresponding percentage figure found in the tables is the marginal tax rate.*

Often, taxpayers simply divide their actual taxes by their income to ascertain their tax rate. Knowing this percentage is not sufficient to show the rate at which the *next* dollar will be taxed, or how much the *next* deduction will save. This concept is shown graphically in Illustration 6.1, which also shows that a taxpayer can actually be in more than one tax bracket.

Margaret is a single status filing taxpayer and has taxable income of $8,000. As the illustration indicates, different portions of this income are subject to different tax rates.

In this example, Margaret is in the 15 percent tax bracket, and she owes $743 in federal taxes. Margaret's total income from all sources may be $10,000 before deductions and adjustments. If the taxes she paid were divided by this total income, the rate would be 7.43 percent ($743/$10,000 − 7.43 percent). However, this percentage is *not* the marginal tax bracket. It shows only what percentage of total income was paid in tax. This rate does

Table 6-2 1985 Tax Rate Schedules—Single Taxpayers

If Taxable Income Is		Then, Tax Is			of the
Over:	But not over:				Amount over:
$ 0	$ 2,390	$0.00			
$ 2,390	$ 3,540	$0.00	+	11%	$ 2,390
$ 3,540	$ 4,580	$126.50	+	12%	$ 3,540
$ 4,580	$ 6,760	$251.30	+	14%	$ 4,580
$ 6,760	$ 8,850	$556.50	+	15%	$ 6,760
$ 8,850	$ 11,240	$870.00	+	16%	$ 8,850
$ 11,240	$ 13,430	$1,252.40	+	18%	$ 11,240
$ 13,430	$ 15,610	$1,646.60	+	20%	$ 13,430
$ 15,610	$ 18,940	$2,082.60	+	23%	$ 15,610
$ 18,940	$ 24,460	$2,848.50	+	26%	$ 18,940
$ 24,460	$ 29,970	$4,283.70	+	30%	$ 24,460
$ 29,970	$ 35,490	$5,936.70	+	34%	$ 29,970
$ 35,490	$ 43,190	$7,813.50	+	38%	$ 35,490
$ 43,190	$ 57,550	$10,739.50	+	42%	$ 43,190
$ 57,550	$ 85,130	$16,770.70	+	48%	$ 57,550
$ 85,130	. . . .	$30,009.10	+	50%	$ 85,130

Illustration 6-1 Tax Brackets

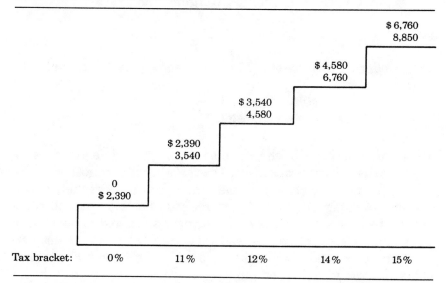

Tax bracket:	0%	11%	12%	14%	15%

not show Margaret that, for every taxable dollar she earned over $6,760, she paid $0.15, or 15 percent, to Uncle Sam.

This is why knowing the marginal tax bracket is so essential. It discloses precisely how painful the tax is and how beneficial solutions can be. The marginal tax bracket is a duel-edged sword. In Margaret's case it reveals that:

- For each additional dollar earned, she must pay $0.15 in taxes.
- For each additional dollar deducted, she saves $0.15 in taxes.

Combined Marginal Tax Bracket (CMTB)

The combined marginal tax bracket is the highest rate on which taxes are collected. This includes not only federal taxes but also the state taxes because most states also tax an individual's income. The following formula is used to find the combined federal and state marginal tax bracket. It is applicable only for those who pay state income taxes and are able to deduct the state tax.

$$F = \text{Federal Tax Bracket}$$
$$S = \text{State Tax Bracket}$$
$$\text{CMTB} = \text{Combined Marginal Tax Bracket}$$
$$F + S\,(100\% - F) = (\text{CMTB})$$

EXAMPLE

If the federal tax bracket is 40 percent and the state bracket is 10 percent, then:

$$40\% + 10\%\,(100\% - 40\%) =$$
$$40\% + 10\%\,(60\%)$$
$$40\% + 6\% = 46\%\ \text{CMTB}$$

(Note: For taxpayers who do not itemize their deductions, simply add the federal bracket and the state bracket together.)

By knowing a client's highest marginal tax bracket, the financial planner can provide an analysis basic to overall planning. The first step is to calculate a client's net cost of borrowing and the net yield of saving and investing. To find this net percentage, a client's tax bracket is subtracted from 100 percent. This aftertax yield is then multiplied by the percentage earned.

EXAMPLE

John is in a 36 percent combined marginal tax bracket (CMTB) and earns 10 percent on his $10,000 savings account. What is his net yield?

Step 1

$$
\begin{array}{rl}
100\% & \\
-36 & \text{CMTB} \\
\hline
64\% & \text{percent retained}
\end{array}
$$

Step 2

$$
\begin{array}{rl}
10\% & \text{percent earned} \\
\times.64 & \text{percent retained} \\
\hline
6.40\% & \text{net aftertax yield}
\end{array}
$$

The sequence is the same for borrowing funds. For example, John has $2,500 in outstanding charge accounts on which the borrowing rate is 20 percent. John's aftertax cost for borrowing is 12.8 percent (1.00 − .36 = .64 × 20% = 12.8%). In this instance, John's aftertax cost for borrowing the $2,500 is 12.8 percent, and yet he is earning only 6.4 percent after taxes on his $10,000 savings account.

It would now be appropriate for a financial planner to discuss this yield discrepancy. If the client's objectives are conservative, then the debt should be paid, because the aftertax cost of borrowing is twice as high as the aftertax yield on savings. The other alternative is for the client to invest the money to achieve an aftertax yield greater then the aftertax cost of borrowing.

FOUR TYPES OF INCOME

To determine the marginal tax bracket, it is important to know precisely the levels of taxable and nontaxable income. Equally significant is determining which types of income are included and excluded from taxation. In this context, four types of income should be taken into account.

Ordinary income. This includes wages and interest which are fully taxable.

Capital gains. Income is taxed only on 40% of the reportable gain if an asset is held for a minimum of six months, when acquired after June 22, 1984, and before January 1, 1988. Assets acquired before or after these dates require a holding period of one year. To be eligible for capital gains treatment, an asset must be held for investment, or be categorized as a certain type of business asset.

Tax exempt. Income from some sources—notably, interest from municipal securities—is exempt from taxation.

Return of capital. No tax is paid when principal, such as loan repayment, is returned. (Interest is taxable, but principal is not.)

Over the years, income has been divided into these categories as the IRC was influenced by a variety of factors. At this point in time, revenue laws have been modified so that their sole objective is not simply raising revenue. Encouraging economic development and social and political goals, as well as the feasibility of enforcement, are now among the basic components of federal tax laws. Consequently, the tax system—not necessarily logic—determines what and when income is taxable.

Includable Income

Internal Revenue Code Section 61 defines all gross income as taxable, unless there are specific exceptions. Therefore, wages, salaries, commissions, bonuses, incentive awards, certain fringe benefits, severance pay, back pay, professional fees, net business income, and *any* compensation for services, are taxable.

The items listed are considered *ordinary income,* and therefore fully taxable. Also included in the ordinary income category are: interest, dividends ($200 excluded for a joint return, $100 for a single), net rental income, royalties, prizes, embezzled funds, gambling winnings, net farm income, net partnership income, pensions, and jury duty fees. Although this list is not complete, it indicates that when in doubt, an item should be included as income.

Capital gains. Ordinary income is classified as fully taxable. *Capital gains* are not. Included in the latter classification are profits from the sale of stocks, bonds, real estate, and other investment assets. Capital assets do not include inventory or property primarily held for sale in a trade or business. Consequently, a person referred to as a "dealer" or one who regularly purchases assets to sell to customers may not be included.

If an investor sells a capital asset that he has held for at least six months, any profits from the sale are called *long-term capital gains* (LTCG); only 40 percent of these profits are taxable. Profits from capital assets held for less than six months are called *short-term capital gains* (STCG) and are fully taxable.

Capital assets held for less than six months and that produce a loss are fully deductible up to $3,000 per year and are called short-term capital losses (STCL). Losses on capital assets held for more than six months are called long-term capital losses (LTCL), and only 50 percent of a loss up to $3,000 is deductible. Thus, it takes $6,000 of long-term capital losses to produce

Table 6-3 Mike's Investments

Date Purchase	Date Sold	Purchase Price	Net Sales Price	Description of Gain or Loss	
2-1-80	4-1-85	$1,000	$2,000	$1,000	LTCG
7-1-84	6-1-85	2,000	4,000	2,000	LTCG
3-1-84	5-1-85	7,000	4,000	3,000	LTCL
9-1-84	2-1-85	5,000	3,000	2,000	STCL

$3,000 in deductions. Losses must be netted against gain first, and any loss over $3,000 per year may be deducted the next year.

As an example of how the capital gains provisions function, Table 6.3 gives information on Mike's investment. The relevant calculations are as follows:

Step 1

Net all long-term capital gains and losses: $3,000 LTCG and $3,000 LTCL = 0.

Step 2

Net all short-term capital gains and losses: $2,000 STCL = $2,000 STCL.

Step 3

Offset negative and positive numbers. In this example, there is a $2,000 short-term capital loss remaining.

It is important to plan a client's sale of capital assets to achieve the greatest tax advantages. Offsetting gains against losses is one technique.

Other includable income. Includable income is extremely important in divorces. Often one spouse pays both alimony and child support. Alimony is considered income, while child support is not. Alimony payments are deductible, but child support payments are not.

One often-overlooked source of income is the cancellation of debt. Canceling a debt may result in income to the debtor, unless the money is considered a gift or a contribution of capital to the debtor, or involves a court-approved bankruptcy. An exchange of services for relief of debt is a taxable transaction.

Even unemployment benefits can be taxable. The base amount for computing taxes is $18,000 for married taxpayers and $12,000 for all others.

Also of great concern is the taxation of Social Security benefits, beginning in 1984. The base amount for computing the tax is $25,000 for an individual and $32,000 for a married couple filing jointly.

Excludable Income

This category is especially appealing to clients because the income discussed is not taxable by the federal government. Sections 101 through 131 of the IRC provide much of the legislative authority for excluding certain items from gross income. There are other exclusions scattered throughout the code.

Life insurance proceeds. Insurance proceeds paid to the beneficiary on the death of the insured are exempt from income tax. However, the amount may be subject to federal estate taxes. If the proceeds are paid for reasons other than the death of the insured, only the amount paid for the contract is free of taxes. (This would include redemption, surrender, or maturity of a policy. For example, a taxpayer terminated a life insurance policy in which the premiums totaled $7,500. If the taxpayer received a cash surrender value of $9,000, the $1,500 difference would be taxed as ordinary income.)

Employee death benefits. The first $5,000 of benefits paid by an employer to an employee's beneficiaries are not taxed. The benefits must be paid due to the death of the employee, and not for past compensation.

Gifts and inheritances. Those who are *given* assets are not taxed. This does not pertain if the asset was given for services rendered or in consideration for future services. Therefore, businesses cannot disguise compensation in this manner. To qualify under this exclusion, the courts have concluded that the payment must be made because "of affection, respect, admiration, charity, or like impulses." (*Robertson* v. *U.C.*, 72 S. Ct. 994, USSC, 1952.) The facts and circumstances of each case will be the determining factor.

This exclusion does not apply to *income* received from the transferred asset whether acquired by gift, bequest, or inheritance. Thus, if an aunt gives stock to her niece, the niece must pay taxes on any future dividends. This is based on the assignment of income doctrine discussed previously.

Dividends and interest income. Dividend income of $100 ($200 for a married couple filing jointly) received from corporate stock from U.S. companies is excluded from taxation. This dividend exclusion does not apply to amounts received from money market funds or credit unions, although these institutions often refer to interest earned as dividends.

Taxpayers may also exclude up to $750 ($1,500 on a joint return) of dividends paid and reinvested in a qualified public utility. This exclusion applies from 1982 through 1985.

Interest received from state and municipal securities is excluded from federal income tax. To obtain a similar exclusion from state income tax, the interest must originate in an individual's state of residence. For example, Iowa residents may exclude from their state income tax return interest from an Iowa municipal bond but not from a Florida municipal bond.

The interest exemption on federal, state, and municipal securities does not extend to any profit received at the time of sale. This gain would be taxable. As an example, suppose a municipal bond was purchased for $1,000 and sold for $1,300. The $300 profit is taxable.

Interest on federal securities, such as Treasury Bills, Notes, or Bonds, is included as income on federal tax returns. At present, there are two issues of U.S. Savings Bonds—Series HH and Series EE. With a Series EE bond most taxpayers may elect to report the interest earned each year, or defer reporting the interest until the bonds are cashed in or mature, whichever comes first. Series EE bonds may be exchanged tax-free for Series HH bonds. When a Series HH bond matures or is cashed in, the previously deferred Series EE interest is taxable. The current interest earned on a Series HH bond is taxable.

Compensation for sickness and injury. The IRC does not include income received from state workers' compensation. Therefore, these payments for job-related injuries are not taxable. The exclusion does not apply to nonoccupational injuries or health benefits. Nevertheless, benefits may be excluded under an employer-sponsored accident and health plan in the following instances:

- Payments for permanent loss or disfigurement of the body.
- Reimbursements for medical costs.

Medical care previously deducted by a taxpayer should be included as income in the year in which it is reimbursed. If benefits are part of a self-insured plan or medical reimbursement plan it must be *nondiscriminatory.* This means that if the plan discriminates in favor of the highly compensated, benefits received by this class of people will be taxable income.

Benefits received from an *employer*-sponsored health, disability, or income insurance plan cannot be excluded from income, unless they fall under one of the above categories. On the other hand, if an *employee* purchases this insurance, the income received will not be taxable. Sometime both the employer and employee pay the insurance premiums, and the benefits are proportionately taxable. For example, 60 percent of disability insurance premiums are paid by the company, and 40 percent are paid by the employee. If the employee receives disability income of $1,500 per month, the employee will be able to exclude $600 ($1,500 × 40%) per month from taxable income.

The IRC also excludes income from damages awarded by a court or received as part of a settlement agreement. The exclusion applies to personal injuries and sickness, whether physical or emotional. Also excluded are awards for slander, libel, invasion of privacy, and breach of promise to marry. Besides compensatory damages, the injured may also seek punitive damages for gross negligence or intentional harm. Awards of punitive damages for personal injury are not taxable, but such awards for loss of income are fully taxable.

Fringe benefits. Insurance premiums paid by an employer for nondiscriminatory medical coverage are not taxable income to employees. However, premiums paid for life insurance are treated differently. While the cost of the first $50,000 of group term life insurance is not included in an employee's gross income, each additional $1,000 of coverage is taxable according to IRS Regulation 1.79-3(d) (2).

For example, an employer pays the premium for $100,000 of group term life insurance for a 38-year-old employee. The premium cost is 11 cents per month. As the calculations show, the employee must include $66 as taxable income.

Selected brackets per each $1,000 of additional coverage are as follows:

Age	Cost per Month
Under 30	8 cents
30–34	9 cents
35–39	11 cents

Coverage: $100,000 - $50,000 / 1,000 = 50
Premium Cost: 12 months $\times$ .11 = $1.32 $\times$ 50 = $66

Other nontaxable fringe benefits include furnished meals and lodging for the "convenience of the employer." These benefits must be furnished on the business premises, and must be a condition of employment. For administrative ease, the IRS excludes gifts from income if an employee can eat or drink the item, and it is of diminishing value—ham, turkey, or a bottle of wine. Fringe benefits such as van pooling and $5,000 in tuition aid are nontaxable through 1985.

Scholarships and fellowships. Scholarships and fellowships are exempt from taxes. The exemption does not apply to the portion of a scholarship or fellowship that represents payment for *required* research, teaching, or other services. This distinction is not always clear. Nevertheless, the primary purpose of the payment must be to further the education of the recipient, not the interests of the grantor. The issue will be resolved with the facts and circumstances of each case.

Personal residence. Taxpayers who are at least 55 years old may exclude up to $125,000 of profits from the sale of their personal residence. This one-time exclusion applies if they have lived in their home for three out of the previous five years. A married couple is entitled to one exclusion, not one for each spouse. Furthermore, spouses who claim the exclusion and later divorce may not claim it again with a new spouse.

The list of exclusions is not complete. Rather, the examples given indicate planning opportunities and potential tax issues. When in doubt, it would be prudent to conclude that an item is taxable, unless there is a specific exemption in the IRC or a courts citation.

DEDUCTIONS

In addition to excludable income, deductions offer another way of minimizing taxes. To determine a client's overall tax situation, financial planners must be aware of what constitutes taxable income. Important components are includable and excludable income, as well as what items are deductible from gross income. Deductions must be specifically provided for in the tax laws. The courts have clarified this in the doctrine of *legislative grace,* by declaring that the extent to which a deduction is allowed is dependent on the IRC.

To resolve any doubt on this issue, IRC Sections 261 through 280 list items that are not deductible. Some of the more common are:

- Expenses and interest incurred to produce tax-exempt income.
- Personal, living, and family expenses (except as provided in the code, such as personal medical costs or casualty losses).
- Personal premiums for life insurance, endowment, and annuity contracts.
- Losses on transactions between related parties.
- Expenditures for bribes, illegal sale of drugs, or any activity in violation of public policy.
- Worthless debts owed by political parties.
- Losses from hobbies to the extent they exceed income from the hobby.

Deductions can be classified as business or nonbusiness expenses. Usually, a business deduction comes under IRC 162, which covers expenses incurred in carrying on a "trade or business." Nonbusiness deductions are often related to the production of income and fall under IRC 212. Personal deductions are allowable expenses without regard to a taxpayer's source of income or employment.

A further delineation includes expenses deductible *for* adjusted gross income, and those deductible *from* adjusted gross income. *Adjusted gross income* (AGI) separates business or investment-type expenses from personal expenses. The latter are *itemized deductions* and are referred to as deductions *from* AGI. AGI includes gross income from all sources, minus allowable deductions and adjustments (also known as expenses from AGI) but before subtracting itemized deductions.

Business Deductions

For deductions to be classified under this category, a trade or business must operate with:

- Regularity—A substantial and consistent amount of time is devoted to business.

- Profit motive—The intent is to receive a gain or produce income. Unless a taxpayer can prove the activity was entered into for profit, it will be considered a hobby. In that case, losses are deductible only up to the amount of income generated by the hobby.

It is also essential for an expense to be *ordinary and necessary*. Ordinary is defined as usual, customary, or normal. Necessary has been defined as "appropriate and helpful" to developing or conducting a trade or business. If the deduction is challenged, the courts will look for the reasonableness of the expenses. The deduction will also be subject to an "all events test," with the court reviewing all actions to determine whether an ongoing business exists.

Under these guidelines, numerous expenses can be deducted if they serve a bona fide business purpose. These would include interest, taxes, repairs, maintenance, current rent, wages, etc.

The deductions listed below are of interest to both business owners and employees.

Bad debts. A deduction is allowed during the taxable year in which it becomes apparent a business debt will not be paid. A debt is worthless if further action will not bring repayment.

Nonbusiness bad debts or personal loans may also be written off in the year they are uncollectable. The maximum deduction for such debts is $3,000 each year. The unused losses may be carried over to the following year.

Office and home expense. To qualify for a deduction taxpayers must demonstrate that their home or part of it is used exclusively and regularly for business purposes. The location must be the taxpayer's normal place of business. For employees, the deduction is permitted if the home office meets the above requirements and is used for the convenience of the employer. In either situation, the allowable expenses attributable to business use of the home may not exceed the gross income generated.

For business owners, all business expenses are deductions *for* AGI. The following expenses are also deductible whether a taxpayer is a business owner or an employee. However, for employees, some expenses may be deductible *from* AGI, while others are *for* AGI. Reimbursed expenses are not deductible unless an employer has included them as reported income.

Transportation and travel expenses. Transportation expenses include taxi fares, automobile expenses, and tolls and parking fees incurred in the course of business or employment. These deductions do not include the cost of commuting to work but do apply to traveling from one job to a second job.

Computation of automobile expense can be based on a percentage of actual expenses for gas, oil, repairs, and maintenance, and depreciation. Taxpayers may also deduct 21 cents per mile driven.

Travel expenses must be incurred while a taxpayer is away from home overnight. This means the individual spends the night somewhere other than his or her "tax home" that is, the principal place of business or his or her residence. Under this category, not only travel, but meals and lodging are also deductible.

Taxpayers should keep their actual hotel bills, because more than simply a night's lodging can be included in the bill, e.g., costs for clothes, cigarettes, and other items. Airline tickets should also be retained to *substantiate* destination.

Entertainment. If these expenses are directly related to or associated with the active conduct of a business, they are deductible.

The key to these much-litigated entertainment deductions is substantiation of expenses. A taxpayer must document:

- Cost—how much.
- Date—when it occurred.
- Place—where, name and location.
- Business purpose—nature of expected business benefit.
- Business relationship of those being entertained to the taxpayer—name, occupation, and title.

Conventions on cruise ships. These are drawing more attention lately. Taxpayers can now deduct up to $2,000 per year of expenses under the following conditions:

- Meetings are directly related to the active conduct of a trade, business, or income-producing activity.
- The cruise ship is registered in the United States and all ports of call are located in the United States.
- The taxpayer includes information statements on the cruise with his or her tax returns.

It appears to be difficult for average taxpayers to deduct these cruise-related costs as investment expenses because they must show how meetings directly aided them in producing income. If the cruise is taken in relation to a trade, business, or profession, it is easier to substantiate the relationship.

Other adjustments. Before arriving at the AGI, taxpayers may deduct moving expenses in conjunction with job transfers or business relocation. Taxpayers may also deduct penalties on early withdrawal of savings, as well as contributions to qualified retirement plans.

Married couples may deduct 10 percent of the lower wage earner's income up to $30,000 of income. The maximum $3,000 deduction is designed to partially offset the higher tax rates for married couples verses single taxpayers.

Nonbusiness Deductions

Under IRC Section 212, Congress has allowed a deduction for all "ordinary and necessary" expenses incurred for:

- Production or collection of income.
- Management, conservation, or maintenance of property held for producing income.
- In connection with the determination, collection, or refund of any tax.

All of these are considered nonbusiness expenses. No deduction can be taken for any amount spent for producing or collecting tax-free income. Expenses incurred in connection with potentially taxable income would be allowed. It is interesting that investment expenses are not deductible as business expenses. Even if taxpayers devote all their time to investments, they are still investors and not engaged in a trade or business.

Itemized Deductions

Expenses in this category are deducted from AGI. They include: *medical, taxes, interest, charity,* and *miscellaneous expenses.*

There are standard deductions that everyone receives regardless of whether or not they itemize their deductions. The standard deduction in 1985 for married couples filing jointly is $3,540, $2,390 for a single head of household. These deductions are built into the tax tables and are indexed so that the base amount will increase with inflation. To itemize deductions, a taxpayer's deductions must exceed their respective base amounts. That is, for a single person, the itemized deductions must exceed $2,390.

There are restrictions on *medical, theft,* and *casualty* expenses. To be deductible, medical expenses must exceed 5 percent of a taxpayer's AGI. For casualty and theft losses to be deductible, nonreimbursable expenses must exceed 10 percent of AGI and must total at least $100 per incident. For financial planning, medical and casualty insurance coverage must be reviewed because both the combination of financial loss and inability to deduct this could prove devastating.

Interest. *Interest* charges are another deductible expense. Interest is one of the most common deductions, because people often purchase major items on credit. Also, many investors leverage their potential profit by borrowing for investment.

It is important to remember that interest payments are deductible only if there is a bona fide indebtedness or obligation to pay. Sham transactions will not be honored, neither will pure tax-avoidance schemes. Court cases have not set definite guidelines in this area. Therefore, the facts and circumstances of each case and the doctrine of substance over form will be the deciding factors.

One of the most common deductions is mortgage interest. Fees paid to obtain a loan are called *points* or *loan origination fees*. These points are deductible if:

- The loan is for the purchase or improvement of a personal residence.
- The fee paid is compensation for use of the money and is common practice at a standard rate.
- The fee is paid separately and not deducted from the loan proceeds.

If the guidelines are not followed, the points are only deductible over the life of the loan.

Interest on credit and charge cards, automobile loans, installment debts, and other consumer financing is also deductible. Limitations will be discussed separately.

Other itemized deductions. *Personal taxes* are a common expense. This includes state income tax, property tax, and sales taxes, all of which are deductible. However, only the person paying these taxes can deduct them. For example, a son cannot deduct state income taxes he pays for his father. Federal income and social security taxes are not deductible by individuals. Employers, however, may deduct these taxes paid for employees.

With *charitable* deductions, an individual who does *not* itemize may claim a deduction of 25 percent of contributions up to a maximum of $300. For 1985 and 1986, the percentage limitation is 50 percent and 100 percent of the amount contributed with no dollar limitation. This deduction is scheduled to expire after 1986.

In 1969, Congress set up an elaborate system for determining which cash gifts versus noncash gifts would be charitable deductions. Cash, property and out-of-pocket expenses are deductible, but personal services are not. There is no deduction to the extent that a donor receives a benefit, such as for purchase of tickets to a charity ball or banquet. In this case, the expenses qualify for a deduction only to the extent that the cost exceeds the fair market value of the benefits received.

To be deductible, a charitable contribution must be made to a qualified organization. Limitations based on who is receiving a gift and the type of gift offered are set forth in IRC Rule 170. Deductions for cash contributions to churches, educational institutions, tax-exempt hospitals, and government and private foundations that distribute all income to public charities cannot exceed 50 percent of a taxpayer's AGI. Deductions for contributions to nonoperating private foundations, veterans' organizations, and fraternal societies cannot exceed 30 percent of AGI. A 30 percent of AGI limitation applies to appreciated capital gains property which is donated to charity.

Finally, the rules go one complicated step further. If property donated to a charitable institution has appreciated in value, is it ordinary income or capital gain? For ordinary income property, such as inventory or stock-in-trade, and capital assets held for less than six months—if acquired after June 22, 1984—deductions are limited to a taxpayer's basis or original cost.

The *miscellaneous* section is the one most overlooked by taxpayers. Miscellaneous expenses are deductible if they are for, or related to, an individual's work, profession, trade, or production of income. Employee expenses are deductible here, with the exception of transportation and mileage, which are deducted to arrive at AGI.

The list of deductions in this category is long. It includes union dues, professional fees, membership dues for business clubs, fees paid to obtain employment, uniforms (including cost and cleaning), special equipment (such as a fireman's boots), and tools with a life of one year or less and repairs to this equipment.

Educational expenses are also included. Taxpayers may deduct the costs of maintaining or improving skills needed in their employment. Also, any courses taken as a condition of retaining employment are deductible, but courses to qualify for a new trade or business are not. Included expenses are tuition, fees, books, and supplies. (Note: for an employee this is a miscellaneous deduction, but for the self-employed it is deductible on Schedule C.)

Other itemized deductions include charges for tax preparation, tax planning, and safe deposit boxes. Investor expenses incurred in producing tax-free income are not deductible. If investment income is taxable, then custodian fees, service charges, and management and analysis fees are deductible. Fees or commissions paid to a broker to purchase investments such as stocks or bonds are added to the purchase price for determining gain or loss.

Once all allowable deductions are determined, the tax rate on net taxable income is determined using the appropriate tax tables. After the tax has been calculated, the next point is to determine whether any credits are available.

CREDITS

Credits are extremely beneficial because they are subtracted, dollar for dollar from the tax owed. The Tax Reform Act of 1984 reorganized, revised, and renumbered code sections dealing with credits. There are now two types: *refundable* and *nonrefundable.*

Refundable credits are recoverable, even though no income tax liability is involved. Examples are credits for withheld wages, earned income credit, tax withheld at the source on nonresident aliens, and gasoline and special fuels credit.

A nonrefundable credit can reduce taxes, but if the credit exceeds the tax owed, no refund is paid. Credits in this category must be claimed in the following order:

1. Credit for the elderly and disabled.
2. Foreign tax credit.
3. Investment tax credit.
4. Political contribution credits.
5. Child and dependent care credits.
6. Target jobs credit.
7. Residential energy credit.
8. Employee stock credit.

The credits used most by individual taxpayers include the following.

Child care credit. This is a specified percentage of expenses incurred to enable a taxpayer to work or seek employment. To be eligible, a taxpayer must maintain a household for a dependent under the age of 15, or a dependent or spouse who is physically or mentally handicapped. The allowable expenses are up to $2,400 for one qualifying individual, and $4,800 for two or more. The credit is based on a percentage of AGI.

Energy credit. This credit is given for improving energy efficiency. Maximum credit is $300, and it applies only to a personal dwelling completed prior to April 20, 1977.

Political credit. Taxpayers are eligible for a tax credit of one half of their political contributions up to $50 for a single person, and $100 for married couples filing a joint return.

Investment tax credit. This credit is usually given for purchase of equipment, either new or used.

An understanding of the complex federal tax structure is essential for reviewing a client's current tax status. The best indicator is the client's actual tax return, unless, of course, it is fraudulent. It is imperative that financial planners examine income tax returns to spot problems and make future tax projections.

REVIEWING THE FEDERAL INCOME TAX RETURN

The IRS has many forms for computing an individual's federal income tax. The two most common federal tax forms—1040 and Schedule A (itemized deductions)—are illustrated in Exhibits 6.1 and 6.2.

From this tax return we learn that both Mark and Rebecca Sikes work and that they have ordinary income of $49,520 from wages. Their planner would want to determine whether any deferred compensation programs were available through their employers. Such programs would give these taxpayers an opportunity to reduce their taxable income.

The next item to determine is the source of the interest earnings which are taxed as ordinary income. Does this interest income represent a significant amount of savings? Or is the interest derived from an asset that could be repositioned?

The $965 state refund on line 10, as well as the federal refund on line 66, indicate that too much is being withheld from the Sikes's paychecks. A current-year tax projection would determine whether any changes should be made.

Exhibit 6-1   Form 1040

Form **1040** Department of the Treasury—Internal Revenue Service U.S. Individual Income Tax Return **1985**			OMB No 1545-0074

For the year January 1-December 31, 1985, or other tax year beginning _____ 1985, ending _____ 19 ____

Use IRS label. Otherwise, please print or type.
Your first name and initial (if joint return, also give spouse's name and initial) — Mark and Rebecca | Last name — Sikes | Your social security number — 325 00 0000
Present home address — 22 Fair Oaks Lane **EXAMPLE**
City, town or post office, state, and ZIP code — Anytown, State | Spouse's social security number — 246 00 000C
Your occupation — Administrator | Spouse's occupation — Salesperson

Presidential Election Campaign — Do you want $1 to go to this fund? [X] Yes [ ] No
If joint return, does your spouse want $1 to go to this fund? [X] Yes [ ] No
Note: Checking "Yes" will not change your tax or reduce your refund.

Filing Status (Check only one box)
1 [ ] Single
2 [X] Married filing joint return (even if only one had income)
3 [ ] Married filing separate return. Enter spouse's social security no. above and full name here. ____
4 [ ] Head of household (with qualifying person). (See page 5 of Instructions.) If the qualifying person is your unmarried child but not your dependent, write child's name here. ____
5 [ ] Qualifying widow(er) with dependent child (year spouse died ► 19 __). (See page 6 of Instructions.)

Exemptions (Always check the box labeled Yourself. Check other boxes if they apply.)
6a [X] Yourself [ ] 65 or over [ ] Blind — Enter number of boxes checked on 6a and b ► **2**
b [X] Spouse [ ] 65 or over [ ] Blind
c First names of your dependent children who lived with you — Lee — Enter number of children listed on 6c ► **1**
d First names of your dependent children who did not live with you (see page 6). (If pre-1985 agreement, check here ► [ ]) — Enter number of children listed on 6d ►

e Other dependents:

(1) Name	(2) Relationship	(3) Number of months lived in your home	(4) Did dependent have income of $1,040 or more?	(5) Did you provide more than one-half of dependent's support?

Enter number of other dependents ►
f Total number of exemptions claimed (also complete line 36) — Add numbers entered in boxes above ► **3**

Income (Please attach Copy B of your Forms W-2, W-2G, and W-2P here. If you do not have a W-2, see page 4 of Instructions.)

7 Wages, salaries, tips, etc. (Attach Form(s) W-2)	7	49,520
8 Interest income (also attach Schedule B if over $400)	8	2,100
9a Dividends (also attach Schedule B if over $400) ____ , 9b Exclusion ____		
c Subtract line 9b from line 9a and enter the result	9c	
10 Taxable refunds of state and local income taxes, if any, from the worksheet on page 9 of Instructions.	10	965
11 Alimony received	11	
12 Business income or (loss) (attach Schedule C)	12	(4,300)
13 Capital gain or (loss) (attach Schedule D)	13	
14 40% of capital gain distributions not reported on line 13 (see page 9 of Instructions)	14	
15 Other gains or (losses) (attach Form 4797)	15	
16 Fully taxable pensions, IRA distributions, and annuities not reported on line 17 (see page 9)	16	
17a Other pensions and annuities, including rollovers. Total received [17a]		
b Taxable amount, if any, from the worksheet on page 10 of Instructions	17b	
18 Rents, royalties, partnerships, estates, trusts, etc. (attach Schedule E)	18	
19 Farm income or (loss) (attach Schedule F)	19	
20a Unemployment compensation (insurance). Total received [20a]		
b Taxable amount, if any, from the worksheet on page 10 of Instructions	20b	
21a Social security benefits (see page 10). Total received [21a]		
b Taxable amount, if any, from worksheet on page 11. { Tax-exempt interest ____ }	21b	
22 Other income (list type and amount—see page 11 of Instructions) ____	22	
23 Add lines 7 through 22. This is your total income ►	23	48,285

Adjustments to Income (See Instructions on page 11.)

24 Moving expense (attach Form 3903 or 3903F)	24	
25 Employee business expenses (attach Form 2106)	25	
26 IRA deduction, from the worksheet on page 12	26	500
27 Keogh retirement plan deduction	27	
28 Penalty on early withdrawal of savings	28	
29 Alimony paid (recipient's last name ____ and social security no. ____)	29	
30 Deduction for a married couple when both work (attach Schedule W)	30	1,000
31 Add lines 24 through 30. These are your total adjustments ►	31	1,500

Adjusted Gross Income
32 Subtract line 31 from line 23. This is your adjusted gross income. If this line is less than $11,000 and a child lived with you, see "Earned Income Credit" (line 59) on page 16 of Instructions. If you want IRS to figure your tax, see page 13 of Instructions ► | 32 | 46,785

Exhibit 6-1 (concluded)

Form 1040 (1985)				Page 2

Tax Compu-tation	33	Amount from line 32 (adjusted gross income)		33	46,785
	34a	If you itemize, attach Schedule A (Form 1040) and enter the amount from Schedule A, line 26		34a	7,110
(See Instructions on page 13.)		**Caution:** If you have unearned income and can be claimed as a dependent on your parents' return, check here ▶ ☐ and see page 13 of Instructions. Also see page 13 if you are married filing a separate return and your spouse itemizes deductions, or you are a dual-status alien			
	b	If you do not itemize but you made charitable contributions, enter your cash contributions here (If you gave $3,000 or more to any one organization, see page 14.)	34b		
	c	Enter your noncash contributions (you must attach Form 8283 if over $500)	34c		
	d	Add lines 34b and 34c. Enter the total	34d		
	e	Divide the amount on line 34d by 2. Enter the result here		34e	
	35	Subtract line 34a or line 34e, whichever applies, from line 33		35	39,675
	36	Multiply $1,040 by the total number of exemptions claimed on line 6f (see page 14)		36	3,120
	37	**Taxable Income.** Subtract line 36 from line 35. Enter the result (but not less than zero)		37	36,555
	38	Enter tax here. Check if from ☒ Tax Table, ☐ Tax Rate Schedule X, Y, or Z, or ☐ Schedule G		38	6,513
	39	Additional taxes. (See page 14 of Instructions.) Enter here and check if from ☐ Form 4970, ☐ Form 4972, or ☐ Form 5544		39	
	40	Add lines 38 and 39. Enter the total ▶		40	6,513
Credits	41	Credit for child and dependent care expenses (attach Form 2441)	41		
	42	Credit for the elderly and the permanently and totally disabled (attach Schedule R)	42		
(See Instructions on page 14.)	43	Residential energy credit (attach Form 5695)	43		
	44	Partial credit for political contributions for which you have receipts	44		
	45	Add lines 41 through 44. These are your total personal credits		45	
	46	Subtract line 45 from line 40. Enter the result (but not less than zero)		46	
	47	Foreign tax credit (attach Form 1116)	47		
	48	General business credit. Check if from ☐ Form 3800, ☐ Form 3468, ☐ Form 5884, ☐ Form 6478	48		
	49	Add lines 47 and 48. These are your total business and other credits		49	
	50	Subtract line 49 from line 46. Enter the result (but not less than zero) ▶		50	6,513
Other Taxes	51	Self-employment tax (attach Schedule SE)		51	
	52	Alternative minimum tax (attach Form 6251)		52	
(Including Advance EIC Payments)	53	Tax from recapture of investment credit (attach Form 4255)		53	
	54	Social security tax on tip income not reported to employer (attach Form 4137)		54	
	55	Tax on an IRA (attach Form 5329)		55	
	56	Add lines 50 through 55. This is your **total tax** ▶		56	6,513
Payments	57	Federal income tax withheld	57	7,900	
	58	1985 estimated tax payments and amount applied from 1984 return	58		
Attach Forms W-2, W-2G, and W-2P to front.	59	Earned income credit (see page 16)	59		
	60	Amount paid with Form 4868	60		
	61	Excess social security tax and RRTA tax withheld (two or more employers)	61		
	62	Credit for Federal tax on gasoline and special fuels (attach Form 4136)	62		
	63	Regulated Investment Company credit (attach Form 2439)	63		
	64	Add lines 57 through 63. These are your **total payments** ▶		64	
Refund or Amount You Owe	65	If line 64 is larger than line 56, enter amount **OVERPAID** ▶		65	1,387
	66	Amount of line 65 to be **REFUNDED TO YOU** ▶		66	1,387
	67	Amount of line 65 to be applied to your 1986 estimated tax ▶	67		
	68	If line 56 is larger than line 64, enter **AMOUNT YOU OWE.** Attach check or money order for full amount payable to "Internal Revenue Service." Write your social security number and "1985 Form 1040" on it ▶ Check ▶ ☐ if Form 2210 (2210F) is attached. See page 17. **Penalty: $**		68	

Please Sign Here

Under penalties of perjury, I declare that I have examined this return and accompanying schedules and statements, and to the best of my knowledge and belief, they are true, correct, and complete. Declaration of preparer (other than taxpayer) is based on all information of which preparer has any knowledge.

▶ Your signature _____ Date _____ ▶ Spouse's signature (if filing jointly, BOTH must sign) _____

Paid Preparer's Use Only

Preparer's signature ▶ _____ Date _____ Check if self-employed ☐ Preparer's social security no. _____
Firm's name (or yours, if self-employed) and address ▶ _____ E.I. No. _____ ZIP code _____

Exhibit 6-2 Schedule A

SCHEDULES A&B (Form 1040)
Department of the Treasury
Internal Revenue Service (2)

Schedule A—Itemized Deductions
(Schedule B is on back)
▶ Attach to Form 1040. ▶ See Instructions for Schedules A and B (Form 1040).

OMB No 1545-0074

1985
07

Name(s) as shown on Form 1040
Mark and Rebecca Sikes **EXAMPLE**

Your social security number
325 00 0000

Section	#	Description	Line	Amount	Total
Medical and Dental Expenses (Do not include expenses reimbursed or paid by others.) (See Instructions on page 19)	1	Prescription medicines and drugs; and insulin	1	175	
	2a	Doctors, dentists, nurses, hospitals, insurance premiums you paid for medical and dental care, etc.	2a		
	b	Transportation and lodging	2b		
	c	Other (list—include hearing aids, dentures, eyeglasses, etc.) ▶	2c		
	3	Add lines 1 through 2c, and write the total here	3	175	
	4	Multiply the amount on Form 1040, line 33, by 5% (.05)	4	2,339	
	5	Subtract line 4 from line 3. If zero or less, write -0- **Total medical and dental** ▶	5		-0-
Taxes You Paid (See Instructions on page 20.)	6	State and local income taxes	6	1,500	
	7	Real estate taxes	7	400	
	8a	General sales tax (see sales tax tables in instruction booklet)	8a	500	
	b	General sales tax on motor vehicles	8b		
	9	Other taxes (list—include personal property taxes) ▶	9		
	10	Add the amounts on lines 6 through 9. Write the total here. **Total taxes** ▶	10		2,400
Interest You Paid (See Instructions on page 20.)	11a	Home mortgage interest you paid to financial institutions	11a	6,100	
	b	Home mortgage interest you paid to individuals (show that person's name and address) ▶	11b		
	12	Total credit card and charge account interest you paid	12	450	
	13	Other interest you paid (list) ▶	13		
	14	Add the amounts on lines 11a through 13. Write the total here. **Total interest** ▶	14		6,550
Contributions You Made (See Instructions on page 21.)	15a	Cash contributions. (If you gave $3,000 or more to any one organization, report those contributions on line 15b.)	15a	1,200	
	b	Cash contributions totaling $3,000 or more to any one organization. (Show to whom you gave and how much you gave.) ▶	15b		
	16	Other than cash. (You must attach Form 8283 if over $500.)	16	200	
	17	Carryover from prior year	17		
	18	Add the amounts on lines 15a through 17. Write the total here. **Total contributions** ▶	18		1,400
Casualty and Theft Losses (See page 21 of Instructions.)	19	Total casualty or theft loss(es). (You must attach Form 4684 or similar statement.)	19		-0-
Miscellaneous Deductions (See Instructions on page 21.)	20	Union and professional dues	20	175	
	21	Tax return preparation fee	21	125	
	22	Other (list type and amount) ▶	22		
	23	Add the amounts on lines 20 through 22. Write the total here. **Total miscellaneous** ▶	23		300
Summary of Itemized Deductions (See Instructions on page 22.)	24	Add the amounts on lines 5, 10, 14, 18, 19, and 23. Write your answer here.	24		10,650
	25	If you checked Form 1040 {Filing Status box 2 or 5, write $3,540 / Filing Status box 1 or 4, write $2,390 / Filing Status box 3, write $1,770}	25		3,540
	26	Subtract line 25 from line 24. Write your answer here and on Form 1040, line 34a. (If line 25 is more than line 24, see the Instructions for line 26 on page 22.) ▶	26		7,110

For Paperwork Reduction Act Notice, see Form 1040 Instructions.   Schedule A (Form 1040) 1985

The loss for self-employed income on line 12 must be reviewed. What is the profit potential for the business as well as its audit potential? Can future tax losses be realistically projected?

Line 26 reveals a minimal contribution to an IRA. It is important to ascertain why the maximum $4,000 contribution was not made. This is especially relevant if line 8 accurately reflects thousands of dollars in a savings account. Line 30 indicates that both spouses were working, and one spouse earned at least $10,000. It would be important to know the stability and potential growth of this income.

The itemized deductions (Exhibit 6.2) reveal that this couple probably has excellent medical benefits and minimal medical expenses. The tax section indicates that they pay state sales tax.

The size of the Sikes's home mortgage interest deduction indicates that the interest rate is lower than current rates. It would be beneficial to determine precisely what this rate is and how much equity they have in their house. The $450 in credit charges is not high, but why should there be any credit charges if the couple has significant savings? The key here is to compare the Sikes's aftertax cost of borrowing and their aftertax yield on savings.

With regard to Mark and Rebecca's charitable and miscellaneous deductions, it is important to determine whether there will be any significant changes in the next year. For example, are there additional noncash items that could produce greater deductions? It would also be useful to see why the couple does not have more deductions directly related to their employment. However, the Sikes's Schedule C (the form for self-employed taxpayers) may reveal they are deducting these expenses in that section.

Overall, this tax return does not reveal significant expenses, such as interest. However, the planner can explore potential repositioning of assets to minimize taxes and maximize retirement or deferred compensation programs. The Sikes are in a 33 percent federal tax bracket. Thus, any deductions would save 33 cents out of every dollar.

CONCLUSION

No one should have to pay more taxes than are necessary. The financial planner can help to minimize a client's taxes through comprehensive tax planning. The following steps should help:

1. Identify taxpayer's position and spot salient issues.
    a. What is the client's tax bracket?
    b. Is the client attempting to reduce, eliminate, shift, or defer taxes?
    c. What are the positive and negative consequences?
2. What are the current IRS and judicial positions in this area?
3. What is the overall impact of using investment vehicles for tax strategy?
4. What are the economic and time factors involved in implementing these alternatives?
5. Are the risks worth the rewards?

When this type of analysis is made, the financial planner will have performed an extremely worthwhile service for the client.

CHAPTER SEVEN.

Essential Components of Tax Planning

DEPRECIATION

Depreciation is the source of many tax advantages, but it can also be harmful. Consequently, it is essential for financial planners to have a thorough understanding of how depreciation operates and when it is no longer beneficial.

There is an assumption that over a certain time, property will become obsolete or simply wear out. To minimize this effect, the concept of depreciation came into play. However, depreciation now has **no** relationship to how long property will last.

Under the old depreciation rules (asset depreciation range), items were scheduled to be deducted over time. For example, as shown in Illustration 7.1, the IRS would argue that certain real estate should be depreciated over 45 years. Taxpayers would argue for shorter lives. The IRS would also argue over the remaining life—commonly called salvage value. Under the old rules, depreciation could not be less than the residual value of the property. Depreciation can only be claimed for the year the property is placed *in service*. When the property was *purchased* is not the determining factor.

Illustration 7-1 Depreciation

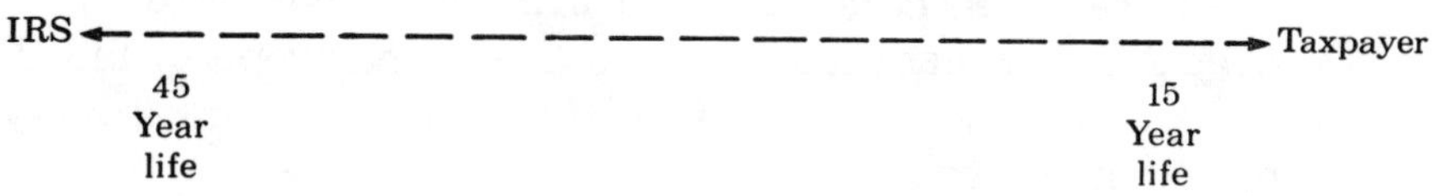

IRS ← — — — — — — — — — — — — — — — — — — → Taxpayer

   45   15
   Year   Year
   life   life

Types of Depreciation

Prior to 1981, there were several different and rather complicated forms of depreciation. The easiest is known as straight-line because the depreciation is calculated by dividing the life of the asset into the cost. Other types of depreciation include sum-of-years' digits, and declining balance. These no longer apply for federal deductions, but are still applicable for many states. Even now, if there is a sale between "related parties" (such as father and son), the old depreciation schedule must be taken. This is also applicable for exchanges to the extent of how much *basis* (the value remaining after depreciation) is carried over.

The new depreciation rules are much simpler. Under the Economic Recovery Tax Act (ERTA), of 1981 a streamlined method called the *accelerated cost recovery system* (ACRS) was devised. The depreciation rules were changed to encourage investing, simplify the laws, and improve productivity through the purchase of new equipment.

ACRS allows taxpayers to depreciate assets over a shorter time period. Again, this is without regard to an asset's real life. Under ACRS, depreciation is calculated by simply using the tables or taking straight-line depreciation. Both methods are referred to as ACRS because they are based on the shorter depreciation lives.

The ACRS tables are constructed by the IRS. The tables begin with accelerated depreciation and switch to straight-line depreciation in later years to produce more deductions. This is applicable only to the 10-year and 18-year tables. Straight-line depreciation may be chosen by taxpayers for several reasons. First, a person may already have enough tax deductions or, unfortunately, losses. The inability to use more deductions would be exacerbated by taking accelerated depreciation. This would produce more tax deductions than straight-line depreciation. By selecting straight-line depreciation, an equal amount of depreciation would be taken over each period.

Depreciation is calculated as follows:

- Step 1. Determine whether the property is real or personal. Real estate is classified as real property; all other property is referred to as personal, such as a car or a computer.
- Step 2. Into what recovery period does the property fall, 3, 5, 10, or 18 years? (Note: The IRS lists the life or recovery period of assets.)

- Step 3. Go to the tables and multiply the percent listed by the cost of the property.

The following are examples of properties classified by recovery period. Table 7.1 shows the ACRS depreciation allowed for each year of a three- and five-year recovery period.

- 3 Years. Automobiles, light-duty trucks, two-year-old race horses, all other horses over 12 years old, research and development equipment.
- 5 Years. Office equipment, furniture, computers, heavy-duty trucks.
- 10 Years. Railroad tank cars, mobile homes, public utility property with an asset depreciation range midpoint of between 18 and 25 years. (The IRS guidelines for the old depreciation rules)
- 15 Years. Qualified low-income housing.
- 18 Years. Public utility property exceeding an IRS-defined life of 25 years and real estate such as office buildings, apartments, and shopping centers.

For example, in Table 7.2, office equipment is purchased for $10,000. To determine the depreciation over a five-year recovery, simply multiply the percentage by the cost of the equipment.

Table 7-1 ACRS

Three-Year Recovery Category		Five-Year Recovery Category	
Year	Percentage	Year	Percentage
1	25%	1	15%
2	38	2	22
3	37	3	21
		4	21
		5	21

Table 7-2 Depreciation of Office Equipment (five-year recovery)

Year	Amount		Percentage		Depreciation Allowed
1	$10,000	×	15%	=	$1,500
2	10,000	×	22	=	2,200
3	10,000	×	21	=	2,100
4	10,000	×	21	=	2,100
5	10,000	×	21	=	2,100

Table 7-3   Depreciation of Low-Income Housing

Recovery Year Is	Applicable Percentage by Month*											
	1	2	3	4	5	6	7	8	9	10	11	12
1	13%	12%	11%	10%	9%	8%	7%	6%	4%	3%	2%	1%
2	12	12	12	12	12	12	12	13	13	13	13	13
3	10	10	10	10	11	11	11	11	11	11	11	11
4	9	9	9	9	9	9	9	9	10	10	10	10
5	8	8	8	8	8	8	8	8	8	8	8	9
6	7	7	7	7	7	7	7	7	7	7	7	7
7	6	6	6	6	6	6	6	6	6	6	6	6
8	5	5	5	5	5	5	5	5	5	5	6	6
9	5	5	5	5	5	5	5	5	5	5	5	5
10	5	5	5	5	5	5	5	5	5	5	5	5
11	4	5	5	5	5	5	5	5	5	5	5	5
12	4	4	4	5	4	5	5	5	5	5	5	5
13	4	4	4	4	4	4	5	4	5	5	5	5
14	4	4	4	4	4	4	4	4	4	5	4	4
15	4	4	4	4	4	4	4	4	4	4	4	4
16	—	—	1	1	2	2	2	3	3	3	4	4

*Use the column representing the month in the first year that the property is placed in service, e.g., January = 1.

Real estate tables.   Real real estate tables are slightly different, permitting depreciation only for the months of ownership. Real estate is divided into at least two categories: (1) low-income housing, and (2) all other real estate, commonly known as 18-year real property. Depreciation on each type of property is shown in Tables 7.3 and 7.4.

Using the example in Table 7.3, depreciation would be calculated as follows:

- Step 1. Select the appropriate real estate table.
- Step 2. Select the percentage figure based on the month the property was placed in service. (In this example, low-income housing was purchased in May. Therefore, the percentage for the first year is 9 percent.)
- Step 3. Multiply the percentage by the amount allocated to the building, but not including the value of the land. (Example: 9 % times $1,500,000 = $135,000.)
- Step 4. Use the same column to obtain the depreciation percentage for each succeeding year. This is shown in Table 7.5.

Table 7-4 Depreciation of 18-Year Real Property (18-year 175% declining balance)

Recovery Year	Applicable Percentage by Month*										
	1	2	3	4	5	6	7	8	9	10–11	12
1	10	9	8	7	6	6	5	4	3	2	1
2	9	9	9	9	9	9	9	9	9	10	10
3	8	8	8	8	8	8	8	8	9	9	9
4	7	7	7	7	7	7	8	8	8	8	8
5	6	7	7	7	7	7	7	7	7	7	7
6	6	6	6	6	6	6	6	6	6	6	6
7	5	5	5	5	6	6	6	6	6	6	6
8	5	5	5	5	5	5	5	5	5	5	5
9	5	5	5	5	5	5	5	5	5	5	5
10	5	5	5	5	5	5	5	5	5	5	5
11	5	5	5	5	5	5	5	5	5	5	5
12	5	5	5	5	5	5	5	5	5	5	5
13	4	4	4	5	5	4	4	5	4	4	4
14	4	4	4	4	4	4	4	4	4	4	4
15	4	4	4	4	4	4	4	4	4	4	4
16	4	4	4	4	4	4	4	4	4	4	4
17	4	4	4	4	4	4	4	4	4	4	4
18	4	4	4	4	4	4	4	4	4	4	4
19	—	—	1	1	1	2	2	2	3	3	4

*Use the month in the first year that the property is placed in service.

Table 7-5 Depreciation of Low-Income Housing

Year	Percentage		Amount		Depreciation Allowed
2	12%	×	$1,500,000	=	$180,000
3	11	×	1,500,000	=	165,000
4	9	×	1,500,000	=	135,000

This process is repeated for each year until the property is sold.

The new depreciation schedule dramatically increases deductions for personal property as well. For example, under the old laws using straight-line depreciation $1 million worth of equipment with a 10-year life, amounts to an annual depreciation of $100,000. The new laws would allow a first year deduction of $150,000 on $1 million worth of equipment, given a five-year life using ACRS. The next year's depreciation would be $220,000.

Table 7-6 Deductions for Personal Property Allowed under the ERTA

Year	Amount of Deduction
1985–1987	$ 5,000
1988–1989	7,500
1990 and later	10,000

The Economic Recovery Tax Act introduced an excellent benefit into the depreciation laws which was minimized by the Tax Reform Act of 1984. Code Section 179 was changed to permit taxpayers to elect to "expense" or deduct the full cost of certain property. Therefore, personal property used in a trade or business can be immediately deducted in the amounts shown in Table 7.6.

These special elections do not apply to property used for investment purposes (e.g., a computer purchased to track personal investments). If the property does not retain its trade or business status over the following two years, then the depreciation must be recaptured as discussed below.

Recapture rules. There is a complex set of rules regarding how much gain a person can keep and how much must be given back in the form of taxes when a depreciated asset is sold. These rules are essential for planners to understand because clients must know what to expect at the time an asset is sold. Knowledge of these rules will also indicate which tax shelters are appropriate.

To determine recapture, the property is assigned to categories depending on the IRS code sections in which it is defined.

1245 property. This includes all depreciable:

1. Personal property, such as cars, machinery, office equipment, and livestock.
2. Patents, copyrights, and leaseholds of 1245 property.
3. Single-purpose agricultural and horticultural structures and petroleum storage facilities.

Code Section 1245 allows taxpayers depreciation benefits that offset ordinary income, but gain is *not* taxed at long-term rates. Therefore, all depreciation under Section 1245 will be recaptured as *ordinary income*, regardless of the type of depreciation deducted or the holding period of the property. The following is an example.

EXAMPLE

Assumptions
Cost of equipment	$10,000
Depreciation taken	6,000
Remaining value (basis)	$ 4,000

A taxpayer sells the equipment at the prices shown in Table 7.7.

In the first alternative, the total amount of depreciation taken ($6,000) was greater than the gain ($4,000). Consequently, according to Code Section 1245, the full amount of depreciation up to the amount of gain received is ordinary income.

Alternative two is a loss. Therefore, there is no recapture of depreciation deductions.

Alternative three illustrates the rare occurrence of personal property selling for more than its original cost. In this instance, 100 percent of the depreciation, or $6,000, is recaptured as ordinary income. The remaining $2,000 of the gain is taxed at long-term capital gain rates.

1250 property. This section applies to depreciable real property such as apartments or office buildings, shopping centers or warehouses.

Recapture rules under this section are less severe than for section 1245 property. Depreciation recapture rules for 1250 property are as follows:

1. If straight-line depreciation is taken, all gain is taxed as long-term capital gain.
2. If the accelerated cost recovery system (ACRS) percentage is used, recapture rules are dependent on the type of property being depreciated.

Table 7-7 Sale of Section 1245 Property

	Alternative 1	Alternative 2	Alternative 3
Sales price	$8,000	$3,000	$12,000
Basis	4,000	4,000	4,000
Profit (loss)	$4,000	−$1,000	$ 8,000

Table 7-8 Recapture of Depreciation on Sale of an Apartment Building

Straight-Line Depreciation		Accelerated Depreciation	
Cost	$100,000	Cost	$100,000
Depreciation	26,667	Depreciation	39,000
Basis	$ 73,333	Basis	$ 61,000
Sale price	$140,000	Sale price	$140,000
Basis	73,333	Basis	61,000
Gain	$ 66,667	Gain	$ 79,000

For residential property (apartments, duplexes, houses) accelerated depreciation in excess of straight-line depreciation must be recaptured as ordinary income. An example is given in Table 7.8. On nonresidential real property (office buildings, shopping centers, etc.), when accelerated depreciation is taken, gain equivalent to the amount of depreciation taken is taxed as ordinary income.

With straight-line depreciation the $66,667 gain is all long-term capital gain. With accelerated depreciation, the excess of the $79,000 gain over the straight-line gain ($66,667) is taxed as ordinary income. In this example, $11,333 is taxed as ordinary income, and $66,667 is taxed as capital gains.

If the same numbers are used, but the real property is an office building, the effects of the recapture rules could be devastating. The first example would be the same because straight-line depreciation was taken. The effect in the second example is dramatic. All depreciation, or $39,000 of the $79,000 gain, is taxed as ordinary income. The remaining profit of $40,000 is taxed at long-term capital gain rates.

It is essential to look at the type of depreciation taken on real estate investments. If nonresidential property is being depreciated using the accelerated method, then the results could be very bad for certain investors. And, if the property is held for less than six months, long-term capital gain rates do not apply. However, in most situations, it would be unwise to pass up the benefits of long-term capital gain for accelerated depreciation on nonresidential property.

Phantom income.   Depreciation does not cause the phenomenon known as *phantom income*. Rather, depreciation gives tax deductions that shelter cash flow and provide excess deductions which shelter other income. However, when depreciation expires, so does its protective cover. The result can be *phantom income*—that is, no cash is received, but there is taxable gain. The following example describes a highly leveraged leasing program that produces phantom income.

EXAMPLE

Equipment costing $100,000 is purchased with a $10,000 down payment and $90,000 is financed with a seven-year, fully amortized loan consisting of a yearly principal and interest payment of $21,000.

In Table 7.9, ACRS five-year depreciation is used. For this example, figures are rounded and maintenance expenses are disregarded. Note that depreciation and interest are deductible. Principal reduction payments are not.

The information in Table 7.9 reveals taxable consequences. Look at the economics. In the first through the fifth year, there is an actual cash profit of $4,000 ($25,000 gross income less the $21,000 loan repayment = $4,000). The problem begins in the sixth year. There are no depreciation deductions in the sixth and seventh years. However, investors are still making the $21,000 loan repayment and receiving $4,000 in cash.

In year six, the only deduction is the $4,000 interest payment ($25,000 − $4,000 = $21,000 taxable gain). In year seven, the taxable gain is $23,000 ($25,000 income less the $2,000 interest deduction = $23,000). Taxpayers must be prepared to pay taxes on money never received. The leasing program originally produced $4,000 in income per year and various tax deductions. When depreciation expired, there was only a small amount of deductible interest expenses.

Considering the time value of money, it is a good idea to defer taxes to the future if a taxpayer:

1. Is prepared for the tax consequences.
2. Will be in a lower marginal tax bracket in the future.
3. Will invest the original cash flow and tax savings to receive the desired aftertax rate of return.

These are essential points in considering many tax-sheltered transactions. Some people can get caught up in the apparent benefits of tax deductions. Many commit themselves to tax shelter programs on the basis of tax deductions only, giving little at-

Table 7-9 Phantom Income

				Year			
	1	2	3	4	5	6	7
Income	$25,000	$25,000	$25,000	$25,000	$25,000	$25,000	$25,000
Depreciation	− 15,000	− 22,000	− 21,000	− 21,000	− 21,000	− 0	− 0
Interest	− 13,000	− 12,000	− 10,000	− 9,000	− 7,000	− 4,000	− 2,000
Principle	8,000	9,000	11,000	12,000	14,000	17,000	19,000
	$ − 3,000	$ − 9,000	$ − 6,000	$ − 5,000	$ − 3,000	$21,000	$23,000
	net loss	net loss	net loss	net loss	net loss	net gain	net gain

tention to the underlying economics of the venture. Just imagine the problems if the equipment in this example did not generate the projected income. In that instance, there would be true economic damage from the very beginning, tax benefits notwithstanding.

DEPLETION

Depletion is to minerals what depreciation is to property. Depletion is a deduction that compensates investors for using up a nonreplaceable asset. In contrast, depreciation is an economic benefit because the property may be appreciating in value. Property will seldom depreciate at the same rate as the decreases given in the ACRS tables.

There are two types of depletion methods.

Percentage depletion. This method computes the allowance by a fixed percentage. The percentage varies according to the type of mineral involved. The allowance for oil and gas was 15 percent in 1984. However, the percentage depletion cannot exceed 50 percent of the taxable income from the property before the allowance. The calculation of percentage depletion is as follows:

Gross income	$1,000,000
Less expenses	650,000
Taxable income	$ 350,000
Depletion allowance	
(15% of $1,000,000)	150,000
Taxable income after depletion	$ 200,000

Note: the depletion allowance is either one half of the taxable income ($175,000, in this case) or the percentage depletion (in this example, $150,000), whichever is less.

Cost depletion. This is computed by dividing the basis (cost) by the estimated number of units of an asset (barrels, tons). Multiply this amount by the number of units sold.

EXAMPLE

A mineral interest was purchased for $2 million. The estimated recoverable reserves are $400,000, and 40,000 units were extracted this year.

$$\frac{\$2,000,000 \text{ cost}}{\$400,000 \text{ total}} \times 40,000 \text{ unit produced}$$
$$= \$200,000 \text{ depletion allowance}$$

The method that produces the greatest benefit should be chosen. However, with timber, the cost depletion method must be used.

Percentage depletion is based on the gross income from the property, regardless of cost. Consequently, if the minerals are extracted, the investor may receive more than the original capital investment. For example, if investors paid $1.5 million for 150,000 barrels of proven reserve, their cost per unit is $10. If 200,000 barrels were extracted, they would have received a depletion allowance exceeding their $1.5 million investment.

BASIS

Basis, the value remaining after depreciation, is an essential element in determining the tax consequences of a transaction. Is an economic loss deductible? How much gain has to be reported? To answer these questions, basis must be subtracted from net sale price. But first of all, a myriad of rules will determine what the basis is in acquiring, depreciating, and selling property.

The first step is to see how the property was obtained. The alternatives are purchase, inheritance, gift, or exchange.

Purchase. In the case of an outright purchase, basis would be the value of what was paid for the property. This includes cash, the amount borrowed, and the value of the property. It must be remembered that *at risk* rules (full recourse financing in all purchases except real estate) apply to determining basis. In addition, the purchase price is not a determining factor in establishing basis if the transaction was contrived. Here, the doctrine of substance over form comes into play.

A comment needs to be made concerning the *related party transaction* regulation. This rule is intended to prevent related taxpayers such as a husband and wife, parents, grandparents, children, grandchildren, or brothers and sisters from creating an artificial loss. Given the possibility of arrangements between such related parties, the purchase price does not establish basis for loss, but only for gain. The basis for a loss is the same one the previous owner-relative had.

EXAMPLE

Ted pays his dad $10,000 for 1,000 shares of stock. His dad's basis is $8,000. If Ted sells the stock for $6,000, he will report a $2,000 loss—$8,000 (his dad's basis) − $6,000 = $2,000.

Inheritance. This code section has been changed several times. At present, the basis for inherited property is the fair market value at the donor's death. This is the origin of the expression, "To get out of a burned-out tax shelter, you have to die!"

EXAMPLE

Maria inherited raw land from a friend. Fair market value was $25,000. Her friend originally paid $5,000 for the vacant land. Maria's basis on this land is $25,000. If she sells it for $25,000, no gain is reported.

Gift. The basis of property received as a gift is the basis when the donor held the property.

Exchange. In the exchange of similar property Code Section 1031 provides for calculating basis by starting with the adjusted basis of the property surrendered in the exchange. Added to this amount is the adjusted basis of assets or boot given, and any gain recognized. The fair market value of the boot received or recognized loss is subtracted.

INVESTMENT INTEREST LIMITATION

Over the years Congress has produced a series of complicated laws regarding what types of interest are deductible. The results affect clients dramatically.

First of all, there are no deduction limitations for borrowing money for a trade or business, or to finance consumer debt, such as a car, home, or student loan. However, when money is borrowed either to finance investments or for certain net lease properties, there are limitations. For example, the amount of investment interest that may be deducted is limited to the following:

- $10,000 is the base amount for married couples filing separate returns. The limitation is $5,000 for each person, plus,
- Net investment income—This is defined as gross income from interest, dividends, royalties, rents, net short-term capital gain from property held for investment, and ordinary income from recapture of 1245 and 1250 depreciation.

EXAMPLE

John has $25,000 in interest expenses. He may deduct up to $21,000 in interest, comprised of the following:

1. Base amount	$10,000
2. Interest income	2,000
3. Dividend income	4,000
4. 1245 recapture	1,000
5. Net short-term capital gain	4,000
Total:	$21,000

The remaining $4,000 may be carried over into the future until it is used.

The assets classified as investments for purposes of this code section include:

1. Stocks.
2. Bonds.
3. Interest paid or incurred by a partnership.
4. Vacant land held for appreciation.
5. Property subject to a net lease, i.e., when business deductions total less than 15 percent of rental income or a lessor is guaranteed against loss or guaranteed a specified return.

A key element in this context is that the law usually classifies ownership of apartment and office buildings as a trade or business. Consequently, this type of real estate is not subject to investment interest limitations has more than 15 percent of gross income as deductible expenses, such as repairs and maintenance.

ALTERNATIVE MINIMUM TAX (AMT)

The alternative minimum tax (AMT) can be described as a "flat tax."

The AMT was originally created to prevent individuals from completely avoiding paying taxes. The tax now involves a rather complicated formula that will snag the unsuspecting. This is true because taxpayers will pay either their regular tax or the AMT, whichever is greater. *Nothing* reduces the AMT, except the foreign tax credit. The following should be of assistance in making preliminary tax projections for using the AMT.

- Step 1. Planners must start with the taxpayer's adjusted gross income (AGI).
- Step 2. Subtract *only* the following allowable deductions from the AGI:
  a. Charitable contributions.
  b. Medical expenses (in excess of 5 percent of AGI).
  c. Casualty losses (in excess of 10 percent of AGI).
  d. Qualified housing interest (special rules).
  e. Other qualified net interest investment.
  f. Gambling losses to the extent gambling income is recognized.
  g. Other categories, such as estate taxes and alternative net operating losses, as well as income included under IRC 667.
- Step 3. ADD any of the following *tax preference* items:
  a. Capital gain deduction (except on principal residence).
  b. Interest and dividends excluded under Sections 116 and 128.
  c. Accelerated depreciation in excess of straight-line depreciation on real property.
  d. Accelerated depreciation in excess of straight-line depreciation on leased personal property.
  e. Amortization of certified pollution control facilities.
  f. Mining exploration and development costs.
  g. Circulation, research, and experimentation expenses.
  h. Percentage depletion in excess of cost depletion.
  i. Incentive stock options bargain element.
  j. Excess intangible drilling costs.
  k. Accelerated cost recovery deductions.
- Step 4. From this final number, subtract $30,000 for a single person, $40,000 for a married joint filing, and $20,000 for a married person filing separately.
- Step 5. Multiply the amount found in Step 4 by 20 percent. This is the AMT.

EXAMPLE

John is single and has an AGI income of $39,000. The only allowable deduction he has is $7,000 of mortgage expense. John sold a lot for $30,000 profit. Consequently, the 60 percent exclusion ($18,000) is a tax preference item. To calculate his AMT:

- Step 1. $39,000
- Step 2. (7,000)
- Step 3. +18,000
- Step 4. Exclusion of $30,000 = Net taxable income for AMT of $20,000
- Step 5. $20,000 × 20% = $4,000 AMT

Now compare the $4,000 AMT to John's regular tax computation. If John's regular tax is less than the AMT, he will still pay the $4,000 amount.

Few clients will escape this tax, so it is important to have an AMT projection made on most clients.

PART THREE

The Investment Environment

CHAPTER EIGHT

The Economy

It is essential for financial planners to be cognizant of the cycles that occur in our economy, as well as current economic theories. Investments usually respond to economic cycles by increasing or declining in value. Thus, the ability to predict future economic conditions can have a profound impact on investment performance. This is one reason the services of economic forecasters are in demand. But predicting economic cycles is easier said than done.

Obviously, recognizing causal factors in economic fluctuations would greatly increase the value of economic forecasting. Knowing just what combination of factors contributes to economic downturns and upturns would be invaluable to the investor. Numerous theories have drawn interesting conclusions, and a few of these perspectives will be highlighted.

ECONOMIC THEORY

Classical Economics

The concept that individuals have unlimited desires and scarce resources is one of the elementary tenets of economics. The 19th-century French economist J. B. Say came up with the theory that "supply creates its own demand." *Say's Law* proposes that there will be sufficient consumption spending to equal the supply of goods. In analyzing a capitalist economy, many prominent economists, now known as classical economists, embraced Say's Law, using it as a foundation for their theories. Classical economists came to perceive capitalism as a self-regulating economy capable of running itself. From this perspective, full

142 / CHAPTER 8

employment was the norm and government assistance was unnecessary to keep the economy humming.

Keynesian Theory

As one can imagine, Say's theory came under significant criticism during the depression of the 1930s. In 1936, the English economist John Maynard Keynes published his economic perspective. He concluded that capitalism is neither self-regulating nor capable of guaranteeing perpetual prosperity and full employment. Keynesian theory rejected classical theories that interest rates control and coordinate the diverse motives of saving and investing by both individuals and businesses.

Keynesians have argued the amount saved can be inversely related to the interest rate (that is, less is saved when rates are higher). As an example, it would take $125,000 in an 8 percent savings vehicle to produce $10,000 of income per year. However, individuals would have to save only $62,500 to achieve an income of $10,000 per year if they could net a yield of 16 percent per annum. Thus, from a Keynesian viewpoint, saving and investing can be at odds, resulting in oscillating levels of employment, total income, and total output and prices. Keynesian theorists also attacked many other aspects of the capitalist economy.

During the Depression, there was significant underconsumption and, at the same time, overproduction. People simply did not have the money to buy, so it was virtually impossible to make cash customers out of the unemployed. This crisis brought the Keynesian theory of employment to a prominent position. The idea that government fiscal policies could exert a stabilizing influence began to be widely accepted. The Keynesian viewpoint contends that government, in effect, can control business cycles. Thus, to offset certain cycles, the Federal Reserve Board, Congress, and the administration manipulate government spending and taxes.

Following Keynesian theory, in a recessionary cycle, government can return the economy to equilibrium by an expansionary fiscal policy. Such a policy puts more money into the general economy through increased government spending, decreased taxes, or a combination of both. The effectiveness of this theory is difficult to measure, and has been the subject of debate since its first implementation by Franklin Roosevelt's administration in the early 1930s.

Monetarism

Nobel Prize winner Milton Friedman and other economists espouse a theory known as *monetarism*. They feel the money supply is the key determinant of employment, output, and price level. In contrast to the Keynesian viewpoint, monetarists believe that government intervention is inefficient and produces negative economic results. Rather than tinkering with the demand aspect of the economy, the monetarists focus their attention on the quantity of money within the economy relative to national output. To sustain steady growth in the economy, monetarists believe that the supply of money must grow proportionately. They see the cost of money (interest rates) as a principal determinant of the level of economic activity, and the supply of money, in turn, as a principal determinant of interest rates.

Phillips Curve

The divergent positions of the Keynesians and monetarists are not the only intriguing theories intended to explain our economic phenomena. During the 1970s and early 1980s, the American economy suffered stagnating employment and output as well as inflation, all at the same time. This unusual combination of unemployment and inflation is often referred to as *stagflation*. The English economist A. W. Phillips attempted to reveal the relationship between inflation and employment in what is known as the *Phillips Curve*. He suggested that the price for full employment is inflation. The Phillips Curve poses a serious political dilemma, because it implies that society must accept a certain level of unemployment to achieve price stability.

Keynesians attempted to explain the Phillips Curve through inflationary expectations, random shocks, and changes in the labor force. However, another perspective suggests that the Keynesian model has overlooked some subtle, yet fundamental, aspects of a capitalist economy. This is supply-side economics.

Supply Siders

The "supply siders" challenge many Keynesian conclusions. These economists state that expanding demand is not sufficient to reinstate full employment. Rather, the changes in the *cost of goods* must be seen as fundamental in determining the levels of both unemployment and inflation. Supply siders see the increase in costs as stemming from an increase in taxes, growth of the public sector, government regulations, and disincentives to work and invest.

One of the chief proponents of supply-side economics is Arthur Laffer. His well-publicized position on the relationship between tax rates and tax revenues is depicted in what is known as the *Laffer Curve*. Laffer believes that lower tax rates will stimulate saving, investing, and working. This would expand the national output and income base, thereby sustaining tax revenues. Many economists reject this prospective and believe that large tax cuts generate large budget deficits, thereby accelerating the rate of inflation.

Economics is not a static science. And no single economist or theory can provide a model that explains current economic phenomena and predicts the future. It is appropriate that economic controversy continues, as societies and economies continue to change and evolve. Future theoretical models will have to take into consideration the structural changes in the United States and the world at large. Readily visible forces of change in the United States include an aging population, an expanding communication base, and migration to the Sun Belt. These will have important implications for consumption, saving, and investment theories. The U.S. economy is also intertwined with the economies of the world. One example of this is the magnitude of foreign debt held by this country's largest banks. Should Third World countries significantly default on their loans, the banking system would suffer and, the principal and purchasing power of savers and investors would be in jeopardy.

These and many additional factors must be utilized in developing future economic models. There is a great need to respond correctly to internal and external economic influences. More importantly, it is becoming essential to learn to manipulate these forces with a much greater degree of finesse than is now possible.

While future economic changes must be anticipated, it is also important to understand the forces that are currently influencing the economy. Perhaps the foremost of these is the Federal Reserve System.

FEDERAL RESERVE SYSTEM

This institution is responsible for the formulation and implementation of U.S. monetary policy. The Federal Reserve System, as it is called is divided into 12 geographical districts. Each district has one central bank and, in some cases, one or more branches, for a total of 24. The fed's governing board is comprised of seven members appointed by the president of the U.S. for 14-year terms. This Board of Governors is assisted by the Open Market Committee, which is comprised of the seven board members plus the presidents of five of the Federal Reserve Banks. There is also a Federal Advisory Council, composed of 12 bankers, each from one of the Federal Reserve Banks. In addition, commercial banks may be members of the Federal Reserve System.

The Federal Reserve acts to fulfill the following responsibilities:

1. **Regulates the Money Supply.** Through policy decisions, the Federal Reserve Board determines the amount of money within the economy.
2. **Supervises Member Banks.** Through periodic reviews and unannounced examinations, the Federal Reserve checks the financial stability of banks that are members of the Federal Reserve System.
3. **Provides for Collection of Checks.** The fed acts as a clearing agent for checks.
4. **Acts as an Agent for the Government.** The Federal Reserve holds the U.S. Treasury's checking accounts.
5. **Supplies Paper Currency.** The Federal Reserve oversees and regulates the economy's supply of paper money.

The fed has devised some yardsticks to define and measure the money supply. The first measure is called M_1. It consists of: Coins and paper money in the hands of the public, and demand deposits (checking accounts).

The next category is referred to as M_2. This is a broader definition of the money supply as it includes all of M_1 plus time deposits (saving accounts and certificates of deposit) at public banks. The latter does not function as a direct medium of exchange, but can be readily converted into currency or demand deposits. There are three other "aggregates" used to describe the monetary supply, however, M_1 and M_2 are the most controversial and most analyzed.

Policymakers within the fed attempt to adjust the money supply and influence the cost of money. This is done to attain the following set of Congressional objectives.

1. A high level of employment.
2. Stability in the general price level.
3. Growing economic activity.
4. Equilibrium in the nation's balance of payments.

The Federal Reserve has three principal tools with which to implement policies.

Open market operations. Through its Open Market Committee, the fed buys and sells government securities in the market. Purchase of government securities increases the money supply, while a sale decreases it.

The discount rate. The Federal Reserve makes short-term loans to commercial banks. The interest that these banks are charged is called the discount rate. If a bank must *pay* more for its funds, it will also *charge* more (i.e., raise interest rates on the loans it issues). Thus, by raising or lowering the discount rate, the fed can influence the level of interest rates within the economy.

The reserve ratio. The Federal Reserve can raise or lower the amount of reserves a commercial bank must maintain. This, in turn, affects the amount a bank has available for loans. If the fed raises reserve requirements, less is available for credit.

The amount of credit available to the public has an influence on the general economy. Reserve requirements impact the availability of credit.

The Federal Reserve uses these techniques to minimize cyclical business fluctuations, keep the economy stable, and encourage investments. To understand this monetary policy, it is necessary to see how commercial banks function in the system.

BANKING SYSTEM

Because they accept deposits and make loans, commercial banks are an essential element in the creation and supply of money. In fact, demand deposits, issued by commercial banks, are the major component of the money supply, comprising 90 percent of all transactions.

Commercial banks can create demand deposit money. The first step in this process is accepting demand deposits in the form of checking accounts. The next step is to determine how much of these deposits a bank will lend to earn profits. However, banks do not make this decision independently. One of the main functions of the Federal Reserve is determining how much a commercial bank may lend and how much it must keep on reserve.

If the system were not regulated, banks could expand the money supply in an inflationary period to obtain a profit. In a recessionary climate, a bank could restrict the money supply to achieve liquidity. Instead, the Federal Reserve attempts to counteract inflationary and recessionary tendencies through its use of *fractional reserve requirements*. Fractional reserves are based on the theory that all depositors will not want all of their money at the same time. (If this does occur, it is known as a "run" on the bank.) Instead, some portion (fraction) of demand deposits will remain in the bank. And this determines the Reserve Ratio as follows:

$$\text{Reserve ratio} = \frac{\text{Commercial bank's required deposit in a Federal Reserve bank}}{\text{Commercial bank's demand deposits}}$$

The reserve limits were legislated by Congress. However, specific ratios are established by the Federal Reserve's Board of Governors and are a powerful, if infrequently employed, method for controlling the supply of money.

Nonmember banks are also required by state law to keep reserves. There is considerable variation in reserve requirements in different states, but the average is about 15 percent.

As an example, say a commercial bank has $100 million in demand deposits. If the reserve requirement is 10 percent, the bank would be obligated to deposit $10 million in the Federal Reserve Bank in its district. If the reserve ratio is 20 percent, the amount deposited would be $20 million. The commercial bank would be able to lend the excess over its reserve requirements, or $80 million with a reserve requirement of 20 percent.

If every bank loaned out the maximum excess reserve, there would be a significant multiplier effect. With this multiplier effect, commercial banks can create money. Table 8.1 shows the expansion of the money supply when the reserve ratio is 15 percent.

Table 8-1 Expansion of Money Supply

Bank	Demand Deposits	Required Reserve	Excess Reserve	Amount Bank Can Lend
A	$100.00	$15.00	$85.00	$85.00
B	85.00	12.75	72.25	72.25
C	72.25	10.84	61.41	61.41
D	61.41	9.21	52.20	52.20
E	and so forth. . . .			

While an individual bank can lend only the amount deposits exceed reserves, the commercial banking system as a whole can lend a multiple of its excess reserves, as the table suggests. The equation for this is:

$$\frac{1}{\text{Required reserve ratio}} = \text{Monetary multiplier}$$

or

$$\frac{1}{15\%} = 6.667$$

In the above transaction, the commercial banking system created over $666.67 in new money. The lower the reserve requirement, the greater the expansion of the money supply.

"Fed watchers" look closely at the expansion of demand deposits, or M_1, and the expansion of M_2 because of the potential for money creation and resulting inflation. While the fed, through the reserve ratio, discount rate, and open market operations, attempts to control swings in the economy, most economists believe the Federal Reserve cannot fine tune economic cycles through monetary policies alone. Rather, there must be a coordinated effort in terms of fiscal policy. Controlling the federal deficit is a prime strategy that many economists advocate. However, the cooperation of the legislative and executive branches is needed for this.

A final major force in the economy is the federal tax structure. The tax system is currently under much criticism and significant changes are being considered in Congress. Planners should bear in mind that any *major* structural changes, such as a *flat tax*, would have a dramatic economic impact and directly affect a client's investments.

CHAPTER NINE

Marketable Securities

Investing in marketable securities has become increasingly popular because many see it as a means to achieve their financial goals. Some invest in these vehicles for long-term growth or to preserve purchasing power. Others require income, while some desire speculative short-term profit. Although investors' expectations differ, financial planners will seek to match specific objectives with the appropriate vehicle. However, selecting the most suitable security is not an easy task, because each investment has different risk and return characteristics.

Marketable securities are often called *financial assets*. The term is used to describe either debt or equity instruments. For clarification, the opposite of a financial asset is a real asset. Real assets—apartments, office buildings, and airplanes—are tangible. IOUs and stock certificates are not, rather, financial assets represent an indirect claim on real assets. They can also be categorized according to who issued the security, such as a government agency or a public corporation.

Marketable securities include many diverse vehicles including government obligations, stocks, bonds, options, and real estate investment trusts. Some are conservative, while others are as risky as rolling dice. What these assets have in common is liquidity. Typically they can be quickly turned into cash at current market value.

The following sections examine various types of marketable securities, as well as their risk and return characteristics.

SHORT-TERM DEBT INSTRUMENTS

Corporations issue short-term debt in the form of *commercial paper*. This type of debt is sold at a discount from face value, and on maturity, investors receive the full face amount. Most commercial paper in the United States has a maturity of less than nine months. If the debt were longer than nine months, the seller would have to go through the expensive process of registering with the Securities and Exchange Commission.

Interest rates on commercial paper are expressed on a yield basis, determined on a face value of $100 and a 360-day year. The equation for determining price is:

$$P = \frac{100}{1 + (ni)/360}$$

where:

P = price.

i = interest rate.

n = period of time.

If an investor were buying 90-day paper to yield 9 percent, the purchase price would be found by the following calculation:

$$P = \frac{100}{1 + (90)(.09)/360}$$

$$P = \frac{100}{1.0225}$$

$$P = .977995$$

The cost of $500,000 in face value would be $488,997.56 (.977995 × $500,000).

A *certificate of deposit* (CD) is another type of short-term debt. These are deposit liabilities of the issuing bank or savings and loan with a maturity date of under one year. They function in a manner similar to commercial paper, except that CDs are interest bearing, while commercial paper is a promise to pay the specified face amount at maturity.

CDs are usually issued in large denominations, from $100,000 to $1 million, although some nonnegotiable, or nontradable, CDs are available for lesser amounts. Negotiable CDs are considered liquid because a strong secondary trading market has evolved over the past two decades.

A *banker's acceptance* is a short-term debt instrument that often originates with international trade. A bank is responsible for paying at maturity. However, the acceptance is backed by the firm issuing the draft. Yield on banker's acceptances is usually a half point higher than on comparable securities of the same maturity.

LONG-TERM DEBT

In addition to the U.S. government, the major issuers of debt in this country are corporations. There are many classifications of corporate debt, commonly referred to as *bonds*. They all involve some variation of the following contractual promises: (1) interest will be paid periodically, and (2) the principal will be paid at a predesignated time.

Usually corporate bonds pay interest semiannually, and mature in from 5 to 30 years. More specifically, each bond will contain the provisions determining interest payments and when or if those payments can be subordinated to other debt.

The issuer may be able to *call* the bond, that is pay off the debt for a stated price prior to maturity. These *call provisions* are for the benefit of corporations and are typically exercised when interest rates fall below the issue rate. Corporations can save by paying the debt off early and issuing new bonds yielding a lower interest. This is not advantageous to investors, because the amount received on the called bond can only be reinvested at a lower interest rate. To compensate investors, a *call premium*, an amount over the face (par) value of the bond, will be paid by the corporation.

Corporate bonds contain further provisions describing how the debt will be repaid. With a *sinking fund*, corporations systematically set aside a fixed dollar amount or a percentage installment to gradually retire the debt. Bonds are retired at a price not higher than par value and any accrued interest. In the open market, bonds will be retired if the price is below par.

Another method of repayment is the *serial* bond. With this alternative, several small bonds are issued with different maturity dates. Each series is redeemed, usually at par, when it comes due.

It is important to see what the corporation has pledged as security to protect the interest and principal payments. One of the more common ways to provide protection is through a *secured*

Table 9-1 Debt Instrument Rating Systems

Moody's	Standard & Poor's	Rating Description
Aaa	AAA	Highest
Aa	AA	High
A	A	Upper Medium
Baa	BBB	Medium
Ba	BB	Speculative elements
B	B	Very speculative
Caa	CCC and CC	Strong default possibility
Ca	C	Default, possibility of political recovery
C	DDD-D	Default, little chance of recovery

bond. This type of debt places a *lien* against specific assets of the issuer. This gives bondholders the legal right to have the pledged property sold to satisfy the outstanding principal and interest. *Mortgage bonds* fit this category, because they are liens against the real property of the corporation. Also included are *collateral trust bonds* which are secured by the stocks and bonds of other corporations.

Unsecured bonds are called *debentures.* They do not involve a lien against specific property. Rather they have a claim on earnings. Along with holders of commercial paper and trade creditors, debenture holders are classified as general creditors. However, in the event of bankruptcy, holders of secured credit must be paid off first.

Several reporting services, principally Moody's and Standard & Poor's, compile and publish data for determining the financial strength of companies and government agencies issuing debt. Through their ratings, investors can determine the level of risk of a specific organization. Lower ratings mean greater risk, so the yield on these risky investments must be high to attract investors. While the information is very helpful, ratings have not always been lowered in a timely manner. An example involved failure to downgrade New York City's municipal bonds when the city came close to bankruptcy in the 1970s. Table 9.1 illustrates the rating system of the two most popular services.

Investors want to know not only the risk of their bonds, but also the expected rate of return. There are several different ways of measuring a bond's rate of return. Some of the most common techniques include the following:

Yield to maturity (YTM). This measurement reveals the rate of return if the bond is held to maturity.

$$YTM = \frac{[(\text{Face value} - \text{Purchase price})/(n)] + [\text{Annual coupon interest paid}]}{(\text{Face value} + \text{Purchase price})/2}$$

where:

n = maturity.

EXAMPLE

A bond with a face value of $1,000 is purchased for $850. It matures in 10 years, and is paying 5 percent interest.

$$YTM = \frac{[(\$1,000 - \$850)/10] + [.05(\$1,000)]}{(\$1,000 + \$850)/2}$$

$$= \frac{\$150/10 + 50}{75} = \frac{65}{75} = 8.67\%$$

Coupon rate. This return is the fixed rate of interest, or nominal rate, stated on the bond. The formula is:

$$\text{Coupon rate} = \frac{\text{Coupon interest per year}}{\text{Face value}}$$

EXAMPLE

A $1,000 bond is paying $95 per year. This yield is calculated as follows:

$$\text{Coupon rate} = \frac{\$95}{\$1,000} = 9.5\%$$

Current yield. The current yield will differ from the coupon rate if the bond is not purchased at face value. The formula is:

$$\text{Current yield} = \frac{\text{Coupon interest per year}}{\text{Current market value}}$$

EXAMPLE

The coupon rate of a $1,000 face value bond is 8 percent. If the bond is purchased for $920, the current yield is:

$$\text{Current yield} = \frac{\$80}{\$920} = 8.70\%$$

Bond prices are quoted daily in the newspapers. An example of a typical quotation is as follows.

BOND	YIELD	VOLUME	HIGH	LOW	CLOSE	NET CHANGE
Chryslr 8s98	11	30	77	75 3/8	75 3/8	—

The abbreviated name of the company, coupon rate, and year of maturity are listed first (Chrysler, 8 percent, due 1998). The yield column lists the annual interest rate (annual interest paid divided by the closing price). The volume figure indicates the number of $1,000 face-value bonds traded that day. Next, the highest and lowest trading prices on the bond for the day are listed as well as the closing or final price. Last, the net change in price from the previous day is listed. Price in this instance is quoted as a percentage of the bond's face value; thus, a price of 77 means 77 percent of $1,000—or $770.

FEDERAL GOVERNMENT SECURITIES

All securities involve risk, most commonly loss of principal or loss of purchasing power. However, the former is not considered a risk with government securities because the federal government has unlimited power to raise and collect taxes, as well as to print new money to pay obligations. This is not true with corporate debt. The fear of bankruptcy is minimal with government securities, making it a popular choice for investments. An additional feature is that interest earned on treasury securities is free of state income tax.

The U.S. Treasury and various other federal agencies issue debt securities to finance expenditures in excess of tax collections or to refinance maturing debt. Since World War II, the federal government has been steadily generating assorted debt instruments. The first type is a *Treasury bill* (*T-bill*), which is marketed through periodic competitive public auctions.

Treasury bills are issued in minimum denominations of $10,000, and are sold at a discount from face value. As is true of all commercial paper, no interest is paid on T-bills, but investors receive the full face value when the bill matures. Most have a maturity of 13, 26, or 52 weeks. There is a very active secondary trading market for T-bills. Therefore, they can be sold prior to maturity. Their value will then be based on current interest rates and length of time until maturity.

The government also issues debt securities with *coupons*. These coupon issues pay interest at regular intervals, as well as face value at maturity. Coupon issues with original maturity dates of 1 to 10 years are called *notes*.

Finally the Treasury also issues *bonds*. Maturity varies, but is usually over 5 years and often as much as 25 to 30 years. There is also an active secondary trading market in government bonds.

The market value of a particular Treasury issue will depend on the original interest rate, prevailing interest rates, and the length of time until maturity. Typically, the longer the time to maturity of an issue, the greater its market value will fluctuate with changing interest rates. This is a phenomenon common to all debt securities that pay a fixed rate of interest.

Federal agencies also issue debt instruments, usually to provide loans for the benefit of homeowners and farmers. The agencies accomplish this by utilizing various intermediaries to actually make or passthrough the loans. Examples of organizations receiving this source of funding include: farm credit banks, federal land banks, federal home loan banks, the Federal National Mortgage Association, (FNMA), and the Government National Mortgage Association (GNMA).

GNMA is a government-chartered and government-owned corporation. It sponsors a program to passthrough cash payments received by a specific pool of government insured and guaranteed mortgages. GNMA guarantees payments to investors regardless of whether a homeowner pays on his or her mortgage. Payments received by investors include interest on unpaid principal as well as a return of a portion of and any prepayments on principal. Consequently, investors must exercise caution in not consuming the total payment. This is because without a reinvestment plan, the total principal is returned on a periodic basis, rather than as a lump sum at the end of the loan period.

FNMA is a privately owned, government-sponsored financial intermediary. It is designed to improve the liquidity of mortgages by buying government-insured mortgages. Purchase is financed by selling debentures and short-term discount notes. The interest earned on the securities FNMA sells, is slightly higher than on Treasury obligations, but usually less than on corporate debt.

Zero-Coupon Government Bonds

This investment is simply a debt instrument sold at a discount from face value. It does not pay any interest or principal until maturity, in contrast to conventional government bonds that pay interest twice a year. However, the unpaid interest on zero-coupon bonds is taxed by the IRS each year. For this reason, zero coupons have become popular for IRAs and pension plans, which are exempt from current taxation.

As is the case with all fixed-income securities, a zero coupon's value is subject to changes in interest rates. However, zero coupons are affected more dramatically than the average bond because they are discounted so deeply (that is, sell at a price well below face, or par, value). As a result a relatively small change in interest yield translates into a significantly large price move. For example, in 1984 when conventional 30-year bonds fell 3 percent, the price of 30-year zero coupons fell 25 percent. The opposite happens when prices increase, so this volatility must not be overlooked.

Municipal Bonds

Debt instruments are also issued by states, counties, cities, and other government agencies. The main attraction for investors is that the interest income from these bonds is *not subject to federal income tax*. Interest may also be exempted by the issuing state. Thus, if a California resident purchased a municipal bond issued by the State of California, the interest would be exempt from state taxes. This would not be the case if the same California investor purchased a bond issued by the State of Illinois.

As a result of the tax-exempt feature of these municipal bonds, yield is comparable to the aftertax rate of return on debt instruments of equivalent risk. Expressed another way, a 9 percent municipal bond is comparable to a fully taxable savings vehicle earning 13.85 percent if the investor is in a 35 percent tax bracket. This yield can be calculated as follows:

$$100\% - \text{tax bracket} = \text{net yield}$$
$$100\% - 35\% = 65\%$$

Municipal bond rate is divided
$$\text{by the net yield} = \text{Equivalent rate}$$
$$9\%/.65 = 13.85\%$$

Therefore, if a client is in a 35 percent tax bracket, receiving 9 percent on a tax-free vehicle is the equivalent of 13.85 percent on a taxable investment.

Municipal securities are divided into several categories, based on the source of funding for repayment. The key subdivisions are based on the risk of default. Therefore, the identity of the issuer is essential.

General obligation. This bond is secured by a priority claim on all revenues received by the issuer. Many of these obligations also require the issuer to levy sufficient taxes to pay off the debt. It is important that this right of first claim is on the revenues of the issuer, not on the issuer's assets. The debt, which has a maturity of from 1 to 30 years, is called a bond. Debts with less than a year to maturity are called notes.

Revenue and authority bonds. State or local governments issue bonds to cover the cost of capital projects, such as bridges, airports or sewer systems. Principal and interest are paid from revenue generated by the specific project, meaning the risk of default can be significant. Examples of default include Calumet Skyway bonds in the Chicago area and the Chesapeake Bay Bridge and Tunnel. In these cases, revenues from tolls and other sources were insufficient to pay off the bonds.

Bonds and other marketable debt are an important part of many investors' portfolios. In addition to these types of securities, many investors diversify by owning a portion of the assets of a company, that is, by purchasing stock.

STOCK

Stocks are securities that represent an equity interest in a corporation. The value of the interest is arbitrarily established when the shares are issued, and is commonly referred to as *par* value. However, as the forces of supply and demand take over, the price of the stock becomes its *market* value. The *book* value of a stock refers to the specific accounting valuation of a corporation's assets.

Stockholders are entitled to a proportionate share in the corporation's net assets and net income. In addition, corporate profits may be distributed as *dividends*. The size of a dividend is based on many factors, including the corporation's earnings and expenses, and the firm's need to reinvest some portion of its profits in operations.

Dividends can be paid in cash or in stock. With stock dividends, the investors receive more shares based on a percentage of their holdings. For example, a 15 percent stock dividend means an investor who has 100 shares of stock will have 115 shares after the dividend is paid. Par value is not reduced. Instead, corporations transfer funds from retained earnings to the capital stock account. Stock dividends are different from *stock splits*. With a split, the outstanding number of shares is increased and the par value of the stock is reduced. This action is done to make the price per share lower and more attractive to investors.

The dividend payouts are declared on the *date of record*. Whoever owns the stock on this date receives the dividend. On the *ex-dividend* day, the day following the date of record, the stock trades without the dividend and the price usually falls by the amount of the dividend. Note that actual payment of the dividend may be several weeks later than the date of records.

Stockholders have the right to vote on the selection of the board of directors, as well as on the sale, liquidation, or merger of the corporation. However, some corporations issue stock that limits or prohibits shareholders' voting rights. The specific provisions are stated in the articles of incorporation or the corporate charter.

There are two major classes of corporate stock: preferred and common. The first class has a priority over common shares for receiving dividend payments, as well as net asset distributions if the corporation is dissolved. In most cases, no dividends may even be paid on the common stock in any year or cumulative years in which the full dividend has not been paid on preferred shares. Holders of common stock traditionally can vote at shareholder's meetings, while those with preferred stock cannot.

Stocks are often categorized according to their investment purpose.

Income. Stocks in this category are purchased for current and future dividends and usually for a specific periodic payout.

Defensive. This category of stocks is used during recessionary periods or when economic activity is declining. These stocks are considered consistent and safe.

Blue chip. Stocks in this group are issued by companies with long-established records of earnings and dividends.

Growth. The current dividend yield on these stocks is low or zero, with profits plowed back into the company to sustain continued growth. Investors expect growth in earnings to be reflected in a growing market value of the shares.

Cyclical. Profits of firms issuing these stocks fluctuate with business cycles. Earnings fall in a recession and increase during expansions. Auto, steel, and capital equipment stocks are in this category.

Speculative. New stock issues or inexpensive "penny" stocks fall in this category. Potential profit is exciting and the potential for loss is tremendous.

Trading

Stocks of public corporations are usually bought and sold on one of the various stock exchanges or in the over-the-counter (OTC) market. Prices of stocks listed on the exchanges are usually quoted in the newspapers as follows:

HIGH	LOW	STOCK	DIV.	YLD. %	P/E RATIO	SALES 100's	HIGH	LOW	CLOSE	NET CHANGE
55⅞	42½	Exxon	3.60	6.7	9	7040	54	52¾	54	+1

The first group of numbers represents the high and low over the previous 52 weeks. The fractions are a percentage of a dollar, so that 42½ means the stock is selling for $42.50. The next column is the name of the stock or an abbreviation. The next column is the annual dividend. In this case, the corporation is paying $3.60 per share. The following figure is the yield, calculated by dividing the dividend by the closing price. The price-earnings ratio in the next column reflects the relationship between the price of the stock and the issuing company's earnings. Here the stock is selling for nine times its earnings. With this example, for the latest 12 months, earnings are approximately $6.00 ($54.00/9). The P/E ratio reflects the market's expectations about the growth and predictability of future earnings. The following column lists the number of shares sold in 100-share lots; in this instance, 704,000 shares were sold. The next columns show the day's high price of $54.00, low of 52¾ or $52.75, and closing price of $54.00, which represents a net increase of $1 from the previous day.

Stocks traded in the over-the-counter market are listed as indicated:

COMPANY	BID	-	ASK	NET CHANGE
Multi Solution	2½		2⅝	—

The main difference in the OTC quote is the Bid–Ask columns. The bid figure is the highest price at which those dealing in the stock will buy and the ask figure is the price at which these people will sell.

Stock Options

Options are contracts for the sale or purchase of an underlying security, usually common stock. The two key elements of an option transaction are the exercise (or strike) price and the expiration date. According to the terms of the option the exercise price is the price at which the underlying security can be bought or sold. The expiration date is the last day on which the option to buy or sell can be executed.

An option to buy an underlying security is referred to as a *call* option and gives the purchaser the right to buy a specific number of shares at the prearranged price by a certain date. An option to sell is known as a *put* option. A put option gives the purchaser the right to sell at agreed-upon terms. To complete these transactions, the option purchaser must pay the option writer an *option premium*. The purchaser, or the holder of the option, pays the premium to the writer for the opportunity of completing the contract. Whether the option to buy the underlying stock is exercised or not, the writer of the option contract will retain the premium.

Table 9.2 further clarifies the roles of the writer and purchaser of the option for both puts and calls.

Options at first appear confusing and seem like gambling because no one knows for certain what the price of the underlying security will be. Options are used by those seeking profits, as

Table 9-2 Option Transaction

	Put Option	*Call Option*
Possessor of option	Ability to sell at the exercise price by the expiration date.	Ability to buy at the exercise price by the expiration date.
Writer of option	Must buy at the exercise price by the expiration date.	Must sell at the exercise price by expiration date.

well as by "hedgers." In the latter case, an option may be bought or sold by the owner of a stock as protection against price fluctuations. Profit is dependent on which way the market price of the security moves prior to expiration of the option. Because a small change in the price of the underlying stock translates into a large percentage change in the value of the option, profits and losses can be large. To increase the excitement level in these transactions, an option can be *uncovered* or *naked*, that is, the writer of the option does not own the underlying securities. There is unlimited potential for loss by the purchaser of a naked option. However, the loss is limited for the writer of the option who receives the premium regardless.

Short Sale

Investors can choose from a wide array of creative strategies to buy and sell securities. Options are simply one of them. Another often-used technique is the *short sale*. While investors often sell stock if they feel the market price will fall, in a short sale they sell shares they do not own. To execute the trade, stock certificates are borrowed and delivered to the buyer. These borrowed certificates must eventually be replaced.

If the market price of the stock goes down, the short seller will buy the stock at the lower price and realize a profit. If the market price goes up, the investor will have to pay a higher price for the stock and may sustain a significant loss.

SECURITIES MARKETS

Each year new securities are issued through the *primary* markets. Typically *investment bankers* are responsible for arranging these transactions. Their function is to raise capital by purchasing new issues from corporations, as well as from state and local governments, at an agreed-upon price. The investment banker will then arrange for the sale of these securities to the investing public at a higher price. The process is also known as *underwriting* a security.

For this effort, investment bankers receive a commission based on the difference between the purchase price and the sale price to the public. If the price to the public is lower than the purchase price or the whole issue is not sold, the investment banker can suffer a significant loss. Some investment bankers under-write a security on a *best-efforts* basis. With this arrangement, they assume no financial liability if all the securities are not sold.

After securities are purchased in the primary market, they are traded in the *secondary markets*. This trading activity takes place on organized exchanges and in the over-the-counter (OTC) market.

The most widely known recognized secondary markets are the New York Stock Exchange, the American Stock Exchange, and such regional stock exchanges as the Pacific Stock Exchange and the Midwest Stock Exchange.

Trading stocks on an exchange is an easy way to liquidate an asset because there is normally a good match of buyers and sellers and cash is usually disbursed to the seller after five business days. A trading exchange is also an auction market, that is, securities are sold by those offering the lowest price and purchased by those offering the highest.

While the stocks of the larger corporations are traded on the New York and American exchanges, there are approximately 30,000 unrestricted and unlisted stocks traded in the over-the-counter (OTC) market. The OTC market is primarily a *dealer market* with hundreds of broker-dealers scattered throughout the country. There is no one central location. In addition, in the OTC market price is determined by negotiation not by auction. In 1971, the National Association of Securities Dealers (NASD) created an automated quotation system, known as NASDAQ, that increased the efficiency of broker quotes for OTC stocks. It made trading in the OTC market more streamlined and less expensive.

The mechanics of buying or selling securities on an exchange requires investors to simply place an order. Types of buy or sell orders include:

Market order. Investors buy or sell at the current market price.

Limit order. Requires the sale price to be no lower than a specific amount and the purchase price not higher than a specified figure.

Day order. If the order is not executed on that day, it expires.

Good till cancelled (GTC). This order has no specific expiration date. It is open until the transaction occurs or is specifically withdrawn.

Stop loss. This becomes a market order to sell when the price of the stock falls to a specified price level.

Stop limit. When the stock price reaches a certain level, this becomes a limit order.

Once there is an order to trade, a buyer or seller must be found. Spending time looking for a trading partner would be expensive, so over the years a category of market traders has developed. Called *security dealers* or investor's specialists, they promote the exchange of securities.

These dealers act as *market makers* by maintaining an inventory of certain stocks they are willing to buy and sell. This enables investors to have their orders to trade a security executed immediately. The cost of completing these transactions is the "spread" between the "bid" and the "ask" price (that is, the difference between the purchase and sales prices). A market maker buys securities from investors at the bid price and sells to other investors at the higher ask, or offer price. A market maker's profit for completing the transaction is thus the spread. Heavily traded securities can have a very small profit spread for the market makers, while thinly traded issues tend to have a large one. On the NYSE there is one designated market maker for each security; on the OTC market, several traders may make a market in a given issue.

Investors must choose how they wish to purchase the securities they want. The first alternative is a *cash account.* With this account, all transactions are paid for in full, usually in five business days. This differs from a *margin account* which allows investors to borrow to purchase securities. Under Federal Reserve Board Regulation T, brokers are permitted to lend investors up to 50 percent of the value of stocks and some bonds, 70 percent for corporate bonds, and 90 percent for U.S. government securities. As with all borrowing, profits as well as losses are magnified.

INVESTMENT COMPANY SECURITIES

A common concern for small investors is the difficulty of purchasing a diversified group of assets in order to minimize risk. However, for small investors, the cost of diversification may be prohibitive. For example, most bonds have face values of $1,000 and are sold in blocks of five units. The typical trading unit of stock listed on an exchange is 100 shares. Trading smaller blocks of stock is disproportionately more expensive. Thus, investors with a few thousand dollars could wind up placing all their eggs in one basket.

Without diversification the risk of loss can be high. Statistically it is more common for one stock to produce a significant loss than for a portfolio of 50 different stocks to all show a loss. In the multistock portfolio, "winners" tend to cancel out "losers," and portfolio performance tends to emulate that of the overall stock market.

Investors with limited funds can diversify by purchasing shares in an *investment company*. An investment company is a corporation or trust through which investors pool their capital to achieve the benefits of diversification and management of their investments. Shares in such a pool represent ownership in many different companies—often in different industry groups. In addition to providing "instant" diversification, these shares are readily tradable or redeemable. Shares in an investment company represent an interest in all the assets of the company. As the market value of those assets fluctuates, so does the value of the shares.

The two most common types of investment companies are *management companies* and *unit trusts*.

Management Companies

The portfolio of securities in these companies is managed on behalf of the shareholders with specific goals in mind. These objectives are described in the investment company's *prospectus*, which also lists the securities actually held by the fund when the prospectus was issued.

Funds can be structured for "aggressive growth," "income," "growth and income," "tax-exempt income," etc. Moreover some investment companies narrow the focus of their activities to investments in specific industry groups, such as information science and medical technology. There are over 500 investment companies to choose from. Thus, it is not difficult for planners to find several with objectives that correspond to those of a particular client.

There are two types of management companies: *closed end* and *open end*.

Closed end. Closed-end companies have a fixed number of shares outstanding that trade in the OTC market. Closed-end funds fluctuate in value and are usually redeemed for a price below the value of the net assets.

Open end. Open-end companies—or *mutual funds*—are so named because they make a *continuous* offering of new shares to the public. As capital comes in from the sale of new shares, it is invested by the fund's managers.

Unlike those of closed-end companies, mutual fund shares do not trade on exchanges or in the OTC market. Rather, shares are *redeemed* by selling them back to the fund—usually at the *net asset value* (NAV). The NAV is simply the market value of the fund's assets, less liabilities, expressed on a per-share basis. Securities regulations require that redemption requests be honored within seven days.

In addition to the current value of the shares, it is important to look at a fund's long-term performance. The prospectus usually includes 10-years of financial data. Of course, for newer funds, a shorter period is listed. To determine performance, start with the fund's NAV for the period and add net income. Then add the gain or subtract the losses. Any distributions from realized capital gains should be subtracted. The result is the NAV for the end of the period. This figure can be compared to the NAV for each year to determine profit or loss. Table 9.3 provides an example of NAV calculation for a mutual fund.

Table 9-3 Net Asset Value of a Mutual Fund

	1983	1984
Net asset value (beginning of the year)	$11.05	$12.49
Investment activities:		
Income	0.99	1.00
Expenses	(0.08)	(0.07)
Net investment income	0.91	0.93
Net realized in unrealized gain		
(loss) or investment	1.88	0.06
Total from investment activities	$2.79	$0.99
Distributions:		
Net investment income	(0.91)	(0.92)
Realized net gain	(0.44)	(0.48)
Total distributions	$(1.35)	$(1.40)
Net asset value (end of year)	$12.49	$12.08

SOURCE: Wellington Fund Prospectus.

The example shows the NAV at the beginning of 1983 as $11.05 and an ending value of $12.49, for an increase of 13.03 percent. In 1984, the beginning NAV was $12.49 and the ending NAV was $12.08, for a loss in NAV of 3.28 percent.

Load and no-load funds. Some mutual funds include a *load*, or sales charge, for the purchase of shares. The maximum allowable charge is 8.5 percent of the *offering price* (the price at which the client purchases the shares). With *no-load* funds, no such charge is involved. To date, there is no statistical information indicating that load funds outperform no-load funds. In the financial press, price quotes for mutual funds are usually shown as follows:

	NAV	Offer	Change
A Fund	9.15	10.00	+ .04
B Fund	12.69	13.87	− .01
C Fund	6.21	6.21	+ .10

Investors could have purchased shares of A Fund for $10 per share. These shares have a net asset value of $9.15. The difference between the cost and NAV figures is the 8.5 percent sales charge ($10 less 8.5% = $9.15). The C Fund is a no-load fund because there is no sales charge. Thus, the NAV and offering price are the same.

Other fees. When selecting funds, planners should be cognizant of *withdrawal charges* and *redemption fees* that are taken out of the proceeds of some funds, both load and no-load when they are redeemed.

Recently a new fee, known as 12b-1, has been charged. This fee stems from a 1980 Securities and Exchange Commission (SEC) ruling that allows a mutual fund to use assets to pay for distribution or sales expenses, such as advertising or mailing material to customers. The SEC has not placed a limit on the percentage involved. Currently 12b-1 funds charge fees ranging from 1 percent to over 2 percent.

Some critics conclude that existing shareholders are financing the growth of 12b-1 funds. The concern of others is the fact that no separate expense category is listed in the prospectus of such funds. So checking for this hidden fee is not easy. However, future SEC regulations may change how the fee is shown.

All mutual funds charge a *management fee*, usually in the range of .05 percent to 1 percent of the total assets of the fund. This fee is a major source of revenues to the investment companies. In return, shareholders receive professional selection and management of a portfolio of securities, safekeeping of certificates, and regular reports and distributions.

Mutual fund selection.   When selecting a mutual fund for a particular client, the planner has two tasks: (1) determining which funds have objectives and risk characteristics that match those of the client; and (2) selecting from this limited group of candidates the ones most likely to perform well in the future. It is the second of these tasks that presents the greater challenge to the planner.

When selecting stock, the characteristics and earnings prospects of particular firms are analyzed. Mutual fund selection comes down to finding those money managers who are better than others at trading securities. Picking mutual funds is like going to a race where bets are placed on the jockeys, not on the horses!

In making decisions about the future, it is often necessary to look to the past. The historical performance of individual funds are documented in several places. Lipper Analytical Services, the Weisenberger Report, the United Mutual Fund Selector, and the Standard & Poor's Stock Guide all track performance over many years. But some funds are so new that past data are not helpful. Also, successful fund managers often move from employer to employer; this information is never available through regular sources.

Dollar-cost averaging.   Besides the obvious benefits of professional management and shareholder services, mutual funds make regular investing of modest amounts both convenient and possible. In this sense they are useful to clients whose financial plans call for channeling discretionary funds into a pool for long-term accumulation. Clients who can discipline themselves to channel funds in this way find mutual funds a fairly painless way to build an investment portfolio over time. Such systematic investing results in *dollar-cost averaging*. Fund share prices fluctuate over time. So committing a fixed dollar amount to purchasing shares on a regular basis results in an *average* purchase price somewhere between the highs and lows. For instance, when share prices are at $10, a $100 purchase adds 10 shares to the portfolio; when prices are at $5, a $100 purchase adds 20 shares. The investor then has 30 shares at an average price of $6.66.

Unit Investment Trusts

As mentioned, there is a second type of investment company. These companies issue redeemable shares that represent an undivided interest in a *fixed* portfolio of specific assets and are called *unit investment trusts*. They are similar to mutual funds in that monies generated through the sale of shares are used to acquire specific assets. Mutual funds, however, are managed— i.e., securities in the funds are traded in response to economic conditions. Unit trusts make no attempt to manage assets, except in unusual situations. Typically, a unit trust will buy a stated portfolio of securities and deposit them with a trustee.

Securities placed in this type of trust include GNMAs, corporate and municipal bonds, preferred stocks, and equity ownership in real estate. The fixed-interest securities are of course, sensitive to interest-rate fluctuations. For example, as interest rates decrease, the value of a unit trust holding bonds will increase and vice versa. Interest and dividends are paid out periodically to unit holders according to their share of ownership. The unit investment trust terminates when the last asset matures.

METHODS OF INVESTMENT ANALYSIS

No matter what type of investment vehicle is being considered, financial planners and clients must decide whether the *price* represents a good value and whether the *timing* is favorable. While price and timing can often be viewed as a single problem, how this matter is considered differs depending on the theoretical perspective of the analyst. In this context, an investment may be analyzed in several ways.

Fundamental Analysis

This method attempts to ascertain the inherent value of a security based on the present value of future earnings. Fundamental analysis involves predicting the level of those earnings by relying heavily on economic data such as earnings, dividends, and growth rates. Divining the future is no easy task, so practitioners study many factors that could affect a security. For example, in analyzing General Motors stock, the analyst would try to predict how the industry would be affected by social and economics changes. The analyst would then move to the particulars of General Motors and attempt to forecast the level of GM earnings and dividends over a period of several years.

The object of all this effort is to determine whether or not GM or another stock was *undervalued*, that is, the market price is lower than the stock's "intrinsic value," which would mean that the stock will increase in value. However, such a determination is no guarantee of success. Other analysts may not agree the stock was undervalued. In addition, significant time delays— before others concur and act upon the information—can lead to uninspiring returns for the fundamental analyst because the stock will not reach its "true" value.

Technical Analysis

This method is based on the examination of patterns, trends, or cycles in the securities market. Technical analysis attempts to predict future prices based on past volume and price changes. Technical analysts believe that all investors have the same information available and that current market prices reflect this information. However, these analysts recognize that there are delays in the spread of new information.

Prompt recognition of early trends or changes in direction could produce profits. Unfortunately, one characteristic of technical analysis is prematurely entering the market before it has reached bottom or selling too long after the market has passed its peak.

This is not to say that technical analysts do not recognize price movements. There is evidence to support the theory that security prices move in cyclical phases and the appropriate response could produce profits. Major procedures used by technical analysts to predict cycles and trends include:

Price-trend method. This is the oldest and one of the most popular forms of cyclical analysis. Much technical information and special jargon is associated with price-trend analysis. There is also significant difficulty in interpreting the information gathered in such an analysis. Because the judgment of the analyst is critical, price-trend methods are often considered one of the weakest methods of technical analysis. Nevertheless, it is often used as evidence in confirming a market trend.

Breadth of market. This technique predicts future prices by analyzing price trends of certain stocks. Measurement involves data from the entire market. It gives equal weight to stocks, regardless of their market price.

Monetary methods. Here, the actions of the Federal Reserve Board are paramount. Such measurements as the money supply, reserve requirements, and discount rates have proved to be strong indicators of potential cycle changes. These measurements reflect the availability and cost of money. This, in turn, can reveal how much business will be able to expand and how aggressive investors are willing to invest. For example, the less expensive debt is, the more inclined investors may be to leverage their securities purchases by borrowing money. This leverage is referred to as *margin debt*, and can be a strong indicator of investor expectations of market prices.

Thousands of intelligent, highly skilled fundamental analysts labor daily in an effort to find undervalued stocks. At least as many individuals pore over charts of stock and commodity price movements in search of hidden buy and sell signals. Their findings are reflected in thousands of brokers' research reports and investment newsletters. Billions of dollars are positioned in the markets by individuals and money managers on the basis of these recommendations. However, the academic community has introduced two theories that challenge the validity of both fundamental and technical analysis.

Efficient Market Theory

This theory contends that with so many people scrutinizing the value of particular securities, it is not possible for prices to stray too far from true value. Because information about a change affecting a particular stock tends to be disseminated among market watchers almost instantly, that information is quickly reflected in the price of the stock. Thus, according to this theory, the search for significantly undervalued stocks in not productive.

Random Walk

According to this theory, security and commodity prices are not predictable. Future prices are statistically independent of past price and volume data. Thus, the patterns sought by technical analysts are not valid predictors of future prices.

The efficient market and random walk theories suggest that a strategy of buying and holding a portfolio of randomly selected stocks will do better than one that is actively managed (when transaction costs are considered). Computers and data-based information on the market have allowed academics to develop strong arguments for this position.

Investment analysts counter that market inefficiencies exist, that prices are governed as much by emotions as by information, and that price patterns are not random.

Within the controversy, yet another theory exists, one that involves not how the market operates, but how to minimize risk.

Modern Portfolio Theory

One of the foremost investment theorists is Harry Markowitz. In his book, *Portfolio Selection*, he laid the groundwork for what has come to be known as the Modern Portfolio Theory. This is a framework by which risk can be reduced through comprehensive and efficient diversification.

The model divides risk into two components: risk due to market fluctuation and risk inherent in a particular security. With this procedure, the goal is to search out securities that (a) have the same level of risk as other investments, but offer a higher expected rate of return, or (b) offer a similar rate of return as other investments at a lower risk. The selection of these types of securities in a portfolio is called *efficient*.

To implement this theory, the planner first determines the client's desired level of risk (or the degree of risk necessary for achieving the client's stated objectives). The next step is to select stocks with the correct risk characteristics. Those with return potential that is not commensurate with the desired level of risk are eliminated.

Eventually, the planner constructs an *efficient portfolio*—one that has the highest possible return for a given level of risk.

This quantitative approach requires the use of graphs, charts, and figures, which may or may not be interpreted accurately. Unfortunately, Modern Portfolio Theory does not take into account the effects of taxation and other interesting variables.

Illustration 9.1 shows an inverse relationship between level of risk and diversification—as the number of securities in-

Illustration 9-1 Diversification and Risk

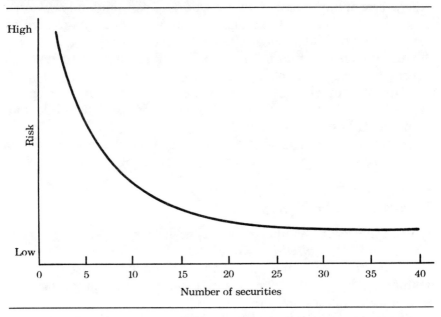

creases, risk declines. This graphic analysis is typical of Modern Portfolio Theory.

As with all scientific approaches, Modern Portfolio Theory is based on quantifiable elements. "Return" is expresssed as a percentage; "risk" is defined by *beta*, a systematic measurement of the relationship between a stock's price volatility and the volatility of the general market. A beta of 1.00 means the risk is average and correlates with overall market risk. In this case, if the market goes up 15 percent, the stock will also increase 15 percent. A beta above 1.00 means more volatility than the market's and more risk. The opposite is true for a beta of less than 1.0.

Betas for particular stocks are derived from past price behavior relative to the market. Betas are available from Value Line and other data sources. By knowing the betas of a portfolio's component stocks, the planner can ascertain the risk level of the overall portfolio.

The tactical significance of betas is important. When a bullish market is expected, portfolios of high beta stocks will perform even better than the market. A portfolio with a beta of 2.00 should do *twice* as well as the general stock market. On the other hand, a pessimistic market outlook calls for betas of less than 1.00.

There is also an *alpha* score that measures how an investment performs as compared to expected volatility. An alpha of 0.0 is considered neutral. If an investment moves up 5 percent, while the market moves up 3 percent, the investment's alpha is 2.0.

Regardless of the technique used, inadequate or inaccurate information and lack of uniformity in disclosure make projecting risks and returns difficult. Many rely on the idea that current and past expectations play a significant role in determining future results.

CHAPTER TEN

Limited Partnerships and Hard Assets

Investments can be made in many different assets: stocks, bonds, rare coins, apartment buildings, grocery stores, etc. But no matter what form those investments take, taxes affect the potential profits in some way. The astute planner knows that just evaluating the economics of an investment is not enough—*after-tax* profit potential must be evaluated.

Some forms of ownership have characteristics that favor tax-sensitive investors. One of these is the limited partnership.

LIMITED PARTNERSHIP

A limited partnership is a legal entity whereby the assets of the partnership are owned by both the limited partners (the investors) and the general partners (the managers of the partnership). The purpose of this type of organization depends on the objectives of the partners and the type of assets owned. For example, a partnership could be designed for asset growth, cash flow for income, or high tax write-offs. Regardless of the purpose, all partnerships pass income and deductions through to the partners because the partnership itself is not a taxable entity.

There are other advantages to owning an asset in a limited partnership as compared to other forms of ownership. Table 10.1 illustrates this comparison.

As the table indicates, an investor would not receive a tax deduction for investing in a corporation. Also, both the corporation's profits and the investor's dividends are taxed. This is usually referred to as "double taxation". On the other hand, a partnership is treated as a direct investment in a business. So all profits and losses are reported on the investor's return.

Table 10-1 Investing through Different Types of Business Ownership

	Form of Ownership		
	Sole Proprietor	*Corporation*	*Partnership*
Deductions flow through to personal tax returns	Yes	No	Yes
Initial capital contribution can be deductible	Yes	No	Yes
Subject to double taxation	No	Yes	No
Personal liability	Yes	No	No (if limited partnership)

An additional consideration is the personal liability of the investors. Investors can limit their liability to their capital contribution by not taking an active role in the management of the partnership, that is, by being classified as *limited partners*.

In order to obtain these benefits, it is essential for investors to be taxed as limited partners rather than as corporate shareholders. The courts have defined what constitutes the characteristics of a corporation and a partnership.

a. *Continuity of life.* A corporation has an indefinite life. A partnership has a specific ending date.
b. *Free transferability.* A corporation has free transferability of interest through public exchanges to sell stocks. There is no such public exchange for partnerships.
c. *Centralized management.* A corporation is run by individuals on its board of directors, and they may or may not own stock in the corporation. The general partners typically run the partnership.
d. *Limited liability.* Shareholders are not liable for corporate activities. Limited partners are not liable for the partnership.

The first two characteristics do not apply to a partnership. To be taxed as a corporation, an entity must have *more* than half of the characteristics mentioned above. To maximize tax deductions and limit liability, many investors seek investments that are structured as limited partnerships. This form of ownership is also attractive because it can provide diversification of assets if investor funds are pooled. With more available money than one single investor would have, several assets can be purchased that, in effect, minimize risk. In addition, leverage can provide funds for further diversification.

Basis

To really comprehend how partnerships are taxed, the concept of *basis* must be understood. Once an investor's basis in the partnership is known, it is possible to determine the maximum tax deductions and gain or loss on the sale or other disposition of the partnership's property.

Basis is composed of:

1. Cash and any property transferred to the partnership by the partners. Note: The partnership's basis in the transferred property is the same as the partner's basis in the property (original cost plus improvements minus depreciation).
2. Accumulated taxable and tax-exempt income from the partnership.
3. Debt. Non-recourse loans if they are *secured* by real estate; recourse loans for all other investment vehicles with financing from an independent organization.

Nonrecourse financing means the investor is not personally responsible for paying the loan in case of default; the lender must look to the sale of the property to pay off the loan. Recourse loans involve other investment vehicles; in these cases, the partner must be liable.

Basis is decreased by the following:

1. Losses.
2. Expenditures that are not deductible by the partnership, such as life insurance premiums and charitable contributions.
3. Amount of depletion and depreciation taken.
4. Amount of cash and adjusted basis of other property distributed. Relief of liability is considered a cash distribution, as well as income from the investment and any proceeds from the sale of an asset.

The following example illustrates how three partners contributed assets with the *same* fair market value, but with a *dif-*

ferent basis. All profits were distributed equally on sale, but each had different tax consequences.

	Partners		
	A	B	C
Contribution:			
Cash	$10,000	$5,000	$0
Fair market (FMV) value of property		$5,000 (FMV $5,000, partner's basis $3,000)	$10,000 (FMV $10,000, partner's basis $6,000)

If ABC sells the partnership for $36,000, the gain is reportable as follows:

$$\text{Sales price} - \text{Basis} = \text{Taxable gain}$$

Partner A:

$$\$12,000 - \$10,000 = \$2,000$$

Partner B:

$$\$12,000 - \$8,000 = \$4,000$$

Partner C:

$$\$12,000 - \$6,000 = \$6,000$$

Finally, it must be remembered, when the dollar basis for each partner is reduced to zero, no further tax deductions can be taken. Investors may not have a negative basis in a limited partnership and take any further tax deductions. (The exception is real estate.)

Over the years, limited partnerships have been structured to produce only tax deductions. These high write-off programs are known as *tax shelters*. Unfortunately, for many investors, the motive of profit got lost, and some cared only about the amount of tax deductions (losses) they could claim. This trend did not go unnoticed by the IRS. To the IRS, the profit motive of a limited partnership and the overall economics of an investment remained high. The IRS published a series of guidelines to help determine which tax shelters are considered abusive. If an investment falls within the abusive category, the tax deductions are disallowed.

The following IRS guidelines may be helpful in determining whether a partnership might be considered "abusive."

1. Is there economic substance to the transaction? Most abusive tax shelters are not engaged in an actual trade or business.
2. Does the client expect to derive a profit for the transaction? When will this profit occur? Most abusive tax shelters do not involve a profit motive.
3. Did the transaction really take place, or is it only on paper? Does reality differ from the transaction reported? Are documents back dated?
4. Who receives the benefits and assumes the actual burdens of ownership? Is this the same person reported as owner?
5. Would a prudent person make this investment? A prudent person is interested not only in saving tax dollars, but also in long-term investment.
6. Is there a promissory note involved? Would a bank loan the designated amount using the same property as collateral? (Nonrecourse loans apply).
7. Is the return of investment derived from the expected tax savings or from the actual return of the capital investment itself? Profit motive is essential.
8. What is there to show for the expenditure other than a tax benefit? Is the asset real or is it contrived or artificial?

The following investment vehicles are often structured as limited partnerships. Obviously, the investment may also exist outside the partnership structure. Nevertheless, all these investments should have one characteristic in common—the potential for making money.

TYPES OF LIMITED PARTNERSHIPS

Real Estate

Real estate has long been the backbone of many investment portfolios. In point of fact, statistics show that more money has been placed in real estate partnerships than in other types of investment partnerships. Motion pictures and television programs have dramatized the fear, excitement, greed, riches, and scarcity factors which this vehicle can produce. This was especially evident in the latter half of the 1970s when an enormous amount of profit was made in real estate.

Whether real estate partnerships are very conservative or extremely aggressive in terms of potential risks, rewards, and tax deductions depends on the use of debt. Real estate is not currently subject to the *at-risk* rules, so financing can be obtained through nonrecourse loans. This type of debt can lead to a great deal of abuse. To minimize inappropriate creativity in financing real estate investments, Congress enacted the *overvaluation rules.* These rules penalize investments that increase the cost of property by creating fictitious nonrecourse debt. Previously, unscrupulous promoters were able to offer high write-offs, such as depreciation and interest deductions, because the basis was dramatically increased through the use of debt. At the same time, the fair market value of the real estate was significantly below the value of the stated nonrecourse debt.

As an illustration, consider the case where Promoter *A* buys an office building under these terms:

Purchase price	$1,000,000
Down payment	300,000
Assumes 9% loan	700,000

The value of the building itself is $900,000, and an 18-year ACRS depreciation is used. If the building was purchased on January 1, the depreciation would be $90,000 the first year.

To create artificial deductions, Promoter *A* restructures the terms and sells the building to the partnership under these conditions:

Purchase price	$3,000,000
Down payment	300,000
Wraparound mortgage	2,550,000

If the value of the building is recomputed to $2.7 million, depreciation under the accelerated cost recovery system would be $270,000 the first year, versus $90,000 under the original purchase price. The financing also produces enormous interest expenses, which will be accrued but not paid. To eliminate this type

Table 10-2 Penalties on
Incorrect Evaluation
of Property

Claimed Evaluation versus Correct Valuation	Penalty
Under 150%	0
150%–200%	10%
200%–250%	20%
250% and more	30%

of transaction and to encourage the accurate valuation of property, Congress enacted the penalties listed in Table 10.2. The penalties are applied to the underpayment of taxes, because the tax shelter produced more deductions than were legitimately allowable.

There are many different categories of real estate, such as raw land, residential property, and commercial property. The key with any type of real estate investment is to remember that the more debt placed on real property, the greater the benefits of appreciation and the greater the risk of loss or need for further capital infusions.

Raw land. The purpose of investing in unimproved property is the potential growth in value. There are minimal tax deductions associated with raw land, unless it is leveraged. For example, land itself cannot be depreciated, but any interest paid due to debt is deductible.

A well-located parcel of raw land in the path of progress can produce an excellent return through appreciation. If the property is leveraged, the profit could be spectacular and would be taxed at long-term capital gain rates. (Note: The holding period must be at least six months if the property is purchased after June 22, 1982. Also, the investor cannot be classified as a dealer, or the gain is treated as ordinary income.)

EXAMPLE

An investor received a hot tip that a large piece of property would be developed as a resort. The property is now selling for $5,000 an acre, but "reliable sources" think the property will be worth $50,000 per acre in one or two years. (It is important to ask why the reliable sources are not investing as much as possible into the land.) Nevertheless, the investor decides to buy 10

Table 10-3 Gain or Loss on Raw Land after One Year

	Situation			
	A	B	C	D
Sale price per acre	$ 50,000	$ 10,000	$ 5,000	$ 2,500
Total sale price	500,000	100,000	50,000	25,000
Down payment	− 5,000	− 5,000	− 5,000	− 5,000
Interest paid	− 6,300	− 6,300	− 6,300	− 6,300
Principal repaid	− 45,000	− 45,000	− 45,000	− 45,000
Profit (loss)	$443,700	$ 43,700	($ 6,300)	($31,300)

acres, by making a $5,000 cash down payment and borrowing $45,000 on a short-term note. The investor is excited about investing $50,000 and watching it appreciate to $500,000. Table 10.3 shows the gain or loss depending on what the land sells for after one year.

If the investor purchased the property during the beginning of the appreciation cycle (Situation *A*), the profit was phenomenal. However, if an overinflated price was paid for the land which was never developed (Situation *D*), then there was a significant loss. Leveraging an investment using "other people's money" can create gains or disasters in all phases of real estate.

Residential property. This category has traditionally been extremely popular with investors. Investments have included single-family houses, duplexes, condominiums, and apartments. The essential element, as with all real estate, is location. Financing terms and management techniques will also determine profitability. Due to significant interest-rate swings, it is increasingly difficult to sell residential property in the short term, so minimum financing arrangements should be for at least 10 years.

Residential real estate is management intensive in that neglect and deferred maintenance will affect the overall value of the property. On the other hand, excellent management will not cure all problems, such as paying too much for an apartment complex.

The tax benefits with residential property revolve around deductions for depreciation and the overall expenses of interest, maintenance, and repairs. It is important to remember that accelerated depreciation in excess of straight-line is recaptured as ordinary income.

Commercial property. Office buildings, industrial parks, and shopping centers fall within this category. One important tax aspect is that if accelerated depreciation is taken on these properties, the gain is taxed as ordinary income.

The stability of tenants is a significant factor in the value of commercial property. If there is excess office space, it is hard to attract tenants. Competition for new occupants can become fierce, and enticements such as free rent affect overall profitability. In some American metropolitan centers, there was enough office space in 1985 to accommodate the needs for over 10 years.

On the other hand, existing leases can produce below-market income. This is important because the income stream is a determining factor in calculating overall yield on the property.

In determining the value of income-producing real estate—whether residential or commercial—many factors and techniques come into play.

Cost. The value of the land, if vacant, is estimated and the depreciated value of improvements is added to obtain the overall value.

Market. Sales data on similar property is used to arrive at the value.

Income. There are several methods of estimating value based on the income of the property. One approach is multiplying the gross rent by a given factor. A more thorough and well-recognized procedure is the capitalization rate (CAP). The CAP rate is determined by deducting the expected vacancy factor and applicable expenses from the anticipated gross annual income. The resulting figure is net operating income, which is then capitalized at an investment yield commensurate with the inherent risk of ownership. The specific capitalization rate used will vary with location. The rate selected depends on the appreciation expected for similar properties, as well as the competitive yields offered by alternative investments. The lower the chosen capitalization rate, the higher the cost of the property. An example of the CAP rate calculation is given in Table 10.4.

The CAP rate selected can produce significant variations in value, so caution must be exercised in determining the appropriate figure. Utilizing historical rates as well as conservative appreciation expectations will be helpful in the selection.

Leasing Investments

Leasing limited partnerships can provide significant benefits and surprises. Investors need to know the purpose of the invest-

Table 10-4 Capitalization Rate

Gross rental income	$3,500,000
Other income	50,000
Less: 5% vacancy	175,000
Less: expenses	
Advertising	100,000
Insurance	225,000
Management	140,000
Payroll	25,000
Repairs and maintenance	75,000
Real estate taxes	35,000
Reserves for replacements	35,000
Utilities	215,000
Miscellaneous	15,000
Total expenses	865,000
Net operating income*	$2,510,000

Net operating income capitalized		
at 7%	$35,857,143	($2,510,000 ÷ 7%)
at 8%	31,375,000	($2,510,000 ÷ 8%)
at 9%	27,888,889	($2,510,000 ÷ 9%)

*Debt service is not subtracted to arrive at this figure.

ment, its tax consequences, the level of risk involved, and the potential yield.

The leasing of office equipment, machinery, and vehicles has become a big part of the national economy. The person or entity owning such equipment is called the lessor. The lessee is the person or business leasing the equipment. Individuals may lease a car because they do not want to purchase, or cannot afford the down payment for a new car. Corporations may lease equipment rather than buying it because they:

- Can minimize the obsolescence factor.
- Can avoid spending the capital necessary to purchase equipment.
- Can better use their money through leasing rather than buying equipment.
- Can enhance their corporate financial statement by leasing.
- Are unable to utilize the tax deductions and credits associated with ownership because they are already in a low tax bracket.

Illustration 10-1 Types of Leasing Limited Partnerships

Conservative — ⌐————. ————⊥————————⊥——— Aggressive

         Income   Combination   Tax Deductions

Why would investors participate in programs designed to lease equipment to businesses? The answer depends on which type of leasing venture an investor chooses. Leasing programs can be structured to produce income or high tax deductions and tax credits or, of course, both. Illustration 10.1 indicates the spectrum of leasing limited partnerships.

Where a specific program falls on the continuum is a direct function of the amount of debt involved. Table 10.5 shows the tax arrangements for the same piece of machinery with and without debt for the first lease year. The example does not include the standard sales charges of limited partnerships.

With Program A, investors receive $22,000 net income after expenses. However, depreciation provides deductions totaling $14,250, leaving taxable income of $7,750. In a 50 percent tax bracket there is $3,875 of taxable income. In addition, there is $10,000 of investment tax credit (ITC), which shelters one dollar for one dollar of taxes owed. Investors in Program A receive a tax-free cash flow and tax benefits according to their percentage of ownership. Cash flows in subsequent years will be sheltered only through depreciation, and the 10 percent ITC is available for the year the equipment is purchased and placed in service. If the credit cannot be utilized then it is carried back three years and any remaining balance is carried forward on the tax return.

With Program B, the investor's total cash contribution is only $10,000 and the net income is $1,000. The tax deductions amount to $31,250, and the ITC is $10,000. The main motivation for investors in Program B is not income, but deductions and credits that would shelter other income.

The tax benefits are received in direct proportion to the percentage of ownership each investor has in the partnership. Therefore, if five limited partners who are in the 50 percent tax bracket each invest $2,000 in Program B, the limited partners would have excess deductions of $1,050 (net income of $22,000, minus interest of $13,000, minus depreciation of $14,250, divided by 5). The tax savings for each limited partner is $525 ($1,050 ×

Table 10-5 Tax Aspects of Limited Partnerships with and without Debt

	Program A (all cash)	Program B (leveraged)
Economic Aspects		
Cost	$100,000	$100,000
Cash down payment	100,000	10,000
Loan	$ 0	$ 90,000
Yearly income	$26,000	26,000
Yearly expenses	4,000	4,000
Debt repayment	0	21,000
(Interest deduction)	0	(13,000)
Depreciation (ACRS)	(14,250)	(14,250)
Investment tax credit	10,000	10,000
Net income	$22,000	$ 1,000
Tax aspects		
Income	$26,000	$26,000
Interest deduction	(0)	(13,000)
Depreciation deduction	(14,250)	(14,250)
Expense deduction	(4,000)	(4,000)
Net taxable income	7,750	(5,250)
Taxable income (loss) in 50% tax bracket	3,875	(2,625)
Investment tax credit	10,000	10,000
Net dollars saved	$ 6,125	$12,625

50% tax bracket) and $2,000 ITC (1/5th of $10,000 ITC) for a total in-pocket savings of $2,525 for each $2,000 of original investment. These limited partners also received their percentage of the $1,000 net cash flow: $200 each.

To obtain all of these tax deductions and credits, the investment must be structured to conform to the requirements imposed by the Tax Reform Act (TRA) of 1984. The concept of "at risk" is especially important to claim the maximum investment tax credit allowed.

At all times, investors must be at risk to the extent of at least 20 percent of the basis of the qualified property. The 20 percent at risk provision includes all cash and the amount of *recourse* financing for which the investor is personally liable. Therefore, nonrecourse financing may not exceed 80 percent of the property basis. However, the remaining financing must be from a "qualified, nonrelated" source, such as a bank, savings and loan, or credit union, because, in theory, lending institutions loan money only to those who will be able to pay it back and go to great lengths to enforce repayment. And, of course, the property must *not* be acquired from a "related" person or entity.

An important feature is that the $10,000 investment interest rules apply. Highly leveraged leasing programs also produce ordinary income, and recapture any phantom income. (Phantom income is described in Chapter 7.)

Table 10.5 presented best-case examples that may not always hold. With leasing arrangements, certain key questions must be answered.

- What is the financial strength of the company leasing the equipment? Without the continued flow of leasing payments, both programs in Table 10.5 would leave the investors in a negative position. However, the B investors would be devastated by debt payments coming directly from their own pockets. Once again, tax benefits are never enough if a deal turns sour.
- How easy will it be to re-lease the equipment in subsequent years?
- How quickly does the equipment lose its value? One essential factor in determining the overall yield is the residual value of the equipment. If the obsolescence factor is high, the remaining value could be less than 10 percent of the original cost.

The economics of a leasing program will always hinge on the level of income that can be generated by the equipment. In a short-term (*operating*) lease, the total income received is less than the purchase price of the equipment. The type of lease is important because of a quirk in the structure of leasing programs: to obtain the investment tax credit, the lease cannot be for more than one half of the equipment's depreciable life.

EXAMPLE

If a machine has a five-year depreciable life according to ACRS, then the maximum time the machine can be leased is two-and-one-half years. This, of course, increases the risk element of a leasing program. Also, to qualify for an ITC, the investors must have operating expenses of at least 15 percent of the equipment's rental income.

The other types of income structure are *full payout,* (meaning the cost of the equipment is paid over the life of the lease), and *net lease.* Individual investor partnerships and Sub-S corporations that place equipment under these type of leases will not qualify for investment tax credit. The rule does not apply to corporations. If partnerships do use full payout leases, they still may be able to pass the ITC through to the lessee and, in turn, negotiate to receive more income for the partnership.

Oil and Gas Programs

A few years ago, a major oil company produced a cartoon commercial showing the difficulty of finding oil. In this advertisement a rather lovable green dinosaur skipped over rocks, slithered, and then slipped through the earth, thereby eluding the oil company. Even though techniques for locating scarce natural resources, such as oil and gas, have improved over the years, these resources continue to be elusive. The formation of oil and gas has occurred over millions of years as animal and vegetable life accumulated in enormous quantities on the sea floor creating thick beds of compressed mud and reservoir rocks.

These organic remains then mixed with mud and sand. When more sediments piled up, the heat and pressure of the upper mud, combined with the salt water and organic material, slowly formed tiny particles of oil. Gradually, some of the oil reached the earth's surface where it formed large pools of tar. The oil that did not reach the surface was trapped by an impermeable layer of rock, called a dome. Not all of those domes have been tapped, so there still remains oil to be discovered.

The problem lies in finding these traps and drilling to the top of the dome. Through the science of oil exploration, these rock formations have become easier to discover. Although oil and gas may be found, the key question remains, "Is the effort commercially productive?"

Promoters may advertise that they have found oil over 90 percent of the time, or their completion ratio is over 90 percent. This information is not sufficient. Rather, it is essential to know what percentage of the oil was actually sold. Was the discovery commercially profitable, and for how long? Or was the well simply closed down after the oil was found? Perhaps the most important question is what potential yield this investment might produce. The degree of risk involved must also be ascertained.

As a result of these considerations, oil and gas investment programs can be divided into the following categories: income, development, and exploration.

Income. With an *income program,* investors purchase existing, producing wells to generate a cash flow. The risk of locating the asset has been eliminated, but uncertainty still remains with regard to the exact amount of commercially extractable oil and gas, and the timeliness of their removal.

The biggest unknown is the future price of these resources. Was the amount paid for the reserves appropriate or excessive? How closely does the cost per barrel or cubic foot compare to the current market price? Since the asset will be extracted over time, how much was the present value of the future benefits discounted? To what level would current prices have to drop before the value of the reserves would start showing a loss? For example, pricing predictions for oil have run from a high of $90 per barrel to $15 per barrel. At the time of this writing, both figures appear to be inaccurate.

The investor seeking income from such a program will receive a cash flow comprised of return of principal as the resource is extracted. At some point the oil or gas reserve will be depleted; therefore, the future appreciation of the reserves is the unknown factor in determining the overall yield the investor will receive. Remember, the profit is dependent on the price of the resource.

Such an income program does not produce tax deductions, and it is not designed for write-offs. However, a portion of the income received is sheltered through the depletion allowance and depreciation of the well's tangible assets (e.g., equipment).

Development. The next category is *development programs.* Under this classification, new wells are drilled in proven reserves or existing wells are expanded. Consequently, a high percentage of wells are successfully completed. However, the return could still be marginal if the well does not pump enough. The potential return is higher than for income programs but, because the well may not be commercially productive, so is the risk.

Exploration. The greatest risk is involved in *exploratory programs.* The potential profits can be astronomical, but the chance of success is approximately 1 in 10 or less.

Because the risk with *wildcatting* is high, investors need more than potential profits to motivate them. Tax benefits provide the added incentive. An initial high level of deductions is allowed in both development and exploration programs for intangible drilling costs (IDC) and costs associated with drilling wells—labor, supplies, fuel, repairs, and hauling. IDCs are not defined as capital expenditures and are currently deductible. However, certain kinds of equipment comprise tangible costs and must be capitalized and depreciated over time. Examples in this category are pipelines, storage tanks, and oil well pumps.

An important consideration with exploratory programs is the structure of the program and how the general partner will be compensated. There are four primary types:

Reversionary interest. With this type of structure, the limited partners pay almost all costs. The general partner receives no revenue until investors have been paid back their entire original investment. A proportionate amount of revenue then reverts to the general partner. It is necessary to determine whether the payout applies to the total program or is on a well-by-well basis. If the latter, the general partner will start receiving revenue before the investors recoup their entire original capital contribution for all wells.

Promotional interest. The general partner usually contributes 10 percent to 15 percent of all costs. In this situation, the tax deductions available to limited partners would be lower because the general partner is paying some intangible drilling costs. The general partner receives an amount at least equal to his or her original contribution.

Carried interest. In this arrangement, the general partner receives, for example, 15 percent of the revenues, while contributing only 1 percent or less of the actual expenses. The incentive for the general partner is to drill and complete wells which will produce income, regardless of the well's potential profit.

Functional allocation. Under this structure, the limited partners pay all the intangible drilling costs. (These are currently tax deductible.) The general partner pays the tangible costs, which are not immediately deductible. The revenue is shared according to the percentage of costs paid or a specific formula.

The major concern with exploratory programs is that investors assume the entire risk of dry holes. Because in most instances the general partner pays only completion costs, he or she knows whether there is oil in the well before putting up any money. However, it is possible to have the general partner guarantee to contribute a minimum amount to the total program.

There has been significant debate over which type of program produces the best results for the investor. The evidence is not conclusive. The criteria for measuring the worth of a program must include the general partner's track record, the amount of upfront organizational fees, how profits are distributed, management capability, and any significant changes in the company.

Research and Development

There is much profit potential in the creation, development, and sale of a new product. As a result, over the last few years, research and development (R&D) partnerships have attracted considerable interest among investors.

Research and development programs are designed to provide the capital necessary to generate a new product or technology that will be commercially successful. Investors contribute the necessary capital and become limited partners. The partnership contracts with a company, usually called the *sponsor,* to do the specific research and development. The sponsor may also be the general partner or may be completely independent.

In return for the capital contribution, the partnership owns the sponsor's new product or technology. Under the terms of a separate contract, the sponsor is granted an exclusive license to market the product in return for which the partnership receives royalties on sales of the product. Usually the partnership also allows the sponsor to reacquire the rights to the technology or product by paying royalties, cash, or stock in the corporation.

From the investors' perspective, it is not sufficient to have a brilliant inventor working on a new product. Rather, it is more important to have positive responses to the following types of questions:

- How advanced is the research?
- What is the experience of the R&D company in this field? What is the company's financial strength?
- Is the company capable of manufacturing and marketing the product, and at a competitive cost?
- Is the end product or technology commercially exploitable?
- What is the competition?
- How and to whom will the product be marketed?
- What is the risk in relationship to the potential reward?
- At what amount will the sponsor be allowed to repurchase the rights to the technology?

In addition to answering these questions, financial planners must keep up-to-date on tax changes affecting R&D programs. Investors have obtained significant tax deductions through the use of creative accrual accounting methods and the use of leverage. However, the Tax Reform Act (TRA) of 1984 requires those involved in a transaction to match the expensing of deductions and the recognition of income. The purpose is to prevent distortions occurring because one entity accured deductions of expenses not yet paid and the other is a cash basis taxpayer (reports income when received). The TRA also provides that expenses can be prepaid for only 90 days, and prohibits investors from claiming deductions for expenses incurred prior to joining the partnership.

In 1982, the Tax Equity and Fiscal Responsibility Act (TEFRA) classified R&D expenses as tax preference items. Consequently using this investment for those subject to the alternative minimum tax would exacerbate the investor's tax problem.

There have been some intriguing success stories and well-publicized fizzles in R&D. The most notable failures included the De Lorean automobile and an investment venture created by Storage Technology.

In an attempt to minimize risk, several partnerships have been formed to invest in several products at once. Diversification through pooling of assets which are invested in a variety of projects is attractive. In any R&D venture, investors must be aware that there is the potential of being treated as a dealer.

With dealer status, profit is taxed as ordinary income. The deciding factor is whether the partnership's purpose is determined to be the sale of technology, rather than the use or licensing of technology. Particular care must be exercised in structuring a multiple-product R&D partnership, so that the investors are not classified as dealers, because investors desire capital gain treatment, not ordinary income taxation.

Cable Television

Investments in cable television have increased dramatically over the past several years. This usually involves the purchase of an existing cable system, because the costs of constructing new systems is generally prohibitive. The investment generates income as the number of subscribers is increased and higher rates are charged because new programs and new services are offered.

Income from cable TV investments can be sheltered through depreciation of equipment and investment tax credits.

Competition for cable systems in large metropolitan areas is fierce, as well as expensive to develop. As a result, cable TV limited partnerships are concentrating on rural locations. In these areas, alternative forms of entertainment may be limited, so that more subscribers will be attracted to the service.

Potential concerns with this type of investment include overleveraging to purchase the system, outdated equipment, and direct competition from satellite TV systems.

Movies, Master Recording, Videos, Books

These types of investment vehicles are usually structured as high write-off tax shelters. Their artistic value or intent is overshadowed by the multiple tax deductions offered.

But things are changing in terms of how attractive these investment vehicles are. Congress has enacted laws that significantly limit the tax benefits of these programs. First, the *at-risk* rules apply in determining the basis for depreciation and investment tax credit. Before the at-risk provisions were applied, the value of the property was often inflated, as in the following example.

EXAMPLE

Sam bought a master recording from a promoter for $250,000. The promoter required a $25,000 cash down payment, and took back a $225,000 nonrecourse loan. This loan could be repaid in a lump sum in eight years, or the master could be returned for a full cancellation of the debt. The calculations under the old and new tax arrangements are shown in Table 10.6.

Under the old laws, Sam would have invested $25,000 in cash and received actual tax savings of $56,250 if he were in a 50 percent bracket. Today, Sam's cash tax savings would be $4,281.

Table 10-6 Inflated Value of Property

	Old Tax Benefits	Current Tax Benefits
Basis	$250,000	$25,000
Investment tax credit	25,000	2,500
Depreciation	62,500	3,563

Recapture and relief of indebtedness should never be overlooked. However, simply focusing on the at-risk rules and the proper use of leverage will help financial planners sift through unrealistic deals. Even as late as 1984, proponents were attempting to circumvent the at-risk rules through the use of leases. Deals were structured so that the organizer purchased, for example, a recording using an enormous amount of nonrecourse financing. The promoter would then pass through the tax benefits of ITC and depreciation.

Not all of these artistic endeavors are without merit. And profit can be made, but the program must be structured for economic gain, not just tax deductions. As always, the essential element is how much money the investor can make.

Animal Breeding and Feeding Programs

If investors are waiting for "Somewhere over the Rainbow," the excitement of owning a race horse cannot be beat. There is always the potential of buying a yearling for several thousand dollars, and later selling stud fees for several million. However, the odds of owning a champion are very small. Every year, thousands of horses never make it past training, but the allure is still strong.

Investors attracted to owning championship horses or cattle must review the risk-to-reward ratio in these types of investments. Knowing the history and the management experience of the promoter is very important. The compensation schedule is also a major consideration, as are the assumptions made in predicting potential profit. Unrealistic inflation factors and cashflow projections produce very disappointing results. For the majority of clients, financial planners will want to diversify in investments other than livestock.

Without significant leverage, breeding and feeding programs will not produce high write-offs. Even cattle feeding programs are not subject to the tax deductions once available. Changes in methods used for accruing expenses and for recognizing income have had a dramatic impact on cattle feeding programs. Finally, cattle feeding programs are simply a deferral of income for no more than one year. Timing the deferral and recognition of income over only one-year cycles can result in a disappointing and costly investment.

HARD ASSETS AND COLLECTIBLES

During periods of inflation, gold, silver, gems, stamps, coins, art, antiques, and other collectibles have produced significant increases in value. In periods of political unrest or economic uncertainty, such investments may also show impressive profits.

Investors who purchase these assets will receive the benefits of long-term capital gains if they hold the investments for at least six months. However, generally speaking, no significant tax deductions are available. For example, gold, diamonds, and art cannot be depreciated. (Antiques used as furniture in a trade or business are depreciable.)

Price fluctuations can be dangerous. For example, gold reached a high of almost $200 per ounce in January of 1975, before declining 50 percent. The metal increased again to over $800 an ounce in January of 1980, before falling to $300 a few years later. Silver also showed a spectacular rise, from $2 per ounce in the early 1970s to over $50 per ounce by the spring of 1980. But it subsequently declined to $5 per ounce.

However, gold and silver are immediately liquid, while there may be frustrating delays in selling other hard assets and collectibles without discounting the price. Bullion may also involve liquidity problems, because it must be assayed prior to resale. This is not typically the case with coins such as the krugerrand, maple leaf, or Mexican 50 peso. However, caution should be exercised in purchasing coins. As an example, a few years ago, a large number of U.S. $20 double eagles were counterfeited in Lebanon. Examination by a coin expert before purchase is advisable.

Rare and/or historic coins are also a popular investment. Value is based on a numerical grading scale created by the American Numismatist Association. Accurate grading is essential because, in addition to the risk of counterfeit, many coins are overgraded. An investor should be able to sell a coin at the same grade at which the coin was originally purchased.

Physical characteristics are basic to evaluating coins. The same holds true for diamonds. The most important feature of these stones include:

- **Carat weight.** The value of a stone increases disproportionately with its weight. For example, a one-carat stone can be worth significantly more than a 0.80 carat diamond.
- **Clarity.** This is the ability of light to pass through the stone without being interrupted by flaws or inclusions. In-

vestment grades include F.L.—Flawless; I.F.—Internally flawless; V.V.S—Very very small inclusions; and V.S.—Very small inclusions.

- **Color.** The most valuable diamonds are colorless or almost colorless. The color of investment grade stones is classified by the letters D through H, with D being the most valuable.
- **Cut.** This is the shape of the stone. A well-proportioned cut can significantly increase the value of the stone.
- **Certification.** The Gemological Institute of America certifies diamonds, while the American Gemological Laboratory typically certifies other gems.

To value rare coins, stamps, art, and/or gemstones, requires considerable knowledge and skill. If financial planners are to recommend these types of investments, more than superficial familiarity is essential. The following questions may be of assistance:

- What is the origin of the appraisal?
- Is the item being purchased from a dealer with long experience and a solid reputation? Has there been a major turnover in the selling organization, and if so why?
- Is there a consistent, reliable, and active market for trading or selling the asset?
- What is the amount of markup or premium on the item?
- Is the potential of appreciation due strictly to inflation, or to either a supply shortage or eager and numerous collectors?
- Can the investor take possession of the asset without enormous risk or cost?
- How dramatic are the economic cycles affecting the specific asset?
- Is the client really investing or simply collecting? Has the investor fallen in love with the asset?

Gold and silver, among the more popular hard assets, have decreased dramatically from their high point in the early 1980s. However, if the public perceives that the United States is changing monetary policy—printing new paper money or eliminating direct ownership or other forms of currency as well as precious metals—then the price of gold and silver will rise dramatically. The threat of inflation also has a positive effect on the value of precious metals.

CHAPTER 11

Due Diligence

The longevity of the financial planning profession will be directly related to the service it provides. Whether a financial planner receives fees or commissions, it is essential that the risks and rewards of various investments be evaluated. One of the more common terms in describing this process is *due diligence.*

Gathering the information for a thorough evaluation is extremely difficult and costly. Financial planning firms and broker-dealers may have their own in-house team to accomplish this task. Nonetheless, financial planners must at some time do their own investigations. The degree and complexity of this endeavor may vary, but planners must still take full responsibility for the investment recommendations they make.

Alternatives to the necessary research are to ignore the questions, to simply trust the opinion of the company's representative, or to trust the opinion of a good friend.

The essential elements and techniques of an investment evaluation include:

- Investigating an offering company—becoming familiar with the company's track record, existing or potential problems, and strengths.
- Calculating the rate of return on previous investments of the offering company and projected potential rates of return.
- Determining the level of risk involved and evaluating alternate uses of money.
- Aligning a product with a client's objectives.
- Reviewing the tax ramifications of the potential investment.
- Monitoring the investment's on-going performance.

Whether individual stocks and bonds or investment partnerships are analyzed, it is necessary to first look at the type of business. What is the economic climate for this industry? Under what circumstances would performance be devastating? How likely is this to occur? Under what type of government regulations does this business function? How will the business be affected by current taxes or the never-ending changes in tax legislation? The questions could continue ad infinitum.

Many resources can be used in evaluating an investment. There are numerous computer software programs that analyze various stocks and bonds. There are also hundreds of newsletters that attempt to forecast market direction, and some recommend individual securities, among the better known are *Dessauer's Journal, Value Line Report,* and the *Zeig Report.* The *Hulbert Financial Digest* ranks various investment services according to their performance over various time periods. The *Stanger Register* and the *Brenovan Reports* analyze limited partnerships.

There are also services that track the performance of mutual funds. Some of the most popular are *Wiesenberger Report, Lipper Analytical Services, United Mutual Fund Selector,* and *Johnson Charts.* Periodicals must not be overlooked. Some of the more important are: *The Wall Street Journal, Financial Planning Magazine, Chartered Financial Analyst Digest, Business Week, Journal of Taxation, The Practical Accountant, Barrons, Forbes, Fortune, Inc.,* and *U.S. News & World Report.*

These lists are not exhaustive, and obviously, no one resource has all the answers. However, by utilizing a variety of sources, financial planners can minimize a client's risk.

Statistical analysis of a company can prove very informative. But, as the numbers are reviewed, a planner must also ask whether the people responsible for past performance are still with the company. If they are not, why not? And what is the experiences of current management? People are a company's strongest resource. Thus, it is necessary to know the backgrounds and levels of experience of key personnel. Also, are key employees being competitively compensated? (What is the industry norm?) The problem of retention cannot be overlooked.

Home-office assistance must also be evaluated. Is the company's sales force so strong the home office cannot keep up with all the orders? Home-office problems can also include inaccurate registration, missing dividend checks, and improper crediting to or withdrawals from accounts, to name just a few. Mistakes will always occur, but frustration is directly related to the responsiveness of home-ofice staff. With other factors being equal, most financial planners will choose to work with companies that minimize logjams.

It is enlightening to review a company's history and how it evolved, as well as the organizations associated with a given company, e.g., accounting, legal and banking firms. Will these associated organizations provide references or documentation? If there is a turnover in outside accounting firms, what is the reason? (Is the company in question simply growing and expanding, or is it displeased with the audit results? Accounting practices should not materially alter investment returns.) Also, are the company's results comparable with those of other companies in the field?

PROSPECTUS REVIEW

Stocks and bonds have been the subject of extensive analysis over several decades. The same is not true of investments structured as partnerships. Yet, over the last 15 years, this form of investing has grown significantly. Nonetheless, these forms of investment must also be analyzed. To begin an analysis of a partnership, the prospectus must be reviewed. This rather thick document should reveal all information necessary to investors. However, unscrupulous promoters may declare that their investments are not structured as partnerships, but as sole proprietorships. If this is done and an investment is not deemed a security, then full disclosure will not be required. The definition of a security can be complex. For example, abusive tax shelters are often sold as sole proprietorships in an attempt to avoid the legal and accounting required in a prospectus. If promoters are attempting to sell products without conforming to security regulations, a planner should obtain a qualified legal opinion. If any doubt remains, contact federal and state agencies that deal with security violations.

With these caveats in mind, this section emphasizes the analysis of investment partnerships, rather than other securities. This is because there are unusual components in these types of offerings. The prospectus is only a starting point, a vehicle to screen out inappropriate investments.

The best place to begin a prospectus analysis is with the table of contents, if it has been included. In addition, the following elements should be examined.

Summary of the offering. This highlights the purpose and terms of the offering. It will reveal whether investors will be treated as general or limited partners. This is important information because investors may enter programs with the idea of limited liability only to find that they have been included as general partners with full liability exposure.

Use of proceeds. From this section financial planners can determine where the money is going. Problems can occur because the terms used are unclear and footnotes do not clarify the questions. Contacting the offering company should clear up the confusion. Once the planner knows exactly where each dollar is going, a comparison can be made. Do other programs have lower fees and commissions? Are the fees realistic? How large are commissions to sales representatives? Are they within a normal range?

Major questions should be raised if the commission structure is abnormally high. How general partners are being compensated should also be noted. Is their level of remuneration within the industry average? Do general partners receive most of the benefits from up-front fees and commissions? On sale, are the profits divided so the investors receive their original investment plus a minimum return *before* the promoters receive their rewards? Is the minimum return comprised of cash or are tax deductions included in this figure?

Track record. This is where financial planners should look to determine how well previous investors have fared. "Plowing through" the record should show planners the amount of benefits received for each dollar invested. This, of course, is easier said than done.

Securities and Exchange Commission regulations do not require listing the results of *all* previous offerings. Furthermore, footnotes explaining the sales price of investments do not show the terms of any mortgages taken back by the partnership. Therefore, on most occasions, to determine the true yield, it is necessary to obtain backup figures dirctly from the promoters. To confirm the reliability of these figures, a *Statement of Authenticity* can be provided by the company's independent accounting firm.

Sometimes there is no track record because none of the previous investments have gone full cycle (acquisition, management, and sale). In such instances, the expertise of the management team will be the deciding factor in terms of how profitable the investment will eventually be. Management's expertise and investment strategy are important.

Management. Within this category, the prospectus will give a brief description of the company's key employees or general partners. It is essential to know whether the general partners have been subject to previous securities violations or fraud charges. This information, as well as the net worth of the general partners, should be listed. Do the general partners have any real assets, or only inflated assets? Any other pertinent information should be obtained from the promoters.

Throughout this "due diligence" process, financial planners must be aware of danger signals. One red flag is a company that does not send information requested. If repeated requests are ignored, investors should be steered clear of the company.

It is also a good idea for financial planners to form a small group to investigate the general partner. This may make it possible to screen out inappropriate investments. This informal association can also save time and review more programs than could one financial planner alone.

Legal opinion. Typically a legal section of the prospectus supports the investment potential in terms of structure and tax deductions. If there are numerous "hedge" words, caution should be exercised. If the legal opinion doesn't "stand for" the investment, why should a finanical planner?

Tax aspects. This section should explain how the investment can be affected by the tax code, regulations, rulings, and court cases. Occasionally, the tax section of a prospectus will consist of 12 to 20 pages documenting why the company should be taxed as a partnership. This, of course, is important. However, if no more than one page is allocated to significant tax issues, financial planners should be extremely wary. Does the prospectus address all the important tax issues? Are questionable tax deductions taken? Are legitimate deductions expensed in one year, rather than amortized over 60 months?

There are sections in a typical prospectus that contain information similar to that described above and, with experience, it will be easy to quickly go through those sections. A careful review of the sections on *Risk Factors* and *Conflicts of Interest* should highlight any unusual problems. It is especially important to know the debt structure and who is responsible for paying the debt. Are there any letters of credit? Is the value of the debt less than the value of the assets held? Will the level of debt prevent a realistic return on investors' money?

Remember that government regulations do not require prior performance to be expressed in compound after-tax rates of return. Adjusted rates of return, shown in Chapter 5, would be the most appropriate. Perhaps some day the regulating agencies will be more responsive, requiring general partners to present all rates of return in the same manner.

The worksheet in Exhibit 11.1 may be used to review a prospectus. This form could be used by a group of planners as part of an informal "due diligence" team, or by an individual planner. It is meant to provide a framework for determining whether further investigation of an investment is warranted.

There are also *suitability requirements* for investment partnerships. These are based on client income and net worth.

Partnerships are categorized as either *public* or *private* offerings. Public offerings must be registered with the SEC. If the investment can only be sold within a specific state, then the offering may be registered with the appropriate agency in that state. (An example is the Department of Corporations in California.) Government agencies do not rule on the merits of any offering. Their purpose is to review the investment to see that all essential information is disclosed.

Private offering.   Private offerings are investment partnerships for 35 or fewer individuals. They do not have to be regis-

---

Exhibit 11–1   Prospectus Analysis Worksheet

PART I. SUMMARY SECTION

1. Name of offeror _____

2. Type of investment, description, and to what financial situations is this best suited? _____

3. Investor qualifications: Net worth $_____ Income $_____
   Federal tax bracket: _____% Other _____

4. Amount of total offering: Total $ _____ Minimum $_____
   Unit size $_____ Installments: _____

5. Blind pool _____ Specified _____ Private _____ Public _____

6. Is there a separate company or agent, such as an escrow company holding the funds? _____

7. Estimate length of the investment. _____

Exhibit 11-1 *(continued)*

PART II. ECONOMIC/FINANCIAL
1. What is the economic environment for this type of investment?

_____
_____
_____
_____
_____
_____

2. Strategy: How sensitive will the rate of return be in these areas:
   Inflation: up/down _____
   Interest rates: up/down _____
   Energy _____
   Government regulation _____
   Tax law changes _____
   Advances in technology _____
   Other _____

3. How much of every dollar raised is actually placed in the investment?
   $_____.

4. Projected internal rate of return _____%
   Adjusted rate of return _____%

5. Track record: Results of prior partnerships:

Program name:	_____	_____	_____	_____
Cash flow:	_____	_____	_____	_____
Tax benefits:	_____	_____	_____	_____
Profit on sale:	_____	_____	_____	_____
Length limited partner to get original investment back:	_____	_____	_____	_____

6. Fee structure:

	Dollar amount	Percentage
Sales commission	_____	_____
Acquisition fees	_____	_____
Organizational fees	_____	_____
Miscellaneous fees (real estate commissions, etc)	_____	_____
Partnership management	_____	_____
Property management	_____	_____

   Reimbursable expenses _____
   Any liquidation fees _____
   _____
   Division of profits _____
      (on termination) _____
   Other fees _____

7. What are the objectives for the use of debt financing?

_____
_____
_____

Exhibit 11-1 (*continued*)

8. What rates are lenders presently charging? _____
_____
Are there any loan commitments at present? _____
At what rate? _____
Under what circumstances would that money not be available?
_____
_____
_____
_____

9. What are the provisions for additional assessments?
_____
_____
_____
_____

10. Unusual risks: underfinancing, development of property, competition,
shortages, etc.: _____
_____
_____
_____
_____

11. General industry practices:
What should an investor be cautious of (e.g., cost allocations, uneven risk
sharing, inflated or unnecessary fees, prominent conflicts of interest, etc.): _
_____
_____
_____
_____
_____

PART III. LEGAL/TAX ASPECTS
 1. Cash or accrual basis of accounting _____
 2. Tax status:
   Court cases on point _____
   Revenue rulings _____
   Opinion of counsel _____
_____
_____
_____

 3. Unusual tax items or structuring _____
_____
_____
_____

 4. Tax track record (actual): Have previous write-offs been accurately projected? _
_____
Tax audit history _____
_____
_____
_____

 5. What type of depreciation is being taken? _____

 6. Amount of investment, interest: _____
_____

Exhibit 11-1 (*concluded*)

7. Amount of tax preference items: _____

8. What is the impact of alternative minimum tax on this investment?

_____
_____
_____
_____

9. What are the projected tax deductions over the life of the program?
   Year 1 _____
   Year 2 _____
   Year 3 _____
   Year 4 _____
   Year 5 _____

tered with government agencies. However, the investor must be given the same information provided with a public offering. The 35-investor limit can be superseded if there are *accredited investors*. Under Regulation D, an accredited investor is one who has at least $200,000 of income or a net worth of $1 million.

INVESTMENT SELECTION

After a planner thoroughly investigates a specific investment, a determination must be made as to whether it is appropriate in a client's investment portfolio. To accomplish this, planners must:

1. Know the client's *specific* objectives and the length of time necessary to fulfill them. Is the client investing for growth, children's education, retirement, or a vacation?
2. Understand the client's investment temperament, including risk tolerance.
3. Match investments with the client's positions in the life cycle: income for those who are retired, growth for younger people.
4. Review the client's investment management skills. Is monitoring and trading stocks a hobby of the client's?
5. Determine how much is available to invest, and whether it is available as a periodic investment or in a lump sum.
6. Identify the economic and tax ramifications of the investment: ordinary income versus capital gains; investments that respond to inflation or deflation.

7. Ascertain how investments relate to the client's total portfolio.

There is no single investment that solves all of a client's financial needs. Nevertheless, dealing with the issues above helps planners determine which investments fit a given client's selection criteria.

The final step is to review the characteristics of specific investments to confirm that they are appropriate. Table 11.1 lists the features of some of the more common investments.

As a summary of the analysis process, the following examples illustrate the steps involved for two different clients.

EXAMPLE

Clients: Retired, ages 70 and 72, risk tolerance is low, taxes are low, they are seeking income.

Investments to consider—high-yielding saving accounts, Treasury bills, and conservative income-oriented stocks and mutual funds.

Investments to avoid—highly leveraged real estate rentals, aggressive growth stocks, oil and gas exploration programs, and leveraged equipment leasing programs.

EXAMPLE

Client: Single, age 38, no dependents, risk tolerance high, high tax bracket, seeking to retire at age 55, desires growth.

Investments to consider—personal residence, real estate rentals, municipal bonds, oil and gas exploration, market-timed growth stocks and mutual funds.

Investments to avoid—low-yielding savings accounts, minimal growth-oriented stocks and mutual funds, treasury bills.

There are no hard-and-fast rules for selecting the most suitable investment. Rather, the characteristics of investments will change in response to the economic climate and new tax laws. Thus, the guidelines will change and be revised as conditions warrant.

In summary, due diligence must emphasize the initial phases of investigation. However, research must continue after a client has purchased the investments. Periodic reviews and assessments of performance in relation to other investment products are essential. This ongoing process will better enable financial planners to assist their clients in achieving financial objectives.

Table 11-1 Characteristics of Common Investments

Asset Description	Income Yield	Growth Potential	Liquidity	Tax Benefits	Management Requirements	Response to Inflation	Response to Deflation	Overall Volatility
Savings accounts	Low–medium	Low	Excellent	Low	Low	Low	Excellent	Low
Treasury bills	Low–medium	Low	Medium–excellent	Low	Low	Low	Excellent	Low–medium
Corporate bonds	Medium	Low–medium	Excellent	Low	Low	Low	Excellent	Low–medium
Municipal bonds	Low	Low–medium	Excellent	Excellent	Low	Low	Excellent	Low–medium
Common stocks	Low–medium	Medium–high	Excellent	Medium–high	Medium	Medium	Low–medium	Medium–high
Mutual funds	Low–high	Low–high	Excellent	Low–medium	Low	Medium	Low–medium	Low–high
Personal residence	Low	Medium–high	Low	Excellent	Medium–high	Excellent	Low	Low–medium
Real estate rentals	Low	Medium–high	Low	Excellent	High	Excellent	Low	Medium
Oil and gas exploration	Low	High	Low	Medium	High	Excellent	Low	High
Gold, silver	Low	High	Medium	Low	Low–medium	Excellent	Low	Medium–high

PART FOUR

Lifetime Planning

Retirement Plans: Qualified Pension Plans; Individual Retirement Accounts; Tax Sheltered Annuities

The retirement plans discussed in this chapter—qualified pension plans, individual retirement accounts (IRAs), and tax-sheltered annuities (TSAs)—provide many benefits. The most advantageous feature is that *all* contributions made to each plan are tax deductible. In addition, these plans provide for tax-free accumulation of assets, so that nothing is taxed until the funds are distributed.

With these exceptional tax benefits, financial planners will typically seek conservative investments that provide a realistic yield for such plans. Selecting a conservative vehicle is important because these assets will comprise part of the client's foundation for retirement. If the foundation is eroded due to the loss of principal or purchasing power, there may not be sufficient time to replace the lost funds. Although planners cannot guarantee the return of principal or yield, they can recommend low-risk investments that minimize potential losses.

The key to selection is long-term growth through steady income or asset appreciation. Consistency in investment performance is more important than sporadically high rates of return.

These plans should not involve investments that produce significant deductions, such as through depreciation or investment tax credits, because the benefits cannot be used in tax-deferred accounts. For example, a $2,000 IRA contribution produces a $2,000 tax deduction. If the IRA is invested in a highly leveraged equipment leasing program, no further deductions, such as for interest expense or depreciation, or any investment tax credits can be taken. Therefore, these additional tax benefits would not be utilized. Ordinarily, high write-off programs produce high risk, which makes them unsuitable for pension plans.

It would also be inapproprite to select investments, such as municipal bonds, that provide tax-free income. There would be no advantage with these types of bonds, because pension plans already accumulate income tax-free. Moreover, the disadvantage in choosing municipal bonds is that the distributions would be taxed. Thus, a traditionally tax-free vehicle would be subject to taxation when the funds are disbursed.

Further, an investment that produces long-term capital gains is not better than one that produces an equal level of ordinary income, because most distributions from pension plans are taxed as ordinary income. (The exceptions are noted later in the chapter.)

The tax advantages as well as the supplemental income they provide at retirement make each of these plans an excellent choice for helping a client reach financial goals. The tax/income combination is rarely surpassed by investments outside of this protective umbrella. Consequently, caution must be exercised in selecting investments that will preserve the client's assets, as well as provide a reasonable rate of return. Get-rich-quick schemes are not appropriate under this umbrella.

Investments planners may wish to consider in funding pension plans include: government securities, conservative stocks and bonds and real estate mortgages, as well as insurance annuities. The values of these investment vehicles may fluctuate, but these investments minimize the risk of loss.

A final consideration in choosing an investment for the plans discussed is liquidity. A certain portion of the assets should always be in liquid investments. This will cover any distributions that have to be made either prior to or at retirement.

At this point, let us examine the different types of plans and who may participate.

INDIVIDUAL RETIREMENT ACCOUNT (IRA)

Thanks to congressional action and mass media advertising, the IRA is the most popular pension plan. Major aspects of the IRA which planners must understand include: who may participate, maximum contributions funding, distributions, and termination.

Participants.   Anyone who has earned income may contribute to any IRA. The income must be salary, wages, alimony, or net taxable income from a business. If the income is subject to Social Security taxes, it qualifies for IRA contribution purposes. One noteworthy exception is a self-employed person who employs his or her spouse. For example, if a wife hires her husband and pays him a salary, the amount paid is not subject to Social Security taxes. However, the husband's wages are taxable and can be used to contribute to an IRA. Income from savings and investments do not qualify.

Maximum contribution and funding.   The maximum sum that can be placed in an IRA is 100 percent of qualifiable income up to $2,000 annually. For a married couple with both spouses working, the maximum is $2,000 in each account, for a combined total of $4,000. With a nonworking spouse, the total for couples is $2,250. This can be allocated in any manner between the spouses as long as each account has a minimum of $250. The full amount does not have to be funded, and future contributions may be skipped whenever desired. However, excess contributions are subject to a 6 percent penalty. For 1985, and thereafter, divorced individuals may include their alimony payments for contributing up to $2,000 to an IRA.

The IRA must be funded by the due date of the tax return, which is April 15. The IRS now allows taxpayers to claim the IRA deduction and submit their return before they make the payment, as long as the account is funded by April 15.

Distributions.   Individuals may receive a distribution from an IRA once a year. The distributed amount can be placed in another IRA within 60 days without being taxed. The IRA custodian, usually a bank or a trust company, provides an important service in any distribution. The custodian must record all transactions and report any distributions to the IRS. The custodian is also required to withold 10 percent of the distribution unless the taxpayer informs them not to do so. The withholding would be especially inappropriate for those who are completing a *tax-free rollover* (an exchange of funds from one IRA to another).

Taxpayers may move IRA money from one custodian to another—never receiving the funds—as often as they wish. This is a *nontaxable transfer.* If clients withdraw their money from an IRA, the amount withdrawn is taxable. A 10 percent nondeductible penalty is levied by the IRS if the distribution is made before the IRA investor reaches age 59½. There is no penalty if the funds are withdrawn due to disability or death of the taxpayer.

Terminations. IRA accounts may be disbursed when an individual reaches age 59½ without incurring any penalties. The money received is taxed as ordinary income regardless of the investment vehicle used for the IRA. The year after IRA investors become 70½, they are required to withdraw amounts prescribed in IRS actuarial tables. For example, Roger is 70½ on December 1, 1985; he must begin a systematic withdrawal from his IRA no later than December 31, 1986. (Those who are married may choose the joint-survivor actuarial table.) Ignoring the withdrawal requirement will cost a taxpayer a penalty of 50 percent of the excess amount remaining in the account.

Miscellaneous rules and regulations. There are several additional considerations involving IRAs, such as:

1. Investors may use a variety of investment vehicles to create an IRA, the exceptions are hard assets, tangibles, and art.
2. Some states have not conformed to changes in federal tax laws so that an IRA is *not* deductible on these state returns.
3. Borrowing from an IRA or using it as collateral is prohibited.
4. Individuals cannot be their own custodians.

Many people are irritated by advertising pushing IRAs and showing a million dollar value in the account in 40 years. These ads emphasize the wrong concept. They overlook the needs of people age 50 and over, who do not have several decades available to accumulate assets. Rather, clients must be aware that, if money is not placed in an IRA, they are going to be paying more taxes. Should clients lack sufficient funds to make an IRA contribution, planners will want to assist them in developing a good cash-flow managment system.

Some individuals believe that an IRA account is not for them because the distributions are taxed as ordinary income when they retire. Certainly, that is one drawback of the program. Yet, *tax deferral* and *time value* must be emphasized. The key is that clients pay less in taxes now, because the IRA lowers taxable income by the amount of the contribution. The money is also compounded much faster when it is not subject to current taxation. Finally, when the IRA funds are distributed, the taxes will be paid with depreciated dollars, because money is worth more today than it will be in the future.

The deferral and tax savings can be seen in the following illustration.

Without Deferral	With Deferral
$1,500 per year	$2,000 per year
9 percent	12 percent
20 years	20 years
$76,740 Total	$144,105 Total

Assumptions:
  Tax bracket: 25%.
  Yearly contribution: $2,000.
  Interest/yield rate: 12%.

Without a qualified plan, the taxpayer earns $2,000, but pays $500 in taxes. Therefore, only $1,500 is saved and the interest is taxable. In a 25 percent tax bracket, the taxpayer can keep only 75 percent of the 12 percent interest, or 9 percent. Yield comparisons should be calculated at the same initial gross rate. The yield on the investments shown is the same whether an IRA is involved or not. For example, the same stock will not perform better or worse because it is in a retirement plan.

The total is significantly different under the qualified plan. However, some have argued that if the amount invested in an IRA is taken out in one payment, the total is less because the taxpayer has been thrown into a higher tax bracket. A more rational perspective would be to consider the amounts to be withdrawn over a number of years so the tax bracket would not increase significantly, if at all. The benefits would still be significantly greater with qualified plans.

TAX SHELTERED ANNUITY (TSA)

TSA programs were created by Congress in 1962 under Internal Revenue Code Section 403(b). These programs are sometimes called tax deferred annuities (TDAs). (An *annuity* is simply a stream of income.) An annuity can be puchased through an insurance company or a mutual fund, but must be specifically designated to qualify under Internal Revenue Code 403(b).

The following are some of the nuances of a tax sheltered annuity.

Participants. Tax sheltered annuities are designed for individuals employed by nonprofit organizations, charitable foundations, or educational institutions. This vehicle is funded through a salary deduction. The contribution must be withdrawn from an individual's check by the employer and sent directly to the selected annuity. At the end of the year, IRS Form W-2 reflects a lower amount of wages.

Maximum contribution. The maximum amount that can be contributed is 20 percent of gross salary. However, there are three formulas for computing a benefit. The one which produces the smallest contribution must be used. Table 12.1 shows the format for the calculation, while Table 12.2 gives the options available.

Distribution. There is a significant difference between distributions from an IRA and a TSA. Clients may withdraw their money from a TSA before age 59½. Currently the 10 percent penalty will not be imposed if the money is withdrawn from an insurance annuity or a mutal fund.

Transfers and rollovers are permitted. As is true with an IRA, withdrawn TSA funds must be reinvested within 60 days of receipt. On disability, retirement, or termination of service, individuals may roll over their funds into an IRA account without any tax consequences. This option may be selected to provide more diverse investments than those provided by an annuity or a mutual fund. At termination there is no special 10-year forward averaging available for this retirement plan.

It is important to note that an annuity is an appropriate vehicle in which to accumulate tax-deferred dollars. Clients may select a fixed-interest-rate account or a "variable" account. The variable account is a mutual fund that invests in the stock market. Consequently, its yield varies with market performance. However, caution must be exercised in selecting an annuity payout for this type of investment.

The concept of "annuitizing". This means clients will receive an income for the rest of their lives. The income is based on the age of the clients and the amount of money in the account. If death occurs *after* annuitizing the annuity, then the principal belongs to the insurance company. For that reason, many people choose to take an annuity option for a *period certain.* This means the insurance company will pay out a lesser benefit, but for a specific minimum period, usually 10 years.

Table 12-1 Basic Exclusion Allowance for 403(b) Plans (contributions to be made through salary reduction)

1. Present annual salary (before salary reduction): $ _____
2. Years of service with present employer as of end of current taxable year: _____
3. Prior tax-exempt contributions by employer to all plans (includes TSA): $ _____
4. _____ times _____ : $ _____
   (LINE 1)　　　　　(LINE 2)
5. _____ times the numeral 5: $ _____
   (LINE 3)
6. _____ minus _____ : $ _____
   (LINE 4)　　　　　(LINE 5)
7. _____ plus the numeral 5: _____
   (LINE 2)
8. _____ divided by _____ : $ _____
   (LINE 6)　　　　　(LINE 7)
9. 20% times _____ : $ _____
   (LINE 1)
10. 1984 dollar limitation: $ _30,000*_
11. Maximum exclusion allowance equals the lesser of lines 8, 9, or 10: $ _____

The exclusion allowance determined on Line 11 above, or in Option A or Option B (Table 12.2) is the maximum which may be contributed to the aggregate of all 403(b) plans. Other "annuity contract" coverage need not be aggregated unless the employee owns or controls the employer or elects alternative Option C.

> This is for sample use only. The prospect may wish to consult with an attorney or tax adviser.

See IRS Publication 590 for further information.

Church employees received revised rules for 403(b) plans which are effective for years beginning after 1981. Pertinent parts of these revisions are:

1. Years of service—treat all years of service with related church organizations as if all were with one employer.
2. Alternative exclusion allowance—if adjusted gross income is not more than $17,000 the maximum excludable contribution is never lower than the lesser of: (a) $3,000, or (b) 100 percent of includable compensation.
3. Special election—if the "basic exclusion allowance" is elected, the following limitations may be chosen: (a) the annual contribution must not exceed the greater of $10,000, and (b) the total of all such annual contributions over the lifetime of the employee must not exceed $40,000.

If this election is made, no other catch-up options may be used during the same tax year.

---

*Adjusted annually by the Secretary of Treasury.
SOURCE: Courtesy of Security Benefit Life Insurance Company.

Table 12-2 Alternative Exclusion Options (for employees of hospitals, educational institutions, home health service agencies, or church organizations.)*

Option A
This option is available only during the year of separation of service.

A. 1984 dollar limitation: $ 30,000†

B. Recalculate line 8 using only the latest 10 years of employment. Ignore service and contributions made prior to 10 years ago.

Maximum contribution is lesser of A or B.

Option B
This option is available during any year of service.

A. Dollar limit: $ 15,000

B. 20% of line 1 + $3,200: $ _____

C. Line 8 amount: $ _____

Maximum contribution is lesser of A, B, or C.

Option C
This option is available during any year of service. The allowance is dependent upon other qualified plan coverage, as follows:

A. If not covered by any other plan, the maximum contribution is the lesser of:

A(1). 1984 dollar limitation, or $ 30,000†

A(2). Line 9 amount. $ _____

B. If covered by another defined contribution plan, the maximum is the lesser of:

B(1). 1984 dollar limitation. $ 30,000†

B(2). Line 9 minus current employer contributions to other defined contribution plans. $ _____

C. If covered by a defined benefit plan, the maximum contribution is the lesser of:

C(1). 1984 dollar limitation. $ 30,000†

C(2). Line 9 amount $ _____

C(3). Amount determined below.

  a. Expected annual retirement benefit $ _____

  b. Lesser of $90,000† or Line 1 $ _____

  c. Line a divided by line c $ _____

  d. 1.25 minus line c $ _____

  e. Line d times line 9 $ _____

To determine past employer contributions and current employer contributions to a fixed benefit plan, proceed as follows:

1. Enter expected annual retirement benefit from employer's retirement plan (other than TSA). $ _____

2. Enter Table A factor, based on retirement age and annuity option (if unknown, use 10 C & L).   × _____

3. Line 1 times line 2, which equals total amount necessary to purchase benefit.   = _____

4. Enter Table B factor, based on total years in plan, as of retirement date.   × $ _____

5. Line 3 times line 4 $ _____

6. Enter annual employee contributions to plan. $ _____

7. Line 5 minus line 6 $ _____

8. Years of past service as of beginning of year. $ _____

9. Line 7 times line 8. $ _____

10. Prior employer contributions to other plans. $ _____

11. Line 9 plus line 10 (enter on line 3 of worksheet) $ _____

*These options are irrevocable. Once an option is chosen, no other option may be used in future years.
†Adjusted annually by the Secretary of Treasury.
SOURCE: Courtesy of Security Benefit Life Insurance Company.

For example, a male, age 63, who has accumulated $40,000 in an annuity account could receive approximately $350 per month for the rest of his life. If he chose a "ten-year period certain," his monthly income could drop to $310 per month.

The key feature is that the income stream is typically not higher than what the individual could receive through investing in government securities. More importantly, once the money is annuitized, the principal belongs to the insurance company. Therefore, clients could not leave these assets to their beneficiaries. Consequently, for clients to retain control over their money it would be more appropriate *not* to select to annuitize an annuity. Tax implications can be minimized through the previously mentioned rollover procedure.

Borrowing. Other benefits of a TSA account include the TEFRA borrowing provision. At this time, 50 percent of an account up to $50,000 may be borrowed. And $10,000 or less can be borrowed, even though it exceeds more than 50 percent of the account. The money must be paid back within five years. The exception is borrowing funds for an individual's personal residence. In this instance, there is no set time in which the money must be repaid.

QUALIFIED PENSION PLANS

As of January 1, 1984, *all* pension plans for sole proprietors, general partnerships, and corporations have the same contribution limits. Thus, the maximum participation in these types of plans is applicable regardless of business ownership. Under TEFRA, Congress attempted to grant parity to the two basic categories of pension plans. Utilizing these qualified plans is now the best way to provide tax deductions as well as to fund retirement objectives. To assist clients in choosing the most appropriate plan, it is necessary for planners to understand how these pension plans operate.

First of all, in selecting a pension plan, the objectives of the owner (employer) and willingness to fund benefits must be known. Furthermore, a pension plan should be designed for today's requirements, as well as the future profitability of the business. It is futile to design a pension plan when the owner (employer) does not wish to share profits or when the minimum level of future profits is undeterminable or looks dismal.

To determine which pension plan is appropriate, salary, age, length of employment, marital status, age of spouse, and commencement of employment must be taken into account. An accurate employee census will reveal the necessary information. This statistical information is necessary to comply with the regulations governing pension plans. ERISA, the 1974 pension reform act, prescribes minimum standards under which employees must be covered in a qualified plan.

Points to consider before selecting the most appropriate pension plan include: coverage, vesting, top-heavy rules, and definition.

Coverage. An accurate employee census will indicate which employees meet the guidlines for coverage. The requirements are as follows:

- An employee must have reached the age of 21.
- The employee must have completed one year of full-time service, defined as at least 1,000 hours per 12-month period. Part-time employees (less than 1,000 hours) do not have to be covered.
- If three years of service is required by the plan, 100 percent vesting is immediate at the end of this period. A plan may not require that the three years of service be consecutive.
- Those who are employed within five years of normal retirement can be excluded from a defined benefit or a target benefit plan.

Furthermore Congress was concerned that some employers would attempt to circumvent the rules in determining which employees must be covered by pension plans. To minimize any discrimination, Congress enacted Internal Revenue Code 410. This law provides mathematical standards with which the employer must comply. The following complicated nondiscrimination rules indicate the number of employees which must be covered:

- 70 percent of all employees or 80 percent of all eligible employees, if at least 70 percent of all employees are eligible to participate.
- All employees who qualify under a classification that does not discriminate in favor of officers, shareholders, or highly compensated employees.

- Employees covered by collective bargaining may be excluded if the union negotiations were done in good faith.

Part-time employees or those who have not met the service or age requirements may be excluded in applying the 70 percent or 80 percent standards.

EXAMPLE

A company has 20 employees, five are part-time, three have worked less than one year, and two are under 21. The 70/80 percent test would be met if at least seven of the employees are eligible and at least six employees (80 percent of seven employees) participate.

Vesting. This is the specified time period over which employees' pension benefits accrue and become nonforfeitable. The vesting schedule, as defined in the Internal Revenue Code, reveals what portion of the pension fund is the employee's should he or she terminate employment or retire. There are three prescribed vesting schedules under the ERISA rules.

Schedule 1. An employee with *10* years of service must have a nonforfeitable right to *100* percent of the accrued benefits.

Schedule 2. Under the graduated 15-year method, an employee must have a 25 percent vested right after five years of service. This increases by 5 percent for each of the next five years, and by 10 percent for each of the following five years. This vesting schedule is shown in Table 12.3.

Schedule 3. This is known as the Rule of 45. With this method, an employee who has at least five years of service and whose age and service together equal at least 45 years must have

Table 12-3 Schedule 2 Vesting

Years of Service	Nonforfeitable Percentage
5	25%
6	30
7	35
8	40
9	45
10	50
11	60
12	70
13	80
14	90
15 or more	100

a nonforfeitable right to 50 percent of the accrued benefits. For each succeeding year of service, the required percentage increases by 10 percent. Therefore, after an additional five years of service, the employee is 100 percent vested. It should be noted that beginning in 1985, breaks in service of less than five years will not require employees to begin their vesting schedule from scratch.

Vesting is only one part of the complexity of pension plans. TEFRA also added the "top-heavy" provisions under IRC 416.

Top-heavy rules. Effective January 1, 1984, a qualified pension plan is classified "top heavy" if:

1. Under defined contribution plans more than 60 percent of the aggregate account balances accumulate to *key employees* (defined below).
2. In a defined benefit plan, more than 60 percent of the present value of the accumulated benefits is designated for the key employees.

If the top-heavy rules apply, then the schedule for vesting increases to:

- 100 percent vesting after three years of service.
- A graduated vesting formula beginning with 20 percent after the second full year of service. The amount increases 20 percent each year thereafter.

In addition, only the first $200,000 of compensation can be taken into account in determining benefits for a top-heavy plan. The minimum benefits for nonkey employees are 3 percent of compensation under defined contribution plans, or 2 percent per year of service, not required to exceed 20 percent of average compensation for the highest five years of compensation under defined benefit plans.

Key employees. As the above indicates, the "key employees" are an important consideration in qualified pension plans. TEFRA defines a key employee as:

- Ten employees owning the largest interest in the company.
- An owner with more than a 5 percent interest.
- An owner holding more than 1 percent and earning more than $150,000 per year.

This could apply to (*a*) 50 officers, (*b*) three employees, or (*c*) 10 percent of all employees, whichever is smaller.

As the rules become more complicated, some individuals seek ingenious ways to circumvent the intent of the IRC. However, the concept of substance over form pertains. Vesting, participation, and qualification requirements will not be subverted by simply establishing a number of companies. Under the *controlled corporation* rules, all employees who are members of a controlled group are treated as employed by a single employer. This prevents a "worst-case" arrangement whereby a corporation artificially sets up pension plans that cover only a few employees and other companies with numerous employees would have no pension plan, although all the companies would be owned by substantially the same group of people.

Qualified pension plans may be divided into two categories depending on whether benefits or contributions define the plan.

Defined benefit plan. Under this program, the retirement benefit is defined. Thus, participants know in advance what benefits they will receive when they retire.

Since the benefit is defined, an actuarial calculation is made to determine what the employer's annual payment will be. The closer a participant is to retirement, the greater the annual contribution. For example, an actuary may determine that an employee who retires at 65 must have $1 million in a pension plan to provide a previously defined income during the employee's retirement years. If the employee is 35, the employer has 30 years to fund the $1 million goal. However, if the employee is 55, only 10 years remain to fund for the benefit, and much more money must be placed into the account annually. This plan is well suited for owners and key employees who are over age 45, because more significant benefits can accrue to them than to younger rank-and-file employees.

The maximum benefit payable under this plan is the lesser of 100 percent of the employee's salary for the highest three years, or $90,000. The $90,000 limitation is actuarially reduced when the retirement benefits begin before age 62. If the benefits begin on or after age 55, the reduction cannot go below $75,000. The percentage of salary selected must apply to all eligible employees, not just to key employees. Separate accounts are not maintained.

The employer is obligated to fund this type of pension plan at the predetermined level. Funding requirements can be extensive. Under extreme hardship, a waiver can be obtained from the IRS.

Investment and actuarial gains in excess of a plan's assumptions must be used to reduce the company's contributions. On the other hand, losses will require more employer contributions.

Defined contribution plans. This classification includes profit-sharing, money purchase, target benefit, HR-10, and 401 (k) plans. A defined contribution plan provides an *individual* account for each participant. Benefits are derived from the amount contributed by the employer to each person's fund, based on a flat dollar amount or a percentage of the salary of the employee. Actuarial calculations are not required to determine the annual contribution.

Profit-sharing plan. This is one of the most commonly utilized defined contribution plans. One reason for its popularity is that each year businesses may decide whether to fund the retirement program. Even if a business earns a profit, it does not have to contribute to the plan every year. However, if an amount is funded for owners or key employees, the same percentage must apply to everyone. If the plan is not funded for several years, the IRS may then classify it as terminated.

The annual maximum amount the employer is allowed to deduct for this type of plan is 15 percent of the employee's compensation. Although TEFRA made several changes in the annual contribution limit (it cannot exceed $30,000), the compensation limits remain the same. The percentage may be increased to 25 percent of salary if the employer maintains additional plans or the employee contributes to such plans.

401(k) plan. Perhaps the fastest-growing deferred compensation arrangement is the 401(k) plan. This program was created by Congress in 1978 and the IRS issued proposed regulations three years later.

Under a 401(k) plan, employees can elect to defer current taxation on a portion of their salary by having the company contribute the reduced amount to a qualified plan. The amount can be matched by the employer. The program is set up under the guidelines for a profit-sharing plan. Consequently, when all segments of the plan are combined, it may not exceed either 25 percent of compensation or $30,000, whichever is less. The employer's contributions may not exceed 15 percent of compensation. The nondiscrimination rules for profit-sharing plans also apply.

The advantages of this program include:

- Ten-year forward averaging on lump-sum distributions.
- Participation by choice through payroll reduction.

- Personal income tax savings.
- Tax-sheltered accumulation.
- Employees can borrow under the TEFRA provisions.
- Hardship withdrawals are permitted under a predetermined company formula.

Congress presumed that higher-paid employees would be more likely to contribute a larger percentage of their compensation than lower-paid employees. To encourage participation, Congress set up a comparative contribution arrangement. The requirements of this arrangement are satisfied under one of the following:

- If the average of the employees receiving the lowest two thirds of compensation put in 2 percent of their salary or less, then the average of the group receiving the highest one third of salary is 2.5 times the rate of the lower group.
- If the lower-paid group contributes between 2 and 6 percent of salary, then the highest one third can contribute 3 percent more of pay than the lower group put in.
- If the lower-paid group averages payments between 2 and 6 percent of salary, then the higher paid can contribute 1.5 times the rate paid by the lower two thirds.

To encourage the lower two thirds' participation in the plan, the employer can match employees' contributions. And all employee contributions are immediately 100 percent vested under this arrangement. This type of program is excellent for large organizations with many participants.

Money purchase plan. This type of plan must specify a fixed contribution formula, usually a percentage of compensation up to a maximum of 10 percent of salary. The contributions must be made even if there are no profits, or an excise tax will be imposed on the employer. The employer may apply for a waiver because of hardship. This amount must be made up within 15 years. The money purchase plan is not flexible as is the profit-sharing program. These two pension plans are often combined to increase maximum contributions to 25 percent.

Target benefit plan. This type of plan is often described as a composite of a money purchase plan and a defined benefit plan. The target benefit begins with a specific retirement benefit, often based on a percentage of compensation. Actuarial calculations are made to determine the initial annual contribution necessary to fund the benefit. This type of plan requires more contributions for older employees because there is less time to achieve the target.

For example, two employees earn $15,000 and will receive the same target benefit at retirement, but A is 20 years old and B is 50 years old. The employer would have to contribute only a few hundred dollars for A but over $2,000 to the account of B. This is because, although the goal is the same, there is more time for the account of A to grow to the desired benefit, so the initial contribution is smaller. An employer would choose this type of plan when salary ranges are similar, but key owners are older than most of the other employees. ERISA classifies this pension as a defined contribution plan, so the 25 percent/$30,000 limitations apply.

Keogh, HR-10.   Keogh and HR-10 plans were originally intended for self-employed persons not covered by other types of pension arrangements. This is no longer a separate classification, although with these plans, employees continue to make their own contributions. Participants may contribute to either a defined benefit or a defined contribution plan. However, with defined contribution plans, TEFRA defines earned income to include salary *less* the amount of the pension contribution. Therefore, the $30,000 limitation applies only when the salary exceeds $150,000. (25% of $150,000 − $30,000 = $120,000; $120,000 + $30,000 = $150,000 total.) The minimum contribution of 100 percent of net income up to $750 applies only if adjusted gross income does not exceed $15,000.

Simplified employee pension (SEP).   This type of pension plan was created by the Revenue Act of 1978. A SEP program is often similar to a defined contribution plan. The main difference with a SEP is the employer provides the retirement benefits by making contributions to employees' IRA accounts in lieu of maintaining a more complicated qualified plan. All qualified employees set up and maintain their own IRAs to which the employer makes deductible contributions. Such contributions are technically required to be included in an employee's gross income, and are deductible by the employee. Employer contributions are exempt from Social Security and federal unemployment taxes if the money is actually contributed to the plan.

To qualify the plan, all eligible employees must participate, and the employer can require participation as a condition of employment.

With a SEP plan, the employer can contribute 15 percent of an employee's compensation up to the first $200,000 of salary. To avoid discrimination, the same percentage must be applied to all participants. This type of plan may be maintained in conjunction with other defined contribution plans, in which case the overall 25 percent limitation applies. Effective January 1, 1984, the provision prohibiting a SEP plan to exist concurrently with a defined benefit plan for Subchapter S corporations and Keoghs, was repealed.

A participant may also contribute 100 percent of compensation, up to $2,000 ($2,250 with a nonworking spouse), to a SEP. Through an oversight in the pertinent legislation, the maximum deduction allowed per employee is $15,000. (Some clarifying action may be taken by the IRS or Congress.)

Reporting requirements are minimal under a SEP program. There are no fiduciary investment responsibilities because there is no trust fund, only participant-maintained IRAs. However, the following requirements must be adhered to:

- The plan must cover all full-time and part-time employees age 21 and over and meet the three-out-of-five-years of service requirement.
- Each participant is immediately 100 percent vested. The employer may not make contributions contingent on future continued employment. Withdrawals by participants must be allowed at any time.
- Amounts contributed must not discriminate in favor of employees who are officers, shareholders, or highly compensated employees.
- If the plan is integrated with Social Security, it must conform to the Internal Revenue Code. Also, the contributions for each participant must bear a uniform relationship to total compensation.

Employee stock ownership programs (ESOP).   An ESOP is a defined contribution plan comprised of a qualified stock bonus plan and/or a money purchase plan. Contributions and distributions consist of company stock, not cash. Contributions may vary from year to year and may be omitted in a particular year.

A corporation offering an ESOP can receive a payroll-based tax credit equal to .75 percent of the company's payroll for the years 1985 through 1987. After 1987 no credit will be available unless the provision is extended by Congress.

Employees are not subject to tax until they receive a distribution of stock from the ESOP trust. Also, employees are not taxed on appreciation of stock until the stock is sold.

This type of plan appears appropriate for a corporation that wants to generate cash and spread ownership among employees.

BORROWING PROVISIONS

Under the terms of TEFRA there are provisions covering a person's ability to borrow from a pension plan. Guidelines do not permit owner-employees to borrow from their qualified plans, previously known as Keogh plans. An owner-employee is defined as one who (a) owns an unincorporated trade or busines or, (b) is a partner who owns more than 10 percent of the capital interest or profit interest in the partnership. An owner-employee who receives a loan from his or her Keogh plan is subject to a tax of 5 percent of the amount of the loan each year. If the loan is not repaid within a specified period, an additional tax of 100 percent of the loan is imposed.

However, TEFRA does allow borrowing from corporate pension plans if the loan is the lesser of (a) $50,000, or (b) one half of the accrued benefit in the employee's account. There is also a five-year repayment requirement, unless loan proceeds are used to acquire, construct, or reconstruct the employee's principal residence.

TAX CONSIDERATIONS

Ten-year forward averaging may be used to reduce taxes on lump-sum distributions from qualified corporate pension plans. However, this provision does not apply to IRA, TSA, Keogh, or deferred compensation disbursements.

Ten-year forward averaging requires all funds from the pension plans to be disbursed the same calendar year. Furthermore, the participant must be in the plan for at least five years. The computation will, in effect, average the amount as if it were received over 10 years, and fewer taxes will have to be paid on the amount received. Plan contributions made prior to 1974 can also qualify for long-term capital gain treatment.

When an employee retires, the planner must determine whether 10-year averaging or a tax-free rollover into an IRA is appropriate. One guideline, of course, involves the time element.

If the retiree will be living on the funds immediately, then 10-year averaging may be the best solution because, overall, less tax would be paid. But if the funds will not be touched for several years, then a tax-free rollover would postpone recognizing the gain. The calculations are specific to each individual and should also be used to determine when the crossover point is reached.

Unrelated business taxable income (UBTI). To prevent tax-exempt organizations from having a competitive edge over businesses that pay taxes, Congress created the UBTI tax. This tax applies to income from any trade or business that is not related to an organization's tax-exempt status. The first $1,000 of UBTI is not subject to tax. Amounts in excess of $1,000 are taxed at rates between 12 percent and a maximum of 50 percent applied to income in excess of $41,000.

CHAPTER THIRTEEN

Social Security and Employee Fringe Benefits

SOCIAL SECURITY

The term "Social Security" is misleading, and even Congress has felt compelled to take steps to make the word "security" more concrete. Heated debate has surrounded the Social Security program, and questions concerning its solvency are likely to continue producing controversy.

For those who will receive Social Security benefits in the near future, government tables list what the benefits will be. For those who are scheduled to retire over the next several decades, the computations will be, at best, guestimates.

One aspect that cannot be overlooked in discussing the problems besetting Social Security is the *length* of retirement. Life expectancy continues to increase. Government statistics show that the fastest-growing segment of the U.S. population, as a percentage, are those in their 80s. For those under age 60 in the year 2000, life expectancy will be over 100 years. Therefore, although no one knows their "expiration date," most people can expect to spend a number of years in retirement.

Planning for this long span of time is a challenge for financial planners. It may also be a disheartening aspect of planning, because the increased life expectancy means that more current income is needed to fund future living expenses. For example, several years ago, the Social Security Administration indicated that retired workers received only an average of 13 checks before they died. As previously stated, this has changed. Now clients must be made aware that funding for longer life expectancies will require more of their money.

Most clients, assuming they are not the beneficiaries of a large endowment or trust fund, cannot rely on one source of income during retirement. For the majority, covering living expenses during retirement will require several sources of income, including retirement pensions, individual retirement accounts, Social Security, and investments. If clients are depending on Social Security to provide the lion's share of retirement income in the future, they may be sadly disappointed. Those near retirement are relatively assured of a certain amount; this is not the case for those with many years to retirement.

Regardless of when a client will retire, the financial planner must assess projected Social Security benefits. First, it is important to look at the cost of contributing to the system. Amendments to the Social Security Act in 1983 were designed to correct projected future deficits by advancing increases in Social Security taxes and reducing or taxing some benefits. Social Security taxes cover Old-Age, Survivors, and Disability Insurance (OASDI) and hospitalization benefits.

The wage base has increased, and now for many individuals, Social Security taxes may be higher than their regular taxes. Clients must be prepared for this new, increased outflow. Therefore, any cash flow projections will have to take this factor into consideration. Current Social Security rates are listed in Table 13.1.

For self-employed individuals, the schedule in Table 13.2 applies.

Self-employed individuals are entitled to a credit against the self-employment tax of 2.3 percent in 1985, and a credit of 2 percent against the self-employment tax in 1986–89. Beginning in 1990, a new system for taxing the self-employed will eliminate some of the disparities between the self-employed and employ-

Table 13-1 Social Security Tax Rates

Year	Combined Rate*	Maximum Social Security Tax†	Maximum Taxable Wage
1985	7.05%	$1,410	$39,600
1986–87	7.15	1,430	indexed to CPI
1988–89	7.51	1,502	indexed to CPI
1990 and later	7.65	1,530	indexed to CPI

*OASDI *plus* hospital.
†The employer must match this amount.

Table 13-2 Social Security Tax Rates for Self-Employed
Persons

Year	Combined Rate	Maximum Social Security Tax	Maximum Taxable Wage
1985	14.10%	$4,935	$39,600
1986–87	14.30	5,005	indexed to CPI
1988–89	15.02	5,257	indexed to CPI

ees. It is noteworthy that the wage base for determining Social
Security taxes must include deferred compensation contributions, such as 401(k) programs. It is especially apparent that the
self-employed may well pay more in Social Security taxes than in
income taxes.

The 1983 Social Security amendments made several other
changes. Notable among these are:

- Automatic cost-of-living increases would be limited if fund
  balances fall below certain levels.
- Social Security recepients under the age of 70 who work
  are subject to a $1 reduction in benefits for every $2 of
  earnings when their earnings exceed a base amount. The
  base amount for 65 year olds was $6,960 in 1984 and will be
  adjusted under the terms of earlier legislation. Beginning
  in 1990, the $1 reduction will apply for every $3 of earnings
  over the base amount.
- More taxpayers will be subject to Social Security taxes, including such previously exempt groups as federal employees (hired on or after January 1, 1984) and employees of
  nonprofit organizations.
- The normal retirement age has been increased via phased-
  in extensions for workers who will reach age 65 after the
  year 2002. For those born after 1937, the age will gradually
  rise in two-month increments to a maximum age of 66 for
  those born between 1943 and 1954. The increase will continue to rise to age 67 for those born in 1960 and later.

One of the most controversial aspects of the Social Security
amendment is the taxation of benefits. A maximum of 50 percent of Social Security benefits can be included as taxable in-

come. Beginning in 1984, the taxable amount of Social Security benefits is the *lesser* of:

- One half of the Social Security benefits, or
- One half of the excess amount of the taxpayer's modified adjusted gross income plus one half of Social Security benefits, minus the appropriate base exclusion.

Modified adjusted gross income is adjusted gross income plus any tax-exempt income, so that income from all sources, except Social Security, is included. The base amount is:

- $32,000 for a married couple filing jointly.
- $0 for a married couple filing separately who do not live apart for the entire year.
- $25,000 for all other taxpayers.

EXAMPLE

John and Jane have an adjusted gross income of $35,000, $5,000 of tax-free income, and $9,000 of Social Security benefits. Their modified adjusted gross income would involve the following:

1. 50 percent of $9,000 (Social Security benefits) = $4,500.
2. $35,000 AGI + $5,000 tax-free income + $4,500 Social Security − $32,000 base amount = $12,500 × .50 = $6,250.

The calculation calls for the lesser of Number 1 or Number 2 to be included in determining taxable income. In this instance, $4,500 is the smaller amount. It is significant that the base amounts are not indexed so that, as inflation advances over the years, an increasing proportion of recipients will be taxed on their Social Security benefits.

It is very important for financial planners to consider the taxability of Social Security benefits when recommending tax-free sources of income.

Potential Social Security benefits can be vital to clients retiring within the next few years. Table 13.3 shows how long employees have to work to be eligible for benefits.

It is important for individuals to check with the Social Security Administration to be sure that they are credited with the proper number of quarters. Corrections can be made only for the

Table 13-3 Quarters Needed
to be Eligible for
Social Security
Benefits

Year at which Age 62 Is Reached	Quarters of Coverage Needed
1985	34
1986	35
1987	36 (9 years)
1988	37
1989	38
1990	39
1991 or later	40 (10 years)

previous three years. To obtain the information, a postcard may be sent to:

Social Security Administration
P.O. Box 57
Baltimore, Maryland 21203

Benefits are correlated to the client's salary and the Social Security wage base. As the wage base is increased, many retirees whose salary did not increase will not receive maximum Social Security benefits. Table 13.4 gives examples of monthly Social Security benefits.

Table 13.4 is used only as an example. It must be remembered that there really is no *one maximum* Social Security benefit for all applicants. Rather, the benefit will be calculated based on the individual's date of birth, lifetime earnings, and the year a person stops working. To accurately determine a client's maximum benefit, use the Social Security Administration's indexing method.

The government has added the following incentives for those working beyond age 65. The current credit is a 3 percent increase for each year a person continues to work over age 65 (1 percent if the person was born before 1917). The increased credit will be phased in for employees born after 1924 at the rate of .5 percent every two years to a maximum of 8 percent for employees born after 1942.

Table 13-4 Maximum Social Security Benefits for Employee Retiring in 1985

The schedule below indicates the monthly amount of the Social Security old-age insurance benefit deductible under an offset pension plan in the case of an employee who terminates service in 1985 for reason other than disability or death and had received maximum Social Security taxable earnings (the Social Security Wage Base) in each calendar year beginning with the year of his 22nd birthday. The amount shown is the amount available at (a) age 65 for years of birth 1920 and later, or (b) actual retirement age for individuals born prior to 1920, exclusive of the delayed retirement credit.

Year of Birth	Type A Pension Plan*		Type B Pension Plan†	
	Class (I)**	Class (II)††	Class (I)	Class (II)
1915	$1,067	$1,115	$1,067	$1,115
1916	1,052	1,098	1,052	1,098
1917	829	853	829	853
1918	796	817	796	817
1919	743	760	743	760
1920	717	730	717	730
1921	725	737	737	748
1922	733	744	754	765
1923	739	748	767	777
1924	736	746	773	782
1925	734	743	779	787
1926	732	741	784	792
1927	729	738	789	797
1928	727	735	793	801
1929	719	733	798	805
1930	712	726	805	813
1931	705	719	812	820
1932	694	713	820	828
1933	681	707	828	835
1934	666	696	835	843
1935	652	683	843	850
1936	639	669	850	858
1937	626	656	858	865
1938	605	634	855	863
1939	584	614	853	860
1940	564	593	850	857
1941	545	574	847	853
1942	527	555	844	850
1943	509	537	840	846
1944	498	526	846	851
1945	484	512	851	855
1946	470	498	855	860

Table 13-4 (*concluded*)

Year of Birth	Type A Pension Plan*		Type B Pension Plan†	
	Class (I)**	Class (II)††	Class (I)	Class (II)
1947	455	483	860	865
1948	441	468	865	869
1949	427	455	869	873
1950	414	442	873	875
1951	400	428	875	878
1952	385	413	878	879
1953	367	395	879	881
1954	349	377	881	881
1955	327	355	871	871

Type A Pension Plan: Considers only earnings received by the employee prior to termination date (i.e., no projection thereafter).

†*Type B Pension Plan:* Assumes projected earnings after termination date to employee's 65th birthday (at rate of $39,600 per annum).

***Class (I):* Employee receives zero or minimal earnings in, or pension plan excludes earnings for, his terminal earnings year (1985 or, for Type B employee born after 1920, year of his 65th birthday).

††*Class (II):* Employee receives earnings of $39,600 in his terminal earnings year.

The amounts indicated in the schedule are computed under the "decoupled formula" method, which is geared to indexed earnings.

Technically, for employees born before 1924 and specifically retiring in the month of December 1985, the benefit in the schedule should be increased by the Social Security automatic cost-of-living percentage which becomes effective for December 1985, eliminating cents from the adjusted result. (Note: For administrative simplification, pension plan sponsors may prefer to disregard this "one-month window" and treat December retirees no differently than other employees retiring in the same calendar year.)

For employees retiring after the month of their 65th birthday (all individuals born before 1920, and some with birth year 1920), the benefit in the schedule should be increased by the Social Security delayed retirement credit—.25 percent for each month thereafter (or 1/12 percent if birth year precedes 1917)—unless the pension plan provides otherwise (e.g., if the accrued benefit under the plan is "frozen" at or about age 65). Eliminate cents from the adjusted result.

For employees whose year of birth is after 1937, the benefit in the schedule (the amount payable at age 65) has been adjusted by the appropriate early retirement reduction, reflecting the increased Social Security normal retirement age effected under the 1983 Social Security amendments.

The benefits in the schedule have been truncated to low dollar amount. Such truncation is called for under the act at the *final* step of the computation process. Accordingly, where the adjustments above apply, the benefit obtained after such adjustment may be slightly understated.

SOURCE: Courtesy of Hansen Reports.

In recent years, Social Security benefits for women have attracted attention. Key issues here involve the amount of benefits and the age requirement. For instance, a nonworking wife under age 60 would not receive benefits if her working husband died and she had no children under the age of 16. This could be a significant burden and should be considered in financial planning.

The California Commission on the Status of Women concluded that Social Security had become the "lifeline for older women." Statistics indicate that almost 90 percent of all women over the age of 65 receive Social Security. For two thirds of them, Social Security is the only income they receive.

Recent changes in the benefits structure now allow divorced women to receive Social Security when they reach retirement age. This applies only under the following conditions:

- The marriage must have lasted 10 years or more.
- Divorced spouses no longer have to wait for their former husbands to retire to collect benefits.
- Divorced wives and widows may remarry *after* age 60, without losing Social Security benefits based on their previous spouse's income.

Hospitalization.   In addition to OASDI, the Social Security program provides hospitalization benefits under *Medicare.* The 1982 tax law extended medicare covevage to federal employees who did not qualify for Social Security benefits. With this change, federal employees became subject to the hospitalization portion of the Social Security tax.

Medicare insurance is for people age 65 or older, those with permanent kidney failure, and certain disabled individuals. Medicare includes both hospitalization and some medical benefits. Hospital coverage is for in-patient care and certain limited follow-up care. The program covers up to 90 days of in-patient hospital care during one illness. Furthermore, each recipient has a lifetime reserve of 60 days of additional coverage after the 90 days have been exhausted. In-patient hospital services include room, equipment, diagnostic or therapeutic services, and medical and surgical services, as well as drugs. It is financed by a portion of the FICA (Social Security) tax.

Medical insurance partially covers doctor's services, outpatient hospital care, drugs that can not be self-administered, and other medical items. Medical coverage is voluntary and is partially paid for through monthly premiums from retirees enrolled in the program and partly through general federal revenues.

Although Medicare covers listed services, the fees charged for these services may be more than the standard Medicare reimbursement. Not many doctors or medical organizations will accept Medicare as payment in full.

Social Security does provide other benefits such as disability coverage and payments to children, under age 18, with a deceased parent(s). It is very difficult to obtain disability payments under Social Security. The purpose of Social Security is to provide supplemental benefits, so this government program should not be looked upon as the sole source of income for the disabled.

EMPLOYEE FRINGE BENEFITS

No one will debate that it is better to receive a tax-free than a taxable dollar. It is particularly apparent when employee benefits are analyzed. Some benefits are taxable, some are not. And whether these so-called "perks" are taxed is an important consideration in financial planning. The planner must also consider whether benefits match the client's objectives and are cost effective. Employee benefits are not a panacea for all financial dilemmas. However, the appropriate selection of fringe benefits can go a long way in assisting clients to reach financial independence or to minimize a financial hardship, such as catastrophic medical bills.

Types of Benefits

First of all, benefits should not be duplicated. For example, if both spouses are covered under separate medical programs, what is the cost of each, if any? Whose coverage would protect dependents at least cost? The answer to these questions may allow one spouse to reallocate medical coverage funds to another benefit. Also important is which selected benefits are tax-free. Many times, employees would be "keeping more" if they sought tax-free fringe benefits rather than a taxable pay increase. As an example, employees in a 40 percent tax bracket keep only 60 percent of their increases in taxable income. Therefore, to pay for $1 of medical coverage, they would have to earn $1.67 before taxes.

The following is a list of tax-favored employee fringe benefits deductible by the employer:

Death benefit. Corporations may pay up to $5,000 on the death of an employee. The money is tax-free to the beneficiaries or the estate of the employee.

Health coverage. Medical and dental plans which do not discriminate in favor of officers or the highly compensated are not taxable to employees under self-insured medical reimbursement plans. Furthermore, medical benefits provided by a licensed insurance company or health maintenance organization (HMO) under a group plan are exempt from the nondiscrimination requirements.

Disability insurance. Employer-paid disability income insurance is another tax-free fringe benefit. However these payments are *not* deductible by a sole proprietor or a partner in a partnership. It may be more beneficial for the client to select another benefit rather than disability insurance, because if he or she is disabled, disability benefits will be taxable.

Nevertheless, under IRC 105, disabled employees who retire prior to age 65 can exclude $100 per week up to $5,200 if their adjusted gross income (AGI) is $15,000 or less. The exclusion is reduced dollar for dollar by the amount AGI exceeds $15,000. Disability payments received from an employee-paid policy are completely tax-free.

Life insurance. The first $50,000 of life insurance is not taxable to the employee. All amounts in excess of $50,000 are taxable, based on the Uniform Premium table in the Internal Revenue Code. TEFRA now requires that these plans be nondiscriminatory. If a life insurance plan discriminates in favor of key employees or officers, then it is taxable to that group. In this case, it would be important to determine whether it would be less expensive for key employees to buy their own protection or be taxed on the company's policy.

Child and dependent care. This can involve a company-sponsored care program or cash payment. No more than 25 percent of the amounts paid or incurred by the employer may be for owners or shareholders who own 5 percent or more of the company. The plan must not be discriminatory.

Qualified group legal services plan. This fringe benefit was scheduled to expire December 31, 1985. Current law requires this benefit plan to be in writing and nondiscriminatory. For those plans which are nondiscriminatory, sole proprietors and partners may make deductible payments. Nonetheless, no more than 25 percent of the benefits may be provided for the owners or shareholders of the company, their spouses and children. Payments may be made only to insurance companies or organizations qualified to provide legal services.

Educational assistance programs. This type of program is also scheduled to expire on December 31, 1985. Up to that time, $5,000 in benefits may be provided tax-free. The plan must be in writing and not discriminate in favor of owners or shareholders. These benefits cannot cover tools, supplies, meals, lodging, or transportation.

Qualified transportation. Allowances for commuter transportation provided by employers is scheduled to terminate December 31, 1985. Such plans, which must be written and nondiscriminatory, do not pertain to sole proprietorships or partnerships. The qualified commuter vehicle must be used 80 percent for transporting employees between home and work.

"Cafeteria" plans. More companies are becoming aware that "one size" does not fit everyone. With this in mind, many companies allow employees to pick and choose among different types of fringe benefits—a so-called "cafeteria package." Some benefits included in these plans have already been mentioned. The IRS has issued guidelines that must be followed for advantageous tax treatment of cafeteria plans under Code Section 125:

- Employees must elect the type and amount of benefit prior to the beginning of the plan year.
- Elections may not be revoked or changed during the plan year unless there is a change in family status, such as birth, death, marrige, or divorce.
- At least one taxable and one nontaxable benefit must be offered.
- Amounts designated for medical, legal, or dependent care that are not used during the plan year will be forfeited. The remaining sums cannot be rolled into a 401(k) plan or into a cash disbursement.
- Dependent care and legal services can only cover expenses for the current year.

Both Congress and the IRS are attempting to minimize some of the tax benefits of employee perquisites. Regardless of the employee benefits available, it is important to determine which benefits meet client objectives, and which benefits cause a gap needing to be filled by another method.

CHAPTER FOURTEEN

Estate Planning

Estate planning is often synonymous with a depressing subject—death. Because of that, clients will often procrastinate rather than address the critical issues involved with this type of planning. Overcoming this psychological barrier requires a great deal of skill on the part of a financial planner. However, motivation may increase as clients become aware of the negative consequences of failing to plan.

Estate planning includes not only the orderly transfer of assets, but also their protection and preservation. Thus, the most appropriate use of assets during life and after death must be considered, as must tax planning. To determine the appropriate path, it is imperative for financial planners to work with an attorney who specializes in this area.

OWNERSHIP CATEGORIES

Estate planning begins with the *titling* of assets (that is, assigning ownership). The form of ownership not only has tax implications, but is also the basis for how assets will be divided if a client dies without a will. In addition, if a client does have a will or a trust, it is important to see whether or not the titling of assets conflicts with these legal documents. In the event of a discrepancy, titling of a specific asset will be the controlling factor. There is also the possibility of an extended and costly court battle to determine the form of ownership.

The various forms of ownership of all types of property include the following.

Tenancy in Common

With this form, two or more individuals own a specified percentage of an asset. The percentage of ownership can be divided in any manner: for example, a person could own 1 percent, or 15 percent, or 89.5 percent of the asset. All coowners can treat their proportionate interest as their own property and sell it, lease it, or use it as collateral, a gift, or a bequest. To minimize legal conflicts, it would be wise to specifically designate in either the actual title or a separate legal agreement, each person's percentage of ownership. Holding title this way does not avoid *probate*, that is, a judicial decision on the disposition of the property. (Probate will be discussed more fully later in this chapter.)

Joint Tenancy

Another form of ownership by two or more persons is joint tenancy with the right of survivorship. As the term implies, when one owner dies,the surviving joint tenant becomes owner of the asset, without the necessity of going through the court process known as probate. Of course, joint tenancy would not be appropriate if your client did not want the other joint tenant(s) to inherit the asset. Furthermore, joint tenancy may leave too much money to a surviving spouse, resulting in a potentially higher federal estate tax.

Joint tenancy is not a substitute for a will. For example, at the death of the final joint tenant or in a common disaster where both die simultaneously, the asset can only pass to the heirs via a legal document (a will or a trust), or through state laws covering the property of those who die without a will. Further, an unintended disinheritance could occur with joint tenancy. Suppose Sarah and Jane are joint tenants with their mother. When the mother dies, Sarah and Jane become the owners of the property. If Jane suddenly dies, Sarah becomes the sole owner. Consequently, Jane's children or a husband could be disinherited. Joint tenancy can also conflict with other legal documents, because there is a presumption in favor of the surviving joint tenant which can only be rebutted in court.

In her will, for example, Sheila indicated that she wanted her brother to receive her interest in a 10-acre parcel of land, but she held title with her husband as joint tenants. To resolve the issue after her death could involve costly litigation, and the result may not be what Sheila would have wanted. This conflict could be avoided by coordinating the titling of assets in accordance with the client's objectives. There are numerous other implications to titling of ownership, but the real key is consistency with other legal documents.

Joint tenancy can be served by one of the joint tenants. For example, if the asset is sold or given away, then the joint tenancy ceases.

Adding a new person to the ownership of assets can have unintended consequences. Under joint tenancy, a potential gift tax return may have to be filed and the unified credit (see below) used if more than $10,000 of value is transferred to any one person. In addition, on the donor's death, the value of the asset is placed in the donor's estate, and taxable gifts over $10,000 are added back to the estate. In effect, under these conditions, the property will be taxed at more than 100 percent of value.

Tenancy by Entirety

This is available only to coowners who are married and do not live in a community property state. As is true with joint tenancy, with this type of ownership, the survivor inherits the property. However, with tenancy by entirety the consent of both owners is needed to end the agreement.

Community Property

This form of ownership is available only to a married couple living in Arizona, California, Idaho, Louisiana, Nevada, New Mexico, Texas, or Washington. These states are known as *community property* states. (All others are *common law* states.)

Community property refers to assets acquired during marriage or voluntarily designated as such. Generally, an individual retains income from independently held property. However, community property laws vary from state to state. As an example, income from independently held property is deemed community property in Texas. Therefore, planners must be aware of the differences in a particular state.

There are important aspects to holding title as community property. For example, each spouse has the opportunity to bequeath 100 percent of their half of the community property assets to whomever they designate. However, the deceased spouse's assets are subject to federal estate taxes if the property is not left to the surviving spouse. Whether community property avoids probate depends on the particular state in which the client resides. There may also be tax advantages to community property arrangements, as the example shows.

FORMULA

Community property assets: new basis is fair market value at death.
Joint tenancy assets: new basis is 1/2 of the (cost) basis plus 1/2 of the fair market (FMV) value at death.

EXAMPLE

Sam and Gwen own stock which they purchased for $14,000 and which is now worth $38,000. If they simply sold the stock while they were both alive, there would be a capital gain of $24,000. As the table below shows, on the death of one spouse, very different results would be achieved depending on whether the property was held as community property or a joint tenancy.

	Joint Tenants	Community Property
Original basis	$14,000	$14,000
Value at time of death	$38,000	$38,000
One half of basis	$ 7,000	
One half of FMV (at death)	$19,000	
100% of FMV (at death)	N/A	$38,000
Total	$26,000	
Gain recognized	$12,000	0

Gain is calculated if the asset is sold after death of the first spouse. The difference arises because the basis for community property is fair market value at death. With joint tenancy, it is one half the basis (cost) plus one half the fair market value ($7,000 + $19,000 = $26,000) at death.

The example reveals that a spouse who holds title as a joint tenant pays a capital gains tax on one half of the capital gains profits. Community property assets receive "a full step-up in basis," but no capital gains tax is paid if, at the time the stock is sold, it is worth $38,000. Therefore, capital gain assets which have appreciated in value before death can receive a full step-up in basis and avoid being taxed on any gain at the death of the first spouse. On the other hand, with assets that have declined in value, joint tenancy would be more appropriate, since only half the loss would be eliminated.

How title is held may not be imperative if the sole asset is a personal residence, one owner is at least 55, and total profit is $125,000 or less. This is because $125,000 of profits from the sale of a personal residence is excludable by law from income taxes under these circumstances.

Separate Property

This arrangement involves married couples and includes property belonging entirely to one spouse. In community property states, this is all assets acquired before marriage, and all gifts and inheritances, even if received after marriage. Separate property is especially important because it determines which assets can be given away during a client's lifetime or transferred after death.

Separate property assets are especially significant during a divorce. Some couples are very careful in designating specific assets as separate property. Those who are not cautious may find that property is not divided as they expected. This can occur if the court does not recognize tracing (or determining the original ownership) of the asset, especially when inheritances are commingled with community property.

In addition, separate property is subject to probate unless it is held in a trust or exempted by statute. Of course, if separate property is held in joint tenancy with another person, say a brother or sister, it will avoid probate.

Common Law Property

Generally, in common law states, property acquired by a wage-earning spouse is that spouse's property. This situation is the reverse of community property states, where there is an automatic equal property division unless the couple has an agreement specifying otherwise.

In common law states, in the event of divorce, there may or may not be an equal division of property. In the event of death, a non-wage-earning spouse's rights are determined according to a variety of legal precepts. For example, some states give the surviving spouse up to a one-third interest in the deceased spouse's property. Once again, the planner must look to the laws of a specific state to determine the property division.

INTESTACY

Titling assets is an important aspect in coordinated estate planning, but it is only the first step. The real key is to determine the clients' objectives. Do they have goals for passing assets to the next generation, or is a charitable beneficiary of primary importance? Because defining these goals is not easy, many clients fail to act. The result is that they die without setting down any formal instructions, that is, they die intestate. The ultimate aversion in planning is dying without stipulating how assets are to be disposed. Because these individuals fail to write down what *they* want to happen, the state—or states—decides.

A classic example is Howard Hughes. In his case, numerous individuals attempted to obtain a piece of the action. The states of California and Texas litigated to gain jurisdictional control of the estate for purposes of collecting inheritance taxes. With proper estate planning, much of the delay and expense, as well as publicity, could have been avoided.

The Hughes case also illustrates the importance of the state of domicile or jurisdictional control. (Domicile is typically defined as a person's permanent home, not necessarily one's current physical residence). The state of domicile will determine who inherits and the rate of tax on the individual's personal property, regardless of its physical location. This alone is an extremely pertinent question, because states levy taxes at different rates. Some states have significantly higher inheritance or estate taxes than others.

Real property—meaning real estate—is subject to the laws of the state in which it is located. For other property, this is not so clear-cut, and with overlapping state laws come increasing complications and costs. Usually, personal property is subject to the jurisdiction deemed to be the domicile of the deceased.

More important in this context, it is unwise for clients to rely on any state to distribute their assets. State-recognized beneficiaries may not be those the client would have chosen. Without planning, the deceased's assets could be divided as follows: one third to the surviving spouse and two thirds to the surviving children. This could unintentionally place the assets in the hands of someone unable to manage them. And, if no relatives can be found, the assets will *escheat,* or pass to the state. Few clients would knowingly give their assets to the state. But without a will and heirs, that is just what can happen.

WILLS

A will is one of the most commonly used devices to transfer assets. There are three categories of wills.

Nuncupative

This is an oral will and involves numerous restrictions. Although these restrictions vary from state to state, they usually apply only to personal property of a minimal amount. The validity of a nuncupative will is also usually limited to those whose death is imminent.

Holographic

Generally, with this type of will the major provisions must be in the client's own handwriting. This document must be signed and dated by the client, but the signatures of witnesses are not required. Many states do not recognize this form of document. The major problem is proving its authenticity, and there could be confusion over what the deceased meant when writing the will. One consequence of this confusion is that these types of wills often become the subject of lengthy litigation.

Formal

Within this category, all the legal requirements must be met. For example, the person who writes the will, usually called the *testator* must:

- Have the legal ability and mental capacity to make a will.
- Be of legal age, generally at least 18 or 21, depending on the state. In some states, an emancipated minor qualifies.
- Be free from undue influence or duress in executing the will.
- Sign the document and have two or three witnesses to the signature. A testator could make "a mark" if he or she is illiterate, or if handicapped, could direct someone else to sign in front of witnesses.

This legal document can provide for orderly transfer of all assets. A client may amend a will by adding *codicils*. If a client has written several wills over a lifetime, only the last one will apply. (An appropirately written will contains a provision revoking all prior wills.) A properly drafted will would contain the following features:

- The name of the *executor* of the estate. This is a person or entity with a fiduciary responsibility to the estate.
- Eliminate the purchase of a bond to cover the potential negligence of a fiduciary. (Bond premiums can be expensive for a small estate.)
- Appoint a guardian for minor children.
- Allow the testator to specifically disinherit children, relatives, or a surviving spouse. This does not include the surviving spouse's one half of community property or, in a common law state, the legally granted statutory share.

Not only does a will give the testator control over how property will be disposed of, it can also plan for uncommon events. For example, the nearly simultaneous death of a husband and wife can cause all the assets to be placed in one of the spousal estates, thereby disinheriting intended beneficiaries. A will can prevent such an unintentional dilemma, and allow the testator's objectives to be accomplished.

PROBATE

To ensure compliance with the deceased's instructions, the will must go through a court proceeding called *probate*. Probate is a process whereby the court supervises the administration of an individual's estate following death. The major purpose of probate is to clear the title of property passing from the deceased to his or her heirs after all debts have been paid.

If the deceased failed to formally designate beneficiaries, then the court will decide who will inherit according to state laws. This process is also designed to see that all legal creditors are paid in full before the assets are transferred. At the end of probate, the heirs will normally receive title to the assets free of creditors' claims, including federal or state taxes. Court supervision and the statutory time limit for creditors to file claims are generally viewed as major advantages. Some major disadvantages include lengthy time delays, public scrutiny, and costly administrative and legal fees. Many states have specific statutory

Table 14-1 State of
California
Probate Fee
Structure

Amount of Estate	Fee
$0–$15,000	4%
$15,000–$100,000	3
$100,000–$1,000,000	2
$1,000,000 or more	1

probate fees. However, some allow for "reasonable compensation." An example of probate fees is given in Table 14.1.

It is important to know that the fees are calculated on the fair market value of the probate estate. Therefore, the fees are *not* reduced because an asset entails debt. For example, Silvia has a probate estate of $600,000 and debts totalling $430,000. At her death, all of her assets are subject to the statutory rates, for a total probate cost of $13,150.

It is also important to know which assets are subject to probate. If title is in the name of one person or tenants in common, the assets will be probated. All assets, with certain exceptions, distributed via a will are subject to this court procedure.

Of course, not all assets are subject to probate. For instance, assets held in joint tenancy or in a trust, as well as life insurance and annuity contracts, are *not* subject to probate. Many states have also simplified procedures for small estates. For example, in California, up to $60,000 in personal property, such as cash and jewelry, may be transferred by a form called an affidavit, without going through probate.

TRUSTS

The word *trust* conjures up a special relationship. With regard to estate planning, a trust is a detailed legal document setting forth specific terms and conditions for the management and disposition of funds and property. The person who creates the trust is called the *grantor, trustor,* or *settlor.*

Trustors may select themselves, an unrelated person, a bank, or a trust company, to oversee, manage, and invest the assets of the trust. This manager is called the *trustee.* The trustee has the fiduciary responsibility to manage the assets in the best interests of the beneficiaries of the trust.

Types of Trust

There are various types of trusts. The key to determining whether a trust is needed and selecting an appropriate form is dependent on the objectives of the individual. Reviewing the following categories will be helpful in deciding whether and when a trust can best be utilized.

Living trust.   This is often referred to as an *inter vivos* trust because it is created during the trustor's lifetime. A living trust:

- Avoids the delay, expense, and publicity of probate.
- Prevents disruption of the income stream.
- Serves as a receptacle of nonprobate assets, such as pension benefits or insurance proceeds.
- Allows for tax planning.
- Selects the state in which the inheritance will be adjudicated.

It is important that assets be transferred to the trust. If a trust is unfunded, the assets cannot avoid probate. Therefore, title to property must be taken in the name of the trust.

There are two types of living trusts: a *revocable* trust and an *irrevocable* trust.

Revocable trust.   As the name indicates, trustors may change the terms and the beneficiaries. The grantor is taxed on the assets placed in this type of trust. The income tax is reported directly on the grantor's individual tax return. However, there is no gift tax on assets transferred to the trust. Upon the grantor's death, all assets in the trust are included in the gross estate. And finally, the new basis for the assets is their fair market value at the grantor's death, or six months thereafter.

Irrevocable trust.   This trust may not be revoked, amended, or altered. Since this is permanent, it is essential for grantors to be certain of actions they take. However, for large estates subject to death taxes, this form of trust has the added advantage of removing assets from the estate prior to death, which means they are not subject to estate or income taxes. However, they may be subject to a gift tax, depending on the value of the assets transferred to the trust.

There are a number of trusts designed to accomplish specific goals. Some of those used more frequently include:

Clifford trust. This is a short-term trust designed to save income taxes. It is classified as an irrevocable trust and must last at least 10 years. All income during the term of the trust is transferred to the beneficiaries. This allows the grantor of the trust to temporarily shift income to a taxpayer in a lower tax bracket. At the end of the trust period, the property reverts to the grantor. This type of vehicle is often used to finance childrens' education or support elderly relatives.

For example, Ralph is in a 50 percent tax bracket and thus must earn $10,000 to provide his son, Carlos, with $5,000 for education expenses. Ralph can transfer the asset to Carlos. Because Carlos is in a lower tax bracket, less income will be lost to taxes. The Treasury Department has proposed that this tax-saving technique be eliminated.

Qualified terminable interest program (QTIP). The QTIP allows the grantor to determine who will receive the property when the surviving spouse dies. A QTIP trust requires that all income received from the trust be paid to the surviving spouse at least on an annual basis for life. This type of trust is often used when a spouse wants to ultimately leave his or her assets to the children of another marriage, but only after the surviving spouse dies. Moreover, it qualifies for the marital deduction, which is discussed further in the next section on federal estate taxation.

Testamentary trust. This type of trust is created only in a will. The trust is operative on the death of the testator, and *does not* avoid probate. At the testator's death, the power to revoke is obviously terminated, and the trust becomes irrevocable.

Establishing a testamentary trust probably will cost less in attorney fees than does an *inter vivos* trust. This instrument can also fulfill certain limited tax-planning strategies. The main disadvantage is that it does not avoid probate.

FEDERAL ESTATE TAXATION

Congress has reduced estate taxation, as Tables 14.2 and 14.3 illustrate, but estate taxes can still be expensive.

To determine the federal estate tax, it is obviously necessary to know the value of the decedent's assets. The guideline for valuation is often defined as the price a willing buyer would pay

Table 14-2 Unified Transfer Tax Rate Schedules for 1985
and Thereafter

If the Amount Is:		Tentative Tax Is:		
Over	*But Not over*	*Tax*	*+ Percent*	*On Excess over*
$ 0	$ 10,000	$ 0	18%	$ 0
10,000	20,000	1,800	20	10,000
20,000	40,000	3,800	22	20,000
40,000	60,000	8,200	24	40,000
60,000	80,000	13,000	26	60,000
80,000	100,000	18,200	28	80,000
100,000	150,000	23,800	30	100,000
150,000	250,000	38,800	32	150,000
250,000	500,000	70,800	34	250,000
500,000	750,000	155,800	37	500,000
750,000	1,000,000	248,300	39	750,000
1,000,000	1,250,000	345,800	41	1,000,000
1,250,000	1,500,000	448,300	43	1,250,000
1,500,000	2,000,000	555,800	45	1,500,000
2,000,000	2,500,000	780,800	49	2,000,000
2,500,000	3,000,000	1,025,800	53	2,500,000
3,000,000		1,290,800	55	3,000,000

Table 14-3 Unified Transfer Tax Rate Schedule for 1988
and Thereafter

If the Amount Is:		Tentative Tax Is:		
Over	*But Not over*	*Tax*	*+ Percent*	*On Excess over*
$ 0	$ 10,000	$ 0	18%	$ 0
10,000	20,000	1,800	20	10,000
20,000	40,000	3,800	22	20,000
40,000	60,000	8,200	24	40,000
60,000	80,000	13,000	26	60,000
80,000	100,000	18,200	28	80,000
100,000	150,000	23,800	30	100,000
150,000	250,000	38,800	32	150,000
250,000	500,000	70,800	34	250,000
500,000	750,000	155,800	37	500,000
750,000	1,000,000	248,300	39	750,000
1,000,000	1,250,000	345,800	41	1,000,000
1,250,000	1,500,000	448,300	43	1,250,000
1,500,000	2,000,000	555,800	45	1,500,000
2,000,000	2,500,000	780,800	49	2,000,000
2,500,000		1,025,800	50	2,500,000

to a willing seller, when neither is being coerced to complete the transaction. However, if there is no active market for the asset, such as the New York Stock Exchange, or an actual sale, determining value can be difficult. The services of an appraiser may be required.

Federal estate tax laws allow the executors to choose the date for appraising the assets. The assets can be valued as of the date of death or six months after death. Whichever date is chosen, the election must apply to all assets.

Federal laws allow real estate valued at $750,000 or less—if used as a farm or a business—to be exempted from appraisal at its fair market value. These assets are exempted from appraisal at their highest and best use value to enable surviving family members to continue operating the farm or business without the burden of normal estate taxes.

EXAMPLE

The following shows how federal estate taxes are applied. If Fred died in 1985, leaving a *taxable* estate of $520,000, the federal taxes would be $163,200. This is calculated using Table 14.2 as follows:

- The tax on the first $500,000 is a flat $155,800.
- The difference between the $520,000 total and $500,000, $20,000, is subject to the tax rate: $20,000 × 37% = $7,400.
- Total tax is the sum of the above, or $163,200.

The next step is to apply the *unified credit* to the amount of tax owed. As do all credits, the unified credit reduces the tax liability dollar for dollar. For the above example, the unified credit for the year 1985 is $121,800. So, Fred's estate would pay $41,400 in taxes. (Regular tax in the amount of $163,200, minus the unified tax credit of $121,800, equals $41,400.)

Table 14.4 shows the unified credit rates and the equivalent value of the estate.

Table 14-4   Unified Credit Rates

Year	Amount of Credit	Amount of Exemption Equivalent
1985	$121,800	$400,000
1986	155,800	500,000
1987 and after	192,800	600,000

Because the unified credit is significant, many clients may not think estate tax planning is necessary. However, it must be remembered that the unified credit does not eliminate any probate fees, nor does it ensure the smooth disposition of assets, or any other client goals. Also, before the most appropriate estate plan is devised, it is imperative to know *what* assets are subject to estate taxation. The first step in calculating potential estate taxes is to list all assets owned by the decedent; this includes certain transfers within three years of the date of death and any retained rights or benefits in an asset.

Tax law requires the list to be all encompassing. However, determining which assets the decedent had an interest in is often difficult. Included is all real or personal property, regardless of location. This is where titling assets is essential in calculating a gross estate. For example, if a married person dies, the value of all separate property is included, as well as one half the value of community property assets and one half of the value of assets held in joint tenancy. However, for joint tenants who are not married, the full value of the property is included in the decedent's gross estate, except to the degree the surviving joint tenant can document his or her original capital contribution. The list of assets comprising the gross estate includes the proceeds of life insurance policies if the decedent names the estate as beneficiary or retains any *incidents of ownership*. (The deceased is considered as possessing an incident of ownership if the right to borrow from a policy, cash in a policy, or change a beneficiary is retained—or if the policy is paid for with the deceased's own funds.) Although life insurance may be included in the gross estate, it is never taxable income to the beneficiaries if received in a lump sum.

Among other items included are *joint and survivor annuities*. Under this type of contract, an insurance company's annuity will pay an income not only to the annuitant, but also to the survivor. This annuity contract is taxable because the annuitant has incidents of ownership at death, namely transfer of the income stream to the survivor.

Retirement plans must also be taken into account when calculating gross estates. These include corporate pensions, deferred compensation, and Keogh, IRA, and TSA plans.

Certain gifts made within three years of death are also part of the estate tax calculation. This includes property the decedent made a gift of, but still retained possession or its enjoyment.

Also included are gifts the deceased retained the power to revoke, alter, amend, or terminate. A reversionary interest in property as well as life insurance policies are also included here.

If a decedent retains *general power of appointment* over assets, these assets would also be part of the gross estate. An example would involve an individual transferring assets to trusts but retaining the right to determine who will receive the trust principal. However, property subject to a *special power of appointment* will not be included in the gross estate. An example of this special power is the right to leave property to a limited class of beneficiaries, such as one's children or designated charities.

DEDUCTIONS

Once all the assets included in the gross estate are determined, all estate tax deductions must be ascertained. Maximizing deductions will lower the net taxable estate, thereby leaving more assets for beneficiaries.

The following are deductible from the gross estate.

Funeral expenses. Included in this category are expenditures for the burial plot; tombstone, monument, or mausoleum; transportation expenses for the deceased to be buried, and any other necessary fees. Some community property jurisdictions require that funeral expenses be an obligation of the community property. If this applies, then only one half of the funeral expenses will be deductible from the decedent's estate.

Administrative expenses. This covers attorney and executor fees. Also deductible are accountants' fees, court fees, appraiser charges, and other settlement expenses.

Taxes. To be deductible, taxes have to be legally owed at the time of death. This applies only to federal and state income and real estate taxes. There is no deduction for estate taxes.

Debts. An individual's outstanding loans at the time of death, including mortgages, liens, and consumer debts, are also deductible.

Charitable contributions. There is no limitation on the amount of property that may be donated from the decedent's estate to a qualifying charitable, religious, or government organization. So, no matter how large the estate, if all assets are transferred to a qualified agency, no estate taxes would be paid. The donation can either be an outright bequest or through certain qualified trusts.

Marital deduction. There is an unlimited deduction for property transferred to the decedent's spouse. No estate taxes are paid on assets left to the surviving spouse. In this case, it is important to verify that the estate planning documents were executed after September 12, 1981, or amended to conform with the unlimited marital deduction of ERTA. This deduction is not allowed where the property passing to the surviving spouse is a *life estate*, that is, the recipient has use of the property but cannot dispose of it. For example, Mary leaves all her real estate to her husband to use, but not to dispose of, for as long as he lives. At his death, all rights to that real estate belong to Mary's children. This type of property does not qualify for the deduction, because the husband does not possess ownership rights at his death. However, if a qualifying terminable interest election is made, then the property will become a QTIP trust, discussed previously.

Once all the deductions outlined have been subtracted from the gross estate, the following apply:

Gifts.   Any taxable gifts made after December 31, 1976, (if not already included in the gross estate), are added to the adjusted gross estate.

Tentative tax.   This involves calculating the tentative tax on the adjusted gross estate using the appropriate estate tax table.

Gift tax.   Now subtract the gift taxes on gifts made after 1976 from the gross estate, or subtract those listed under Taxable Gifts, if the estate tax rate schedule in effect at the decedent's death had been applicable at the time such gifts were made.

Unified tax credit.   Subtract the unified tax credit from the amount of tentative tax.

Credits.   From the net tax determined, subtract any of the following credits, if they apply:

1. Credit for gift tax paid on gifts made prior to 1977, if they were included in the gross estate.
2. Credit for state inheritance or death taxes.
3. Credit for federal estate tax paid previously.
4. Credit for foreign death taxes.

The procedure is illustrated in the following example.

EXAMPLE

Maria was a single California resident who died in 1985. Her burial was simple, costing $500. She owned a home with a fair market value of $225,000 and a mortgage of $30,000. Her personal property totaled $70,000 and her outstanding debts were $10,000. In addition, she had an IRA valued at $10,000, her company's pension benefit valued at $80,000, and a $100,000 insurance policy with her estate as beneficiary. In her will, she left all of her assets to her relatives, except for a $1,000 gift to a local charity. She had made no previous gifts.

After careful review of the information provided, Maria's federal estate taxes can be calculated as follows:

Step 1. Gross estate

Item	Fair Market Value
Home	$225,000
Personal property	70,000
Qualified plans	90,000
Life insurance	100,000
Total	$485,000

Step 2. Allowable deductions

Item	Amount
Funeral expense	$ 500
Administrative expense	10,850
Mortgage and debts	40,000
Charitable contribution	1,000
Total	$52,350

Step 3
Subtract the deductions from the gross estate and compute tentative tax using the correct table. (Note in this example, no prior gifts to noncharities were made.) Therefore:

```
$485,000 – $52,350 = $432,650
$432,650   Net taxable estate
– 250,000  Base tax table amount
$182,650   Subject to a tax rate of 34%

Tax on $250,000 is:  $ 70,800
Tax on $182,650 is:    62,101
Total tax is:        $132,901
```

Step 4

Subtract the unified estate tax credit. (Note: for 1985, the amount is $121,800). Therefore:

$$\$132,901 - \$121,800 = \$11,101$$

In the example, Maria's estate is subject to federal estate taxes of $11,101. If she died in 1986, the unified credit would then be $155,800, and there would be no federal estate taxes.

When a client's taxable estate assets are not subject to death taxes, the client may avoid "bothering" with estate planning. However, financial planners would be foolish to agree with clients in this area. An excellent example of the foolishness of doing nothing involves couples who rely on the unlimited marital deduction to avoid federal taxes. In this case, there is no estate tax on the death of the first spouse, no matter how large the estate, if the surviving spouse receives the assets. However, when the surviving spouse dies, significant taxes may be paid if the taxable estate is above the unified credit limit.

It is also important for planners to keep in mind the concept of the probate estate. In the above example, the home and personal property could be the only assets subject to probate if proceeds from qualified plans and life insurance are paid to a designated beneficiary other than the estate. Nevertheless, all of these assets are still part of the gross estate for the purpose of calculating federal estate taxes. Consequently, the probate estate may be different from the gross estate.

Assume, for example, that Bob dies in 1986 and leaves all of his assets to his wife, Denise. She will die in 1988, leaving an estate with a taxable value of $700,000. Given the above example, the estate will pay $37,000 in death taxes.

It is often said estate taxes are taxes of neglect. Perhaps the same can be said of various administrative fees which can be avoided or minimized with competent legal advice.

GIFTS

Congress has modified the tax on gifts to relatives and friends. At this time, everyone may make a gift of up to $10,000 a year to any person without paying any gift tax or filing a tax return. A married couple may make a gift of up to $20,000 per year, per person.

Using such gifts can have dramatic results. Suppose for example, Margaret and Dave, who are in a combined 45 percent tax bracket, gave their daughter Kelly $20,000 per year for 10 years. They would have transferred over $200,000 of assets from their gross estate. In addition, any interest and appreciation would then be taxed at Kelly's 16 percent bracket. Therefore, if the interest alone amounted to $20,000, Kelly would have paid $3,200 in taxes. If her parents hadn't given her the money, they would have paid $9,000 in income taxes. Margaret and Dave can choose to make gifts outright or through a trust document. In either case, these clients must decide whether it is appropriate to transfer $200,000 of assets to their daughter.

The unified estate tax credit may also be used to avoid any gift tax. Over the years, Congress has modified the gift tax rates. At present there is no difference between the rates for estate and gift taxes. The tables are the same.

An important aspect of estate planning is making gifts of assets to friends, relatives, or charitable organizations. With the latter category, it is possible for a client to donate assets to a nonprofit group, retain some form of benefits, and receive a tax deduction. In estate planning there are two major methods of nonprofit contributions to consider:

Charitable remainder trust. The client donates assets to a charity and receives an income from the charity. Based on the life expectancy of the donor, the residual value is calculated to produce a current tax deduction. At the time of the client's death, the assets belong to the charity.

Charitable lead trust. The charity receives the asset with all rights and benefits. After the death of the donor, the asset reverts to the donor's designated beneficiary.

Making a charitable gift can be an excellent way for clients to minimize taxes and serve a worthy cause. A detailed discussion of the specific ways to make gifts to charities or to children is, however, outside the scope of this book.

Financial planning is an exhilarating and constantly changing field. This book is only the beginning. It should be considered a foundation to which more technical and specific information can be added.

Each topic covered in this text is extremely important to financial planners. However, some areas can be given a higher priority because clients demand it or planners choose to specialize in the area. In such instances, the particular discipline will have to be studied in greater depth than this book can provide.

As planners increase their knowledge base and experience, it will be easy to quantify clients' goals or calculate investment yields. With repetition, these computations will become familiar to the planner and facilitate the decision making required to reach financial objectives.

Taxes, of course, are a major area of concern to clients. Financial planners must become familiar with the impact of taxes and develop strategies for minimizing their effects on a client's financial situation. Consistency and stability are not the trademarks of taxation. Rather, an ever-changing set of laws, regulations, and court cases will require that planners strive to stay up-to-date. The same can be said for investments. The changing economic scenario can provide unwelcome surprises for the unprepared.

With a coordinated investigation of a client's current net worth, a risk management analysis, and retirement and estate planning, financial planners can help the client begin planning for financial goals and present the client with viable alternatives for achieving success.

Those planners who desire to be specialists must first be generalists. By using a multiple but integrated approach, planners will be able to provide a systematic analysis of a client's needs. In addition, alternatives can be more concrete and specifically tailored to every clients' goals. Although this is not an easy or quick task, with training and experience, financial planning can be a rewarding profession.

INDEX

A

Accelerated Cost Recovery System (ACRS), 124, 129, 186
Accredited Investors, 204
Adjustable Life, 45
Adjusted Gross Income (AGI), 110, 111, 114, 115
Adjusted Rate of Return (ARR), 95
Administrative Expenses, 254
Alpha Score, 173
Alternative Minimum Tax (AMT), 136
American College in Bryn Mawr, 7
American Institute of Certified Public Accountants, 7
American Stock Exchange, 162
Animal Breeding and Feeding Programs, 193
Annual Compound Rate of Return, 91
Annuitizing, concept of, 214
Annuity, 74, 213
Assets, 27
Assignment of Income, 98
At Risk Rules, 134
At-risk, 179
Automobile Coverage, 59
Average Annual Rate of Return, 90

B

Background of Financial Planning, 6
Bad Debts, 111
Balance Sheet(s), 26, 28
Banker's Acceptance, 151
Banking System, 146
Basic Tax Doctrines, 98
Basis, 134, 176
Benefit Period, 56
Beta, 172
Blue Chip, 158
Bonds, 151, 155, 198

Books as Investments, 192
Borrowing from a Pension Plan, 226
Breadth of Market, 169
Brigham Young University, 7
Broker-Dealers, 11, 196
Budget, 36
Business Deductions, 110
Business Risk, 30
Buy Option, 84

C

Cable Television, 191
Cafeteria Plans, 238
Calculate a Retirement Need, 86
California State University (San Diego), 7
Call Option, 160
Call Premium, 151
Call Provisions, 151
Capital Gains, 103, 104
Capitalization Rate (CAP), 182
Carried Interest, 189
Cash Account, 163
Cash Equivalent Doctrine, 98
Cash Value Life, 43
Cash-Flow Management, 34
Casualty and Liability Protection, 59
Category, 27
Certain Gifts, 253
Certificate of Deposit (CD), 150
Certified Financial Planner (CFP), 7
Characteristics of a Corporation, 175
Charitable Contributions, 254
Charitable Deductions, 114
Charitable Lead Trust, 258
Charitable Remainder Trust, 258
Chartered Financial Analyst (CFA), 7
Chartered Financial Consultant, 7
Child Care Credit, 117
Child and Dependent Care, 237

Claim of Right Doctrine, 98
Classical Economics, 141
Clifford Trust, 249
Code Section 179, 128
Codicils, 246
Coins, 194
Coinsurance, 58
Collateral, 152
College for Financial Planning in
    Denver, 7
Collision, 60
Combined Marginal Tax Bracket
    (CMTB), 102
Commercial Paper, 150
Commercial Property, 181
Common Law Property, 244
Common Law States, 242
Community Property, 242
Community Property States, 242
Comparison Cost for Term Insurance, 51
Comparison Cost for Whole Life, 51
Compound, 68
Compounding, 68
Comprehensive, 60
Comprehensive Medical, 59
Conflict of Interest Matrix, 10
Conflicts of Interest, 8, 200
Congress, 115, 142, 213, 218
Constructive Receipt, 98
Corporate Bonds, 151
Cost, 51, 182
Cost Depletion, 133
Cost-of-Living Adjustment, 56
Coupons, 155
Coverage, 218
Credit Cards, 32
Credits, 116, 255
Cyclical, 158

D

Data Gathering and Analysis of
    Financial Statements, 13
Date of Record, 158
Day Order, 162
Dealer Market, 162
Death Benefit, 237
Debentures, 152
Debit Ratio, 32
Debit and Deficits, 36
Debt(s), 31, 254
Decreasing Term, 42
Deductible, 58
Deductions, 109
Defensive, 158
Defined Benefit Plan, 221
Defined Contribution Plans, 222
Definite Loss, 40
Department of Corporations in
    California, 201

Depletion, 133
Deposit Term, 43
Depreciation, 123
Development Programs, 188
Diamonds, 194
Disability Costs, 55
Disability Insurance, 237
Discount, 74
Discount Rate, 146
Dividends, 157
Dividends and Interest Income, 106
Dollar-Cost Averaging, 167
Domicile, 245
Double Coverage, 54
Drake University, 7
Due Diligence, 196

E

ERISA, 218
Economic Hardship, 40
Economic Recovery Tax Act (ERTA),
    124, 128, 255
Economic Risk, 30
Economic Theory, 141
Economy, 141
Education, 6
Educational, 115
Educational Assistance Programs, 238
Educational Needs, 78
Effective Rate, 75
Efficient Market Theory, 170
Elimination Period, 55
Employee Death Benefits, 106
Employee Stock Ownership Programs
    (ESOP), 225
Endowment, 44
Energy Credit, 117
Escheat, 244
Estate Planning, 5
Estate Tax Planning, 253
Evaluating an Investment, 197
Ex-dividend Day, 158
Exchange, 135
Excludable Income, 106
Executor, 247
Expense, 111
Expense Patterns, 37
Expenses, 34
Exploratory, 188

F

FICA, 235
Federal Advisory Council, 145
Federal Agencies, 155
Federal Estate Taxation, 250
Federal National Mortgage Association
    (FNMA), 155
Federal Reserve Banks, 145

Federal Reserve Board, 142, 170
Federal Reserve System, 144
Financial Assets, 149
Financial Planner, 240
Financial Planning, 3, 259
Financial Planning Firms, 196
Financial Planning
    Questionnaire, 14
Financial Statements, 26
Formal, 246
401(k) Plans, 222
Fractional Reserve
    Requirements, 147
Friedman, Milton, 143
Fringe Benefits, 108, 236
Functional Allocation, 189
Fundamental Analysis, 168
Funeral Expenses, 254
Future Value, 67
    of a Dollar, 67
    of One Dollar per Period, 70
    of Growing Annuity, 81

G

GNMAs, 168
Gemstones, 195
General Obligation, 157
General Partners, 174
General Power of Appointment, 254
Generally Accepted Accounting
    Principles, (GAAP), 28
Georgia State University, 7
Gift(s), 135, 255, 257
Gift Tax, 255
Gifts and Inheritances, 106
Goal Accumulation Works, 78
Gold, 194
Golden Gate University (San
    Francisco), 7
Good Till Cancelled (GTC), 162
Government National Mortgage
    Association (GNMA), 155
Grantor, 248
Growth, 158
Guaranteed Renewable, 56

H

H-P 12C Calculator, 76
HMO, 237
HR-10 Plans, 222, 224
Hard Assets and Collectibles, 194
Health Coverage, 237
Health Maintenance Organizations
    (HMOs), 57
Holographic, 246
Homeowners, 60
Hospital and Surgical, 58
Hospitalization, 235

I

Incidents of Ownership, 253
Includable Income, 104-105
Income, 32, 103, 158, 182
Income Program, 188
Income Stream, 54
Income and Expense Statement, 26, 32
Income Recognition, 98
Incontestability Clause, 41
Indemnify, 41
Individual Retirement Account
    (IRA), 70, 90, 209, 210
    Actuarial Tables, 212
    Distributions, 211
    Maximum Contribution and
        Funding, 211
    Participants, 211
    Terminations, 211
Inheritance, 135
Institute of Certified Financial Planners
    (ICFP), 6
Insurable Interest, 40
Inter vivos Trust, 249
Interest, 65, 66, 114
Interest Rate Risk, 30
Interest Rates, 75
Interest-Sensitive Life Products, 44
Internal Rate of Return (IRR), 91
Internal Revenue Code (IRC), 97, 212
    Section 61, 104
    Section 105, 237
    Section 125, 238
    Section 162, 110
    Section 212, 110
    Sections 261-280, 110
    Section 403(b), 213
    Rule 170, 116
Internal Revenue Service (IRS), 90, 97,
    117, 123, 177
International Association for Financial
    Planning, 6
International Board of Standards and
    Practices for Certified Financial
    Planners, 7
Intestacy, 244
Investment Bankers, 161
Investment Company Securities, 163
Investment Interest Limitation, 135
Investment Tax Credit, 117, 123, 177
Investment Yield Analysis, 89
Irrevocable Trust, 249
Itemized Deductions, 110

J-L

Joint Tenancy, 241
Joint and Survivor Annuities, 253
Keogh Plan(s), 224, 226, 253
Key Employees, 220

Keynes, John Maynard, 142
Laffer Curve, 144
Laffer, Arthur, 144
Large Groups of Homogeneous
    Exposure, 40
Lease Option, 85
Leasing Investments, 182
Leasing Programs, 184
Legal Opinion, 200
Lessor, 183
Liabilities, 28
Liability, 59
Life Insurance, 237
    Proceeds, 106
Limit Order, 162
Limited Partnership, 174
Liquid Assets, 27
Liquidity, 27
Liquidity Risk, 31
Living Trust, 249
Load and No-load Funds, 166
Long-term Debt, 151
Long-term Capital Gains (LTCG), 104
Louisiana, 242
Low-Income Housing, 127

M

M 1, 145, 148
M 2, 145, 148
Major Medical, 58
Management, 200
    Fees, 167
Management Companies
    Closed End, 164
    Open End, 165
Margin Account, 163
Marginal Tax Bracket, 99
Marital Deductions, 255
Market Makers, 163
Market Order, 162
Market Risk, 31
Market Value, 157
Marketable Securities, 149
Markowitz, Harry, 171
Master Recording, 192
Maximum Benefits, 56
Measureable Loss, 40
Medical Coverage, 235
Medical Protection, 57
Medical Reimbursement, 107
Member Banks, 145
Midwest Stock Exchange, 162
Modern Portfolio Theory, 171
Modified Adjusted Gross Income, 231
Monetarism, 143
Monetary Methods, 170
Monetary Policy, 145
Money Purchase Plan, 223
Money Supply, 145

Mortgage Bonds, 152
Motion Pictures, 178
Movies, 192
Multiplier Effect, 147
Municipal Bond, 107, 156
Mutual Funds, 197
    Selection, 167

N

NASDAQ, 162
National Association of Securities
    Dealers (NASD), 11, 162
Net Asset Value (NAV), 165
Net Present Value (NPV), 93
Net Worth Statement, 27
New York Stock Exchange, 162, 252
Newsletters, 197
Nonintentional, 40
Nominal Rate, 75
Noncancelable, 56
Nondiscriminatory, 107
Nonbusiness Tax Deductions, 110, 113
Nontaxable Transfer (for IRAs), 211
Nonspeculative, 40
Notes, 155
Nuncupative, 246

O

OTC Market, 165
Objectives, 4
Offering, 199
Office and Home Expense, 111
Oil and Gas Programs, 187
Old-Age, Survivors, and Disability
    Insurance (OASDI), 229
Open Market Committee, 145
Open Market Operations, 146
Opportunity Cost, 65
Option Premium, 160
Ordinary Income, 103, 128
Ordinary Life, 43
Over-the-Counter (OTC), 159, 162
Overleveraging, 36
Overvaluation Rules, 179
Ownership, 240

P-Q

Par Value, 157
Payback, 90
Payment, 67
Pension Plans, 217
Percentage Depletion, 133
Permanent Life, 43
Personal Residence, 109
Personal Taxes, 114
Phantom Income, 130
Phillips, A. W., 143

Phillips Curve, 143
Points or Loan Origination Fees, 114
Political Credit, 117
Political Risk, 31
Portfolio, 204
Present Value, 66
  of One Dollar, 72
  of One Dollar per Period, 73
  of a Growing Annuity, 81
Price, 168
Price-trend Method, 169
Private Offering, 201
Probate, 241, 247
Profit-Sharing Plan, 222
Promotional Interest, 189
Prospectus Review, 198
Purchase, 134
Put Option, 160
Qualified Group Legal Services
  Plan, 237
Qualified Pension Plans, 209
Qualified Terminable Interest Program
  (QTIP), 250, 255
Qualified Transportation, 238
Quantifying Life Insurance
  Coverage, 47

R

Random Walk, 170
Rates, 229
Raw Land, 180
Real Estate, 178
Real Estate Investment Trusts
  (REITs), 11
Real Estate Tables, 126
Recapture Rules, 128
Redemption Fees, 166
Refundable and Nonrefundable, 116
Registered Investment Advisor
  (RIA), 10
Related Party Transaction, 134
Research, 7
Research and Development, 190
Reserve Ratio, 146
Residential Property, 181
Retirement Plans, 253
Return of Capital, 103
Revenue and Authority Bonds, 157
Reversionary Interest, 189
Revocable Trust, 249
Risk Factors, 30, 200
Risk Management, 5
  Insurance, 39-61
Risk of Death, 42
Risk of Disability, 53

S

SIPC, 11

SRI International, 7
Say's Law, 141
Say, J. B., 141
Schedule C, 121
Scholarships and Fellowships, 109
Secured Bond, 151
Securities Act of 1940, 11
Securities and Exchange Commission
  (SEC), 10, 150, 199, 201
Security Dealers, 163
Self-Insured Plan, 107
Self-Employed, 121
Self-Employed Taxpayers, 121
Self-Insurance, 39
Separate Property, 244
Serial Bond, 151
Settlor, 248
Short Sale, 161
Short-Term Capital Gains (STCG), 104
Short-Term Debt Instruments, 150
Silver, 194
Simplified Employee Pension (SEP), 224
Single Limit, 60
Sinking Fund, 151
Social Security, 228
Social Security Administration,
  228, 232
Speculative, 159
Split Limit, 59
Stagflation, 143
Stock, 157
  Options, 160
  Splits, 158
Stop Limit, 163
Stop Loss, 163
Straight-Line Depreciation, 124, 129
Sub-S Corporations, 187
Subchapter S, 225
Subrogation, 41
Substance over Form, 99
Suitability Requirements, 201
Supply Siders, 143
Supreme Court, 98
Surviving Spouse, 241
Survivors, 228

T

Target Benefit Plan, 223
Tax Aspects, 200
Tax Bracket, 99, 236
Tax Deductions
  itemized, 110, 113
  non-business, 113
Tax Deferral and Time Value
  (IRAs), 212
Tax Deferred Annuities (TDAs), 213, 253
Tax Equity and Fiscal Responsibility
  Act, 191, 220, 222, 223, 226, 237
Tax Exempt, 103

Tax Planning, 123
Tax Reform Act (TRA) 1984, 191
Tax Shelters, 177
Tax Strategies, 99
Tax Structure, Fundamentals, 97
Tax Sheltered Annuity (TSA),
    209, 213, 253
  Borrowing, 217
  Distributions, 214
  Maximum Contribution, 214
  Participants, 214
Taxable Estate, 252
Taxable Income, 99
Taxation Risk, 31
Taxes, 254
Technical Analysis, 169
Television Programs, 178
Ten-Year Forward Averaging, 226
Tenancy by Entirety, 242
Tenancy in Common, 241
Tentative Tax, 255
Term, 42
Testamentary Trust, 250
The Tax Reform Act of 1984, 116
Time, 66
Time Value
  Concepts, 65
  Equations, 66
Timing, 168
Titling, 5, 240
  Assets, 245
Top-heavy Rules, 220
Track Record, 199
Tracking Expenses, 35
Trading, 159
Transportation and Travel
    Expenses, 111

Treasury Bill (T-bill), 107, 154
Trust, 248
Trustee, 248
Trustor, 248
Trusts, 248
1245 Property, 128, 129
Types of Trust, 249

U

U.S. Government, 151
U.S. Savings Bonds, 107
U.S. Treasury, 154
U.S. Treasury Department, 97
Umbrella Liability, 61
Unified Credit Rates, 252
Unified Tax Credit, 255
Uninsured Motorist and Medical
    Payments, 60
Unit Investment Trusts, 168
Universal Life, 44
Unrelated Business Taxable Income
    (UBTI), 227

V-Z

Variable Life, 44
Vesting, 219
Videos, 192
Whole Life, 43
Wildcatting, 188
Wills, 246
Withdrawal Charges, 166
Wright State University, 7
Years, 46
Yield to Maturity (YTM), 153
Zero Day Qualifies, 56